Twayne's United States Authors Series

Sylvia E. Bowman, *Editor*

INDIANA UNIVERSITY

O. Henry

 77

O. HENRY
(WILLIAM SYDNEY PORTER)

by **EUGENE CURRENT-GARCIA**

Hargis Professor of English and American Literature
Auburn University

TWAYNE PUBLISHERS
A DIVISION OF G. K. HALL & CO., BOSTON

Library of Congress Catalog Card Number: 65-12997

For

ALVA AND THE CHILDREN

ISBN 0-8057-0368-3

MANUFACTURED IN THE UNITED STATES OF AMERICA

Contents

Chapter

	Chronology	13
1.	Life	17
2.	O. Henry's Southern Literary Heritage	48
3.	O. Henry's Western Apprenticeship	68
4.	Bagdad—The New York Stories	95
5.	O. Henry's Technical Achievements	135
6.	Reputation and Revaluation	156
	Notes and References	167
	Selected Bibliography	182
	Index	188

About the Author

Born and reared in New Orleans, Lousiana, Professor Eugene Current-Garcia attended Tulane University and took the A.B. and A.M. degrees there in 1930 and 1932. He continued graduate work in English at Harvard University, taught for a number of years at the University of Nebraska, and later returned to Harvard to complete his studies for the doctorate in American Civilization. Before receiving his Ph.D. in 1947, he served for a time in Nicaragua as Director of the English-teaching Program sponsored by the United States Department of the State in that country; later he taught for several years at Louisiana State University. Since 1947 he has served continuously, except for two interruptions, as professor of American literature at Auburn University. During the year 1953-54 he attended Princeton University as a Ford Foundation Fellow, and from 1956 to 1958 he held the Chair of American Literature as Fulbright Lecturer at the University of Thessaloniki, Greece.

Besides his various published articles on Southern frontier humor and other topics, Dr. Current-Garcia is co-author of the following books: *American Short Stories* (1952), *What Is The Short Story?* (1961), and *Realism and Romanticism in Fiction; An Approach to the Novel* (1962).

Preface

THE PROBLEM of doing justice to O. Henry's achievement is that of steering a safe middle course between the "Squills" of fatuous adulation and the "Chalybeates" of pompous dismissal—to pilfer one of his own many ludicrous distortions of classical reference. For O. Henry is one of those rare writers who, long after their brief candle has gone out and the critics have brushed them aside, still bring pleasure to millions of readers the world over. How then can one hope to judge fairly or to appraise accurately the writings of one who is at once so popular and yet so dated in his contribution to a developing form of literary art?

On one hand, it can be pointed out that, within the short span of a decade or so, O. Henry produced nearly three hundred stories that captured the fancy and touched the hearts of countless newspaper and magazine readers of his own time; that most of these same stories, translated into many languages in scores of foreign editions during the past fifty years, are still read and enjoyed throughout the civilized world; that many of them—in radio, television, and motion picture adaptations—have been and still are equally popular with millions more; and that the impact of these tales made itself felt not only in the commercial area of book sales and publication rights but also in the realm of literary art. The pseudonym "O. Henry" has become a symbol to represent a recognizable species of short story writing. These are facts, easily documented.

But, on the other hand, it must also be pointed out that a great many, if not indeed nearly all, of these same stories fall below accepted, lasting standards of first-rate literature; that many were written hastily and carelessly, by an author who often relied upon cheap and tawdry effects to put them across; that most lack intellectual substance and depth; and that all are "seared with trade; bleared, smeared with toil" in the effort to create a product that would appeal to a mass market. These, however, are critical opinions, matters of taste that cannot be so readily or incontrovertibly proved in the court of world opinion.

And so, somewhere between the facts on the one side and the consensus of literary criticism on the other lies the mystery of O. Henry's rightful place in America's literary hall of fame. This book cannot pretend to locate the exact spot where his niche should be carved. It can only attempt, thanks to the help received from many others, to tell briefly who O. Henry was, what he wrote about and how he wrote it, and why I believe that, flawed as it is, much of what he wrote bears the stamp of individuality that insures permanence as well as transitory popular appeal.

One secret of O. Henry's staying power may be found in the representative quality of his stories. They are above everything else indubitably American in language, attitudes, and spirit; for the voices of Americans, native and naturalized, recognizably speak through them. Another secret of their continuing appeal may be found in the pervasive humor that supports them: a brand of humor often gauche, smart-alecky, overripe, and also thoroughly American. A third quality, hard to define yet plainly felt in them as something transcending national boundaries, is a kind of basic human sympathy for the common joys and sorrows of mankind that appeals to the romanticist in each of us.

If we disregard the many stories and sketches O. Henry wrote for his *Rolling Stone* and the Houston *Post,* his total output of short stories numbers more than 250. As catalogued in Clarkson's *Bibliography,* these appeared in thirty-four different magazines between 1899 and 1910; and they were eventually issued in thirteen volumes under the aegis of Doubleday, Page and Company, beginning with *Cabbages and Kings* in 1904 and concluding with *Waifs and Strays* in 1917. To attempt to follow the chronology of either the volumes or the individual stories would be pointless since many of O. Henry's earliest written stories were not published until near the end of his life, while many of the last ones he wrote dealt with experiences dating back to his earliest memories. But his stories do fall naturally into several well-defined spatial categories that clearly reflect experiences gained during the major periods of his career—his childhood in North Carolina, his youth in Texas, and his maturity in New York.

The plan adopted for treating O. Henry's work in this book is therefore the following: after a short summary of his life in chapter one, the next three chapters deal with the types, themes, and other special features of his stories which are related to the three major phases of his experience and to those experiences associated with his prison years. Because O. Henry was born and reared in the South, where he imbibed many of the traditional values of that section during the bitter transitional years of the Reconstruction Era, the earliest influences upon his writing were drawn from a Southern literary heritage—specifically, the humorous tall tale of the Old South and the local-color story of the post-Civil War period. These matters are treated in chapter two. Similarly, as shown in chapter three, the fourteen years O. Henry spent in Texas and the three more years he served in the Ohio Penitentiary influenced his work in other ways, chiefly by extending his range and by sharpening his perceptions. But the impact of New York City upon him during the remaining ten years of his life climaxed his career, not only by stimulating his most productive and distinctive efforts, but also by establishing his world-renowned reputation. These New York stories are discussed in chapter four.

No attempt has been made to summarize or to evaluate all the stories in each of the foregoing groups. Rather, in each group those stories which in my judgment reveal the most characteristic features of O. Henry's art have been examined critically and compared briefly with others of their type in an effort to appraise their literary worth. Chapter five concludes this critical analysis by discussing the structural and technical characteristics of the O. Henry stories as a whole; and chapter six summarizes briefly the growth and decline of O. Henry's reputation as an influence upon the developing form of the short story in American literature.

EUGENE CURRENT-GARCIA

Auburn University

Acknowledgments

For the preparation of this book I owe a debt of gratitude to many persons who offered both aid and encouragement. Thanks are due first to my colleagues, Walton R. Patrick and Carl Benson, and to Professor Sylvia E. Bowman, for patiently reading my manuscript and for suggesting many improvements in it; second, to Peggy Walls, who typed several versions of it; third, to the staff members of the Auburn University Library, who helped me obtain research materials not available here; fourth, to the Administration of Auburn University for granting me a leave of absence from teaching duties during the writing of the book; and finally to my wife, whose critical acuity is responsible for whatever stylistic aberrations it may have managed to escape. Its errors, however, either of omission or commision, are wholly mine.

I am indebted also to many others who made it possible for me to examine and use original source materials which have deepened my experience and, I hope, enriched this study. Among these I must include specifically Professor Gerald Langford of the University of Texas, not only for having written a fine biography of O. Henry which saved me many hours of scholarly toil, but also for offering his generous assistance in enabling me to obtain a microfilm copy of the entire Greensboro Collection of manuscript materials; Miss Olivia Burwell, Librarian of the Greensboro Public Library, who graciously placed these materials at my disposal and granted permission for securing them in microfilm copy; the members of her staff, who likewise gave me unstinting assistance; Mrs. Elsie Stephens Arnett, author of *O. Henry From Polecat Creek,* who gladly supplied many intimate details from her capacious storehouse of Greensboro lore; and Mr. and Mrs. Calvert R. Hall, through whose generosity I was enabled to meet, at the O. Henry Centennial Celebration, numerous Greensboro officials and members of the Porter family, as well as to examine historic relics assembled for that occasion.

For permission to quote extensively from the works of O. Henry and that of his first biographer, C. Alphonso Smith, I express appreciation to both the firm of Doubleday and Company and, particularly, its Permissions Editor, Miss Dorothy M. McKittrick, who generously supplied a large quantity of important factual data. For similar permission granted to quote from other writings, I also offer sincere thanks as follows: to Mr. Upton Sinclair personally for permission to quote from his privately printed play, *Bill Porter: a Drama of O. Henry in Prison;* to the Macmillan Company, for permission to quote from Mr. Langford's *Alias O. Henry;* to the firm of Harper and Row, for permission to quote from F. L. Pattee's *The Development of the American Short Story* and from Claude Simpson's introduction to *The Local Colorists;* to E. P. Dutton and Company for permission to quote from *The Confident Years* by Van Wyck Brooks; and to the editors of the *Texas Review,* the Shakespeare Association *Bulletin,* and the *Classical Journal,* for permission to quote brief passages from scholarly articles published in those journals, as cited in detail in the footnotes. Finally, I should like to acknowledge my indebtedness to all other O. Henry scholars, especially to the authors of unpublished master's theses not here individually cited, for these earlier labors contributed much to the enhancement of my own.

Chronology

1862   William Sydney (earlier spelled *Sidney*) Porter born, second son of Dr. Algernon Sidney and Mary Jane Porter, at Greensboro, North Carolina, on September 11.

1865   At mother's death, moves with father and brother into home of Aunt "Lina" and Grandmother Porter.

1867-   Develops fondness for literature and drawing under Miss
1876   "Lina's" tutelage.

1879   Begins working in Uncle Clark's drugstore as pharmacist apprentice.

1881   Licensed as practicing pharmacist by North Carolina Pharmaceutical Association, August 30.

1882   Leaves home as guest of Dr. and Mrs. James Hall on visit to their four sons in southwest Texas.

1882-   Remains as house guest of Mr. and Mrs. Richard Hall on
1884   their cattle ranch in La Salle County; gains intimate knowledge of cattle raising in raw frontier country and develops talents as cartoonist.

1884-   Moves to Austin, living as house guest of the Joseph
1886   Harrell family; keeps up his interest in sketch-writing and drawing.

1887   After whirlwind courtship marries Athol Estes, step-daughter of P. G. Roach, prominent Austin grocer; begins work as draftsman in Texas Land Office, headed by Mr. Richard Hall, Land Commissioner of Texas.

1888   Son born but dies shortly after birth.

1889   Second child, Margaret, born; Athol dangerously ill.

1891   Loses post in Land Office as result of Richard Hall's failure to achieve gubernatorial nomination and replacement as Land Commissioner; secures post as teller in First National Bank of Austin.

1894   Begins publication, in March, of his own humor weekly, *The Rolling Stone,* which survives exactly one year;

obliged to quit bank job in December because of shortages disclosed in his accounts; indicted to stand trial in following July.

1895   Grand jury returns no-bill, apparently closing case; but bank examiners secure orders from Washington to reopen it in following year; secures job as feature writer on Houston *Post,* turning out many sketches and short stories during ensuing six months.

1896   Arrested in Houston (February); en route to stand trial in Austin, flees to New Orleans and thence to Honduras; secures in both places abundant material for treatment in later fiction.

1897   Returns to Austin in January. Athol, desperately ill, dies on July 25. Awaiting trial, moves with Margaret into her grandparents' home; continues writing and receives publication acceptance of first story, "Miracle of Lava Canyon," from McClure Company in December.

1898   Tried and found guilty, February; with motion for appeal rejected, begins serving, in April, five-year sentence for embezzlement at Federal Penitentiary in Ohio.

1898-   Launches professional career as short story writer; pro-
1901   duces while a prisoner more than a dozen stories published in national magazines; released on good behavior after serving shortened term of three years.

1901-   Lives for short time with Roaches and daughter Margaret
1902   in Pittsburgh; writes features and stories for *Dispatch* and for New York magazines.

1902   At urging of Gilman Hall, editor of *Ainslee's,* moves to New York; quickly gains fame in magazine world under new pseudonym of O. Henry though largely unknown to public.

1903   Signs contract with New York *Sunday World* for weekly feature short story; produces over one hundred of these during next two years, achieving nation-wide fame.

1904   Publishes first book, *Cabbages and Kings,* a loosely unified collection of stories based on his Central American experiences.

1906   Publishes, in April, *The Four Million,* a collection of twenty-five of his most famous New York stories; brings him world-wide fame and popularity.

1907   Marries childhood sweetheart, Sara Lindsay Coleman; attempts unsuccessfully to combine normal family life with furious writing activity.

1907- Publishes, despite flagging energies, seven more volumes
1910   of collected short stories; collaborating with F. P. Adams, attempts unsuccessfully to write plays based on his stories.

1910   After serious illness of over six months, dies at Polyclinic Hospital, New York, on June 5; buried in Asheville, North Carolina.

1910- Five more posthumous volumes of his stories published
1920   by Doubleday and Company.

1916   First authorized biography, written by C. Alphonso Smith, published by Doubleday.

1920- Literally scores of translations made and publication
1955   rights to his works sold in many foreign countries; millions of volumes sold throughout the world, particularly in Soviet Russia, despite declining reputation among American scholars and critics.

1957   *Alias O. Henry,* most fully-documented biography published, attempts to restore him to rightful place as *minor* American classic.

1962   Centennial memorial of his birth celebrated with appropriate fanfare at Greensboro Public Library on September 11; centennial commemorative stamp issued in his honor by Soviet Russia.

CHAPTER 1

Life

I *Greensboro Years*

WILLIAM SIDNEY PORTER, better known to millions
under his pen-name, O. Henry, the most popular short
story writer in American literary history, was born near Greensboro, North Carolina, September 11, 1862.[1] Though many later
experiences elsewhere found expression in his voluminous output,
no accurate judgment of his work can be made without taking
into account his early years in this small community of the
South during the bitter period of the Reconstruction. Recent
scholarship has shown that family life, friends, schooling, the
work he did as a youth—all had an important bearing on his
career;[2] and, while these influences cannot alone explain either
his phenomenal success as a writer or his dismal failure as a
man, it will be seen that they contributed much to the paradoxical dualism of his development. For, like the ultimate value of
his writings which still charm the masses though the critics
scorn them, Porter himself remains an elusive, enigmatic figure
who defies analysis and explanation. But the source of this two-
fold mystery may be traced to his grandmother's cottage on
West Market Street, where the three-year-old, motherless boy
went to live with his father and older brother in 1865.

Will Porter came of respectable, though not wealthy, middle-
class stock. His father, Dr. Algernon Sidney Porter, a prominent
physician of Guilford County, had inherited both his professional
bent and his genial devotion to the sick from his sturdy grandparents, David and Eunice Worth, who had established there
in 1820 the first general hospital in North Carolina.[3] Will's
mother, Mary Jane Virginia Swaim, the daughter of William
Swaim, editor of the Greensboro *Patriot,* enjoyed as a young
girl all the advantages of a well-to-do household, having graduated with honors from the Greensboro Female College in 1850.
Reputedly "quick of wit" (she delivered on her graduation a
commencement essay, "The Influence of Misfortune on the

Gifted"), she evidently passed on to her son a gift for repartee as well as an artistic temperament and a certain instinctive shyness.[4] At the time of her marriage to "Dr. Al" in 1858, the young couple seemingly possessed all needed ingredients for a useful, contented, prosperous future: a home of their own provided by her stepfather, an extensive medical practice—"the biggest in Guilford before the Civil War"—and the genuine affection of everyone. For, long after his death, Dr. Al was to be remembered warmly as "the best loved physician in Greensboro . . . kind to everybody, to children as well as grown people."[5]

Misfortune, however—foreshadowed in his mother's schoolgirl essay—began darkening Will's path almost before his birth. The onset of the Civil War doubled and redoubled the numbers of wounded, both Federal and Confederate, who, besides his regular patients, required Dr. Al's attention after the Edgeworth Seminary was converted into a military hospital. As the times grew increasingly harsh, his income fell off inversely in proportion to the overburden of work placed upon him. And finally, to cap the climax of the war's end, which meant the destruction of a way of life for the whole South, his wife died six months to the day after giving birth to their third son. The doctor's world had collapsed and with it, apparently, his desire to compete: he gave up his home; moved to his widowed mother's house; and gradually abandoned his practice to others and the discipline of his two sons, Shirley and Will (the youngest, David, died in infancy), to his mother and to his maiden sister, Evelina. Soon withdrawing into a solitary world of his own, "the father of Will's earliest memories was a man who had already lost his grip."[6] Within a few more years he had become obsessed with the problem of perpetual motion, spending most of his days, as one acquaintance recalled, "in his barn with his machines and his bottle, oftentimes sleeping as much as one-half of the time. And this continued until his death."[7]

On the other hand, a contrary and far stronger influence upon Porter's early life came from his aunt, "Miss Lina," a forceful disciplinarian who served not only as his surrogate mother for the next seventeen years but also as the best teacher he ever had. Under her tutelage—she kept a private primary school as one means of providing the family income—young Will learned respect for the written word as well as for the essentials of creative art. Obviously a born teacher, she inculcated in her

young charges a love of learning by making them active par-
ticipants in the learning process: among the devices she employed
regularly was that of beginning an original story herself and
then calling upon each of her pupils in turn to develop it by
contributing a part. Others included field trips in the spring,
when she took them on wild-flower hunts; and her annual
"exhibition," to which their parents were invited to watch them
perform. Regularly throughout the school year, even on Friday
nights, she read to them, guiding and stimulating their minds
through the example of good literature. Thus, however in-
adequately prepared Miss Lina may have been to teach Latin
and algebra of the upper levels, there is no doubt that her
enthusiasm and discipline were the forces that aroused Porter's
youthful passion for reading and his later desire to create.

As he himself testified many years later: "I did more reading
between my thirteenth and nineteenth years than I have done
in all the years since, and my taste at that time was much better
than it is now, for I used to read nothing but the classics.
Burton's 'Anatomy of Melancholy' and Lane's translation of 'The
Arabian Nights' were my favorites."[8] Had Porter been granted
the benefit of a formal university education—the one thing
which he said repeatedly he would have "given his eyes" to
possess and which he drove himself mercilessly to provide for
his daughter[9]—this early passion for literature might well have
drawn him into a scholar's path and the quiet security of
academic halls. Instead, he remained largely self-taught after
leaving his aunt's supervision; and although the wealth of literary
allusions in his stories reveal an astonishingly wide acquaintance
with the works of standard authors from Homer, Chaucer, and
Shakespeare to Tennyson and Henry James,[10] his many references to their works and others, including the Bible, usually
betray a familiarity with quotable phrases rather than a scholar's
depth of insight. Nevertheless, the most noteworthy talent that
Porter's wide reading sharpened to a fine point was his fondness
for and discriminating use of the individual word. If a concord-
ance of O. Henry's works were ever prepared, it would show
that he possessed one of the largest vocabularies among modern
writers of English. Too often, perhaps, he used it ostentatiously;
but, more frequently than not, he used it effectively.

Whether Porter attended any other school besides his aunt's,
which he left in 1876, is not quite clear. His latest biographer

cites evidence that he was registered in the Greensboro public school as a high school sophomore during that year and the next,[11] but the records for those years appear to be defective or incomplete: moreover, none of his boyhood companions, including his first biographer, Professor C. Alphonso Smith, makes any conclusive reference to such schooling. Smith states positively that William received no other schooling beyond his fifteenth year;[12] whereas his older brother Shirley has said simply that William's "school days ended when he was 17 years of age [and he] entered the drug store of his uncle, W. C. Porter, to learn the business."[13]

In any event, there is ample evidence to show that his Uncle Clark's drugstore, a social hang-out for the town's leading "characters" and men of substance alike, provided an educational resource second only to that of Miss Lina's. There the youthful Porter, "a red-cheeked, black-haired boy, about five feet six inches tall"—as described by a contemporary[14]—quickly but unobtrusively learned the tools of the trade and many other things besides. That he mastered thoroughly the techniques and secrets of the pharmacopoeia is readily discernible in his expert use of professional terminology in such stories as "The Love-Philtre of Ikey Schoenstein," "Let Me Feel Your Pulse," "At Arms with Morpheus," "A Ramble in Aphasia," and in numerous others.[15] But his qualifications are also officially established in the records of the North Carolina Pharmaceutical Association, where his name appears "on the first list of druggists" registered on August 30, 1881, the date on which all practicing pharmacists were required by state law to have a license.[16]

During the three years that Porter worked in his uncle's drugstore, he found time for numerous other activities besides pill-rolling and soda-jerking. In the clearing behind the store he could often take a hand at horseshoe pitching or pistol practice (he became an expert marksman); or he could, in other idle moments share in the chess game continuing at all hours in the back room. With his fiddle, he could join the serenading parties of young lads who entertained the college girls on summer nights; or occasionally he could relieve boredom by playing youthful pranks on unwary customers, such as surreptitiously adding syrup to a specimen of urine submitted for analysis and displaying in alcohol a snake allegedly extracted from a man's stomach.[17] More significantly, he could develop further a second

talent acquired in childhood and encouraged by Miss Lina—
that of cartoon drawing, a skill that made young Will a local
celebrity; for he was said to be able to capture so graphically
the lineaments of townsfolk who entered the store that they
could be unmistakably identified. The originals of many of
these drawings are among the most highly prized relics housed
in the Greensboro Public Library. Two in particular reveal
Porter's native wit as well as his draughtsmanship: one depicts
the interior of the drugstore with Uncle Clark, behind the
counter, glumly observing two customers rifling his cigar case
while a third stalks across the cigar-butt-littered floor bearing
a liquor-filled pitcher; the other is a portrait of the well-known
carpetbagger, Judge Albion Tourgée, wearing wings as he takes
flight from Greensboro in 1879 after an unwelcome sojourn
there of thirteen years.[18]

Most important for Porter's future career as a writer, he was
meeting people and storing up during these drugstore years
countless impressions of their personal oddities, mannerisms,
gestures, and modes of speech which were later to be reflected
in his stories. Thus, the matrix for his characterizations was set
in Greensboro. For it is not only in such well-known tales as
"A Municipal Report," "A Blackjack Bargainer," or "The Rose
of Dixie" that recognizable Greensboro types are to be found;
they also appear repeatedly but thinly veiled in stories ranging
in settings from New York to Central America.[19] Porter's drugstore years, like his school days have doubtless been overideal-
ized in the recollections of aging cronies, as recent biographers
agree;[20] yet it seems obvious that he was enjoying himself, as
young men will, while his talents rapidly matured, for the
nostalgia expressed in his correspondence with Sara Coleman
twenty-five years later bears this out.[21] At the same time, it
is also apparent that he found the daily grind of the drugstore
an agonizing drudgery[22] and his health and home life unsatisfactory.[23] When Dr. James K. Hall and his wife invited
Porter to accompany them as their guest on a far-away visit to
their four sons in Texas, he took the offer and left, happy to
escape from the hometown to which he never returned except
for brief visits in 1890 and 1891 after his father and grandmother
had died.[24] His few letters extant from that period give no
indication that he felt obligated either to them or to his
Aunt Lina.

II *Texas Years*

Texas was already a storied land of "Wild-West" romance when Porter went there—a strange setting indeed for the shy, delicate, rootless youth whose personal interests, though still unchanneled, centered upon artistic things rather than upon such rugged outdoor activities as cattle roping and branding. And the family under whose hospitable roof he was to spend his next two years had contributed notably to that romantic legend of the West. Lee Hall, eldest of the Greensboro doctor's sons, had long since acquired a nation-wide reputation as a fearless leader of the Texas Rangers, symbolic scourge of desperadoes and outlaws;[25] but by 1882, when Porter came under his wing, he had married and left the Rangers to become manager of the Dull Brother's huge cattle ranch in La Salle County, with his three brothers assisting in its management under his supervision. Triumphantly engaged at this time in the fierce warfare between cattle ranchers and fence-cutting thieves and sheepmen, Lee Hall naturally assumed heroic stature in Porter's imagination, and he reappeared in later stories disguised as a bold champion of law and order.[26] Porter, however, spent his time—on the whole an uneventful, leisurely period, though rich in the variety of new impressions it afforded him for story materials—in the small household of Richard Hall, who with his young wife Betty, a small child, and an assortment of ranch hands, was managing one of his brother Lee's sheep ranches that was forty miles from the nearest, ramshackle town of Cotulla.[27] Here, Porter adopted the pattern of life that was to mark his future course and dependency—of irresponsibility toward practical affairs on the one hand, as opposed to a singleminded attachment to literature and writing on the other.

Porter's experiences at the Richard Halls resembled those of his romanticized troubador, Sam Galloway, a privileged, footloose guest welcome at lonely ranches, who pays his way by singing and playing his guitar.[28] Though Porter quickly mastered the rudiments of the cowboys' profession and was accepted by them, he did not often take part in their routine labors of herding and branding. The only duties he regularly performed were riding fourteen miles each week to Fort Ewell for the mail, baby-sitting the Halls's youngster during their infrequent absences, and serving as substitute cook in the intervals between the departure of one cook and the hiring of another. For a young man of twenty it was a lonely life in the wide-open spaces, with only an occasional flirtation to relieve the tedium; yet Porter's extant letters to old friends in Greensboro show little nostalgia or homesickness.[29] What they do show, rather, is that he filled his long stretches of leisure with an extensive program of reading; for he soon absorbed not only the Halls's slender stock of books but new arrivals in the mails, plus those in a sizable private library belonging to a lawyer friend in Cotulla.[30] His rich literary diet again included not only the standard English poets, novelists, and historians but, more significantly, Webster's dictionary, which he reputedly carried about with him and studied by the hour. It was this fondness for and, facility with words, expressed in delightfully witty, sometimes bizarre or caustic turns of phrase and epigrammatic flourishes, that endeared him to his associates; and they likewise admired the readiness with which he picked up Spanish, French, and German.

Porter also found time during these two years for excursions to Cotulla and to Friotown, cultural meccas of the area, to mingle at dances and outings with varied ranks of their pioneer society—from colorful members of the cattle aristocracy down to the more raffish types that patronized the saloons.[31] But these were infrequent diversions. During most of his free time he busied himself rather with the problem of developing further the two lines of artistic interest opened in childhood—drawing and writing. As a consequence of certain juvenile extravaganzas composed in Greensboro, he learned from his friend, Dr. Beall, of his election to honorary membership in a North Carolina reading society—and promptly celebrated this distinction by writing another humorous sketch in reply.[32]

His fame as a draughtsman also spread, even to Texas, and resulted in a more ambitious, though abortive project, when he was professionally engaged to draw illustrations for a book of memoirs written by a mining prospector named Joe Dixon. For three weeks the two men worked closely together at the Hall ranch, where Dixon had sought out Porter at the suggestion of a friend in Austin, John Maddox, who had offered to underwrite the cost of illustrating and printing the book because he had heard of "a young fellow here . . . who can draw like blazes." While turning out some forty drawings, Porter so fascinated his older collaborator that he later remembered Will vividly as "a taciturn fellow, with a peculiar little hiss when amused . . . [who] could give the queerest caustic turn to speech, getting off epigrams like little sharp bullets."[33] Their joint effort came to nothing, however, for Dixon decided that his book was worthless and pitched the manuscript, drawings and all, into the Colorado River; but while Porter's first professional job thus aborted, the contact established through it with Maddox paid dividends later when he went to Austin after the Halls had liquidated their holdings in March, 1884.

Years later, in an interview with C. A. Smith after Porter's death, Mrs. Hall remembered him as a youth lacking in "physical and moral courage" and as feeling "no sense of responsibility or obligation or gratitude" either to family or friends.[34] This judgment was based on daily observation over an extended period, and its merit was borne out by a similar pattern of behavior in the years ahead after Richard Hall became Land Commissioner of Texas and once again provided employment for Porter in his office. Yet the Halls felt genuinely protective toward him and introduced him to another Greensboro family, the Joe Harrells, who had become prominent Austin citizens and who in turn welcomed him warmly into their capacious household.

Virtually as a member of the family, Porter lived with the Harrells for nearly three more years, apparently contributing toward his support little but his engaging personal charm. This, however, sufficiently assured his acceptance, especially by the Harrells's younger sons, one of whom recalled affectionately that Porter had been "just like a brother to me."[35] Taking great delight in his feats of word definition (reputedly he could never be stumped for the spelling and meaning of words chosen at random from Webster's unabridged), his witty repartee, sketching, verse writing, and mimetic performances, the Harrell boys introduced Porter to their friends and thus launched his career among Austin's socially élite. A young buck of twenty-two, with a covey of admiring damsels to be dazzled by his versatility, Porter thrived in this milieu; for Austin at this point was not, like Greensboro, a village of two thousand souls but the capital, and the fourth largest city of the state, and already bursting with activity.

Within a short time after his arrival, Porter made gestures toward settling down to work. A registered pharmacist armed with references from North Carolina testifying to his qualifications, competence, and moral character, he readily obtained employment as drug clerk in a local pharmacy. But once again, within a few months the routine demands of this labor proved less attractive than sporadic attempts at light verse and skit writing. He abandoned the job and found nothing remunerative to do for the next two years, except as an occasional volunteer relief clerk in the Harrells' cigar store. His repeated references to money in letters to his friends in Greensboro suggest that his lack of it was a sore point.[36] Yet he apparently made no further efforts to earn an income; and, since the Harrells not only provided his board and lodging but even offered to send him to an art school in New York—an offer he declined for unspecified reasons—one can only conclude that he preferred to remain contentedly secure in a sheltered atmosphere. Like a charter member of Dickens' "Finches of the Grove," he managed somehow to fill the role of gay young bachelor about town; for he engaged in amateur theatricals, joined a quartette and a succession of church choirs, serenaded the ladies with music and song, and, perhaps not infrequently, sampled the wares of some of the city's forty-three groggeries.[37]

Porter's first steady employment began in the fall of 1886, when John Maddox (who had picked him to illustrate Dixon's book) found a place for him as bookkeeper in the real-estate firm of Maddox and Anderson, a job Porter held until the following January and gave up then only in order to take a more congenial one as draughtsman in the new Land Office headed by Richard Hall. Though totally inexperienced, Porter received the not inconsiderable salary of $100 a month and was thoroughly coached in his duties by Charles Anderson—another in the lengthening string of benefactors captivated by his charm—who would in the future repeatedly go out of his way to help the young man by finding other jobs for him, providing him and his bride with free housing, and vouching for his character in time of trouble. Anderson himself later testified to Porter's seriousness of purpose at this juncture, noting especially the rapidity with which he mastered the details of bookkeeping.[38]

Quite possibly, Porter's decision to apply himself at last was prompted by his expanding social life and by his desire to strengthen his competitive position as a suitor. For two years he had flitted about gaily, indulging himself in numerous flirtations but gradually centering his attention after 1885 on a spirited young high school girl from Tennessee, Athol Estes, whose stepfather, P. G. Roach, ran a prosperous grocery business. Porter's campaign, however, was not to be easily won. For, although his talents and natural endowments made him desirable in the eyes of Athol's coterie of young girl friends, her mother, understandably enough, thought him "too sporty" and backed his rival, the son of a wealthy German family named Zimpelmann, whose prospects as a husband appeared vastly more promising. The titillating tale of Porter's courtship and marriage has been amply told from many points of view.[39] Suffice it to say here that Porter prevailed. Romantically sweeping up his bride, despite her torn dimity skirt and the ill-omen of a Friday afternoon, he dragooned the Andersons into supporting the conspiracy, secured a license, overcame the scruples of a reluctant minister, and took his new wife to Anderson's home, leaving him to mollify the raging Mrs. Roach at midnight (July 1, 1887).

By a grim coincidence, Porter's married life was to be as sad as that of his parents, but it lasted somewhat longer. Like his "enskyed and sainted mother," his nineteen-year-old wife, Athol, was a young woman of wit and high spirits, who is said to have stimulated and encouraged him in his ambition to become a writer and who delightedly shared his joys on receiving the first small checks his published skits occasionally brought in. But, like his mother too, Athol was not physically strong: her first child, a son born in 1888, lived but a few hours; and she herself, having inherited tuberculosis to which her own father had succumbed, survived her second child's birth by only seven years of declining health. She died before reaching thirty.

Porter's four years as a draughtsman in the Land Office were probably the happiest of his entire life. His $100-a-month job meant security, if not luxurious comfort; and it also afforded him ample time to continue his sketching and writing. As seen in several stories written years later, notably in "Bexar Scrip No. 2692" and in "Georgia's Ruling," Porter obviously enjoyed and profited by the contacts and expanded horizons his work now provided; for the Land Office teemed with life and with new problems incident to the settling of new territory in the West. He liked and was liked by his fellow workers, though most of them recalled later the odd combination of his reticence and flashing wit. He was reconciled to his wife's parents, the

Roaches, who became very fond of him and gave generous support in times of stress. He also enjoyed the confidence and good will of a wide circle of friends, particularly the Andersons and the Halls, who loaned him and Athol their comfortable home in the summers.[40] During these four years, and even later as misfortunes piled up, Will and Athol evidently shared many gay, carefree moments in Austin society.

But ill luck, when it came, took its toll repeatedly. Barely surviving the birth of her second child, Margaret, in 1889, Athol never fully recovered thereafter, despite her mother's constant care and her trips to Nashville and Greensboro for health and relaxation. Then, in January, 1891, Porter's job at the Land Office folded when Richard Hall, having lost his bid for the gubernatorial nomination in the primary, also lost his post as Land Commissioner. Shortly afterwards Porter obtained another $100-a-month job—again through his friend Charles Anderson's influence—as teller in the First National Bank, a job that was to bring him both disaster and fame.[41]

Though he had but little bookkeeping experience, Porter apparently worked satisfactorily during the nearly three years he held this job. Whether he performed diligently is another matter, as he seems to have kept up his inveterate sketching and skit writing during banking hours; yet he might have prospered indefinitely had not lax banking practices and his own incapacity for managing his affairs proved his undoing. The unsystematic, indeed highly irregular, banking methods prevalent in Austin at that time are nowhere better dramatized than in Porter's own story "Friends in San Rosario," which tells how the president of one bank temporarily embarrassed for funds circumvents the federal bank examiner by making an unethical appeal to his friend, the president of another bank.[42] But these practices alone would not likely have ruined Porter, had not mounting domestic troubles, his own personal weaknesses, and his determination to run an unprofitable newssheet enmeshed him by the end of 1894 within an inexorably tightening web of ruinous circumstances.

In March, 1894, Porter fulfilled a long-felt aim to publish his own humor paper by buying a cheap printing press and the rights to a scandal sheet, *The Iconoclast,* owned by a ruffian named William Brann. Porter and his partner in the venture, James P. Crane, renamed their paper *The Rolling Stone,* changed it from a monthly to a weekly, and began issuing it the following month. Although never a commercial success, the paper survived exactly one year, reaching a peak circulation of 1,500; but the fact that Porter managed to run it at all while holding down a full-time job was in itself a remarkable feat. He filled its eight pages each week with humorous squibs and satirical barbs on persons and events of local interest; moreover, he carried the load virtually single-handed. He produced most of the contents, which included some surprisingly well-finished fiction; and he even attended to the mechanical tasks of typesetting and printing. Crane, however, soon left Austin for greener pastures in Chicago, and the various others whom Porter enlisted as aides in editing and in printing were of little help. Thus, though he worked tirelessly, even jubilantly, to keep it rolling, *The Rolling Stone* became a millstone, dragging him deeper into debt and eventually into degradation. Yet, in this ephemeral little paper—his first body of work—are to be found the origins of his later themes, plots, methods, and style.[43]

In his efforts to shore up the sagging prospects of *The Rolling Stone,* Porter borrowed heavily from his father-in-law and other friends, apparently with too little concern as to how their money would be repaid if the paper failed. He also became involved with shady characters, shady deals, and shady ladies. By frequenting the numerous barrooms and gambling houses of Austin, he precipitated stormy scenes at home. Sometime during the year 1894 he evidently began taking funds he needed from the bank and altering his accounts with the idea of readjusting them later upon replacing the money. Whatever the details of these manipulations may be—they lie buried under a mountain of conflicting evidence, making the truth hard to get at—the fact is that toward the end of the year the shortages in Porter's books stood revealed and he was obliged to give up his job in December. The worst was yet to come, however; for, though Mr. Roach and others agreed to make up most of the shortage (a sum in excess of $5,000) and though the bank officials were apparently satisfied to let the matter drop, the federal bank examiner insisted upon prosecuting the case at the grand jury hearing to be held the following July.[44]

During the six months prior to the trial, Porter remained out of work and lived on the generosity of his father-in-law, earning only such small sums as occasionally published squibs brought in. He tried to keep *The Rolling Stone* alive by proposing to his former partner Crane to move the paper to Chicago; and, when that proposal failed, he even took on as co-editor a phony Englishman named Ryder-Taylor to manage a branch office of the paper in San Antonio. But all was to no avail. The poor little humor sheet quietly rolled its last on March 30, 1895, and it was soon forgotten until O. Henry's world-wide fame a few decades later made it a collector's item. As the trial approached, Porter seems not to have felt unduly apprehensive; and, when it opened, such strong testimony of his innocence was set forth by friends and even by officers of the bank to counter the charges of embezzlement brought against him by F. B. Gray, the bank examiner, that a no-bill was rendered by the grand jury. This apparently closed the case in his favor, leaving him free, if somewhat shaken, to choose among several jobs elsewhere. The first of these, an offer to edit a humorous paper in Washington, which came through the influence of his friend Crane, Porter had to decline after planning to take it, when Athol's condition abruptly worsened; but upon her recovery later in the summer, he providentially received another offer to serve as a fill-in writer for the Houston *Post,* which he gratefully accepted, even at the poor starting salary of fifteen dollars per week.[45]

When Porter left Austin to fill this job, he may have thought that his troubles in the bank case were over; but he reckoned without the persistence of the bank examiners, whose determination to reopen the case resulted in orders from Washington to re-submit it at the next session of court in February.[46] Meanwhile, however, Porter again demonstrated in Houston his ability to win friends among influential people through his charm, wit, courtesy, and dedication to his work. Though his duties on the *Post* were at first varied and unclassified, he quickly rose in his publisher's estimation; and he received advances in salary up to the limit of twenty-five dollars weekly paid to *Post* reporters after he began running a daily feature column called "Some Postscripts," which resembled the kind of anecdotal humor he had written for *The Rolling Stone.* His special value to the paper at first lay in the many satirical barbs and political cartoons he turned out, but soon his major appeal to the public came from the longer sketches he began writing, many of them incorporating themes, plots, and situations which reappeared later, polished and elaborated upon, in some of O. Henry's most famous stories.[47]

In the nearly sixty pieces definitely identified as Porter's work, his facility for ringing changes on the familiar O. Henry themes of mistaken identity, false pretense, misplaced devotion, nobility in disguise, and the bitter irony of fate can be seen in embryo, along with such sentimental types as the sensitive tramp, the ill-starred lovers, the starving artist, and the gentle grafter. Long before he reached New York, therefore, to delight millions with such tales as "The Enchanted Kiss," "While the Auto Waits," "Roads of Destiny," "The Door of Unrest," "The Caliph and the Cad," and numerous others, both the basic structure and tone of his stories, as well as the attitudes responsible for them, were being shaped in the *Post* sketches by the harsh realities of his Texas experiences from which there could be only vicarious escape.

In mid-February he had been arrested in Houston and taken back to Austin; and, though quickly released on a $2,000 bond (signed by his father-in-law and another close friend) and granted a continuance, enabling him to return to Houston to prepare a defense and help care for his prostrate wife, now in July the inevitable trial had to be faced. But Porter could not face it. Despite the goodwill and support of friends in both cities, most of whom believed him innocent and thought that his trial would be a mere formality, he had apparently prepared no defense whatever nor made plans of any sort except at the last moment when, ostensibly entrained for Austin, he switched instead toward New Orleans and shortly thereafter skipped the country. This act of desperate folly, exposing the tragic flaw in Porter's character, at once marked the climax of his career in Texas and opened the road of destiny he chose to follow.

III   *Shadowed Years*

Whether Porter's sudden flight was premeditated or impulsive as his apologists argue—again the evidence is mixed—when he reached New Orleans with the $260 loan raised for his trial expenses by friends on the *Post*, he evidently had no detailed plans for the future, except possibly to evade the law by remaining outside the United States until freed by the statute of limitations. Little is definitely known of his activities during the few weeks he spent in New Orleans, but casual acquaintances later recalled that he mingled unobtrusively but convivially with newspapermen while working for one of the dailies. That he kept in touch with his family by sending notes and drawings to Athol through an old friend is also on record,[48] incidentally supporting the possibility that his wife had known beforehand of his intention to flee. But the clearest evidence of both his state of mind and his experiences at this point may be inferred from the several stories he later wrote with a New Orleans setting—particularly the one entitled "Blind Man's Holiday," the hero of which, a remorseful gambler-embezzler "on the lam," paralleled his own case precisely.[49] More significantly, as an instance of Porter's sharp eye and ear, other stories in this group such as "Cherchez la Femme," "The Renaissance at Charleroi," and "Whistling Dick's Christmas Stocking" show how unmistakably he could recapture in swift, flashing phrases the distinctive features of the locale: the lights and shadows, the flowered paths and local customs, the architecture and dim interiors of public buildings and little cafes, the speech rhythms of native Creoles—the very atmosphere of the Vieux Carré. Yet Porter lived there but a short time before sailing to Honduras, where he remained for the rest of the year.

Porter's experiences in Honduras, like all his others elsewhere, are shrouded in legend and myth, the most romantic versions of which are to be found in his own stories. Nearly thirty of these written in after years appeared in various popular magazines, and about twenty of them, reworked and tied together, were published in 1904 as his first book, *Cabbages and Kings*. As a record of what actually happened to Porter they are, of course, wholly unreliable; but one of their special artistic merits, shared by most of his other stories as well, is their high concentration of realistic detail, captured chiefly in descriptive and dialogue passages. Almost equally unreliable, however, is the allegedly authentic account of his wanderings all round South America written by Al Jennings, a notorious train robber who first met Porter in Honduras and later knew him both in prison and in New York.[50] But even more dependable sources give only conflicting reports of his whereabouts and actions. It is known that he corresponded fairly regularly with Athol through third persons; that he received messages from her and others; that he found life there a blessed relief from the troubles at home; and that to the bitter end he held out hopes of bringing his wife and child to live with him. But the hopelessness of all this escapism Porter had to acknowledge when news came that Athol was dying; with borrowed funds, he returned home in January to face his trial at last.

The year 1897 must have been the grimmest in Porter's sad life, notwithstanding the many bitter moments that lay ahead for him. Yet ironically, it was also the year that first brought him promise of the national fame to come when in December the McClure Company accepted his story "The Miracle of Lava Canyon"; but Athol would not live to know of this good fortune.[51] Because of her serious condition at the time of his return to Austin, the court granted him the privilege of a new bond and another continuance of trial until after her death; but, although she rallied temporarily under the daily care and companionship of her husband and her parents, her end came on July 25. Throughout the ten years of an increasingly tortured married life her loyalty and her faith in Porter's innocence, as well as in his future fame, had never slackened. Now with a young child to support and the uncertainties of the ordeal facing him, perhaps Porter's sole consolation, apart from the genuine love and comfort he could bestow on little Margaret, was the knowledge of steadfast support given him by her grandparents. Having made room for both in their home, as well as a separate area for Porter to work in, the Roaches not only sheltered and fed him but kept alive his hopes and encouraged his efforts to write during the rest of the year.

Porter's trial opened in February, 1898. To the four original indictments brought against him and charging him with the embezzlement of over $5,500, two more were added as a result of his having attempted through flight to avoid prosecution. Many of Porter's apologists, determined to exonerate him, have argued that this latter charge, a technicality, was the sole reason for sending an innocent man to prison; that he was accordingly made a scapegoat, the victim of a gross miscarriage of justice, in order to vindicate the harshness of federal authorities, if not actually to shield other guilty superiors. Such a mass of confused, incomplete, erroneous, and distorted testimony has been thrown up in this effort to absolve him that the full truth may never be known. On the other hand, in what appears to be the most thorough and impartial analysis of all the available documentary evidence in Porter's case,[52] it seems obvious not only that he was guilty but also that he received a perfectly fair trial, in which all the charges against him were established to the satisfaction of the jury and of many others besides. Thus, according to Langford (125), "the traditional claim that there was a miscarriage of justice in Porter's trial is a myth." For, though the burden of testimony in his favor may be summed up in the phrase "Negligently, perhaps; criminally, never,"[53] those who follow this line of reasoning have either overlooked or ignored much damaging evidence proving beyond reasonable doubt that Porter, despite his own protestations of innocence, deliberately took the money himself and altered his account books to conceal his theft.[54]

That his actions were clearly not those of a typically hardened criminal is, of course, another matter altogether. Quite possibly, as one of his fellow clerks testified, he had no intention of keeping the money when he began taking small sums to invest in cotton futures, with the idea of restoring them later and using the profits to support *The Rolling Stone*. If so, the question of his moral guilt or innocence, though difficult to determine absolutely, is perhaps nowhere more sympathetically weighed than in Langford's observation that Porter's behavior as a bank teller had followed the same pattern set up for him during his boyhood and youth in Greensboro, at the Halls's ranch, and in the homes of the Harrells and Andersons: "His reaction to financial temptation, as to marital stress, had been less that of the responsible adult than that of the overprotected child. . . . With neither problem had he come to grips realistically. In the matter of the embezzlement he had not let his right hand know what his left hand did. His handling of money throughout his life is a clear indication of how he was unable to change or grow, and this immaturity is reflected in his writing. It was a cruel destiny for one with the natural endowments which Porter had" (126).

Perhaps the court likewise sensed the irony of this cruel destiny. In any event, Porter was given the lightest sentence possible under the prevailing terms of the law—a term of five years, which his good behavior would reduce to three; and, though the finality of even this sentence was a terrible blow to absorb, his reaction to it followed the same pattern of helpless immaturity noted above. Withdrawing still further into himself,

Porter continued to protest his innocence in letters to Mrs. Roach; yet he had done nothing to help his lawyers defend his own case and, significantly, when later in prison he came to write stories closely paralleling his predicament, they were to be singularly lacking in any note of bitterness or protest.

When Porter entered the Ohio Penitentiary as Prisoner Number 30664 in April, the only strongly positive aims he seems to have had were a determination to blot out the past and a desire to continue his writing. Whether he deliberately falsified his age with a view toward future concealment of his prison record is uncertain, but Dr. John M. Thomas, the prison physician who befriended him, later observed that he had "never known a man so deeply humiliated by his prison experience."[55] At first Porter threatened suicide and avoided his fellow prisoners almost entirely, studiously guarding against all mention of his family to anyone; yet almost from the first his quiet reserve won their respect, while his knowledge of pharmacy earned him a favored post as night druggist and provided relative comfort and freedom to pursue his writing. Gradually he became inured to his plight by withdrawing into a realm of fiction, keeping up an elaborate pretense on the one hand in a long series of charming letters to little Margaret[56] (who was never told the real reason for his absence), and producing on the other fourteen of the senti-mentalized tales that were later to bear the unmistakable stamp of the O. Henry style.[57]

In his letters to the Roaches he occasionally lowered the mask enough to describe graphically the horrors of prison life as he found them: "... misery and death and all kinds of suffering around one all the time. We sometimes have a death every night for a week or so. Very little time is wasted on such an occasion ... the next day the doctors have a dissecting bee and that ends it. Suicides are as common as picnics here. ... They cut their throats and hang themselves and stop up their cells and turn on the gas and try all kinds of ways. Most of them plan it well enough to succeed. ... These little things are our only amusements."[58] But these and other inhuman brutalities suffered by the prisoners—such as punishment by means of high pressure hosing in the face and beatings to the point of insensibility; rancid food purchased by bribing prison officials; and neglect even to the extent of being carted off to the morgue while still alive—generally left Porter too stunned to comment openly about them. When his fellow prisoners urged him to expose these conditions in his writings, he is said to have replied that, since he was not a reporter, the prison and its shame were not his responsibility, and that he would never speak of crime and punishment or try to remedy "the diseased soul of society. I will forget that I ever breathed behind these walls."[59]

What Porter might have done with his talent had he chosen to rival Upton Sinclair or Lincoln Steffens in the muckraking era can only be surmised. Instead, he stuck to his fiction, and his success in blotting out of memory his prison experiences can best be seen by the complete transformation he gave so many of them in his stories. For regardless of where, when, or how his pen name was first picked up, "O. Henry" was literally born during Porter's three-year stretch in prison.[60] Not only the fourteen stories written and published during this period (beginning with "Georgia's Ruling" in 1900) were the product of his prison career, but many others published later also grew out of yarns and anecdotes told him by his fellow prisoners. The Jeff Peters stories in *The Gentle Grafter*—as well as many of those involving the exploits of Texas outlaws and other forms of banditry in *Heart of the West, Roads of Destiny, Options,* and still other volumes—came originally from the same sources. The most famous of all these is, of course, "A Retrieved Reformation," the tale of a light-fingered safe-cracker, Jimmy Valentine, later to be dramatized with phenomenal success, though not to Porter's financial aggrandizement, in motion pictures and on the stage.[61]

The fact that Porter launched his professional career while in prison is significant in several ways. He derived a large volume of story materials from his fellow prisoners, and, though relatively uncommunicative himself, he was no solitary recluse. For the same personal warmth that had attracted friends and supporters among prominent Texans won him friendship and respect among the officials and prisoners alike. As Al Jennings later recalled, "They were all fond of the nimble-tongued, amiable dignity that was Bill Porter's. Everyone wanted to make him a present as he was leaving."[62] But the fact that Porter stored up and produced so many stories during his prison years also shows how diligently he was working at his craft throughout the long nights. A notebook he kept during this period discloses that some of his most popular stories—such as "The Enchanted

Kiss," "A Fog in Santone," and "The Emancipation of Billy"—drew as many as ten or more rejection slips before finding a publisher; others, however, gained immediate acceptance.[63] But the most striking indication of his professional growth is found in the prison stories themselves. For although the style of these fourteen stories is not markedly different from that of either his earlier or later work, "they do testify," as Langford has pointed out, "to the results of a remarkably thorough self-discipline in a form which previously he had attempted only casually or spasmodically—the short story proper, or rather the short story as it was to flourish through his influence. The fourteen prison stories show almost the full range of O. Henry . . ." (150).

Moreover, this writer continues, in many of these stories there is a significantly prominent autobiographical element, as eight of them are concerned with the same basic idea: "the vindication of a character who has in some way forfeited his claim to respectability or even integrity. . . . and the plot invariably turns on the regeneration of an admitted delinquent, not on the vindication of a character who is blameless" (*ibid.*). Whether or not the forfeiture of integrity had become for Porter a compulsive idea and these stories embodying it, an oblique effort to confess—as Langford surmises—the mere fact that this autobiographical vein is discernible to the probing scholar but artfully concealed from the average reader shows how fully his art of the short story had been developed. Porter entered the Ohio Penitentiary an amateur, but he came out three years later as O. Henry, the professional literary artist.

IV New York Years

When Porter stepped out of prison and into the twentieth century, he had but nine years to live, years that would be packed with new sensations, adventures, and personal triumphs, bringing him to the pinnacle of success as the self-anointed Caliph of Bagdad-on-the-Subway. Yet, they were also to be years of intense suffering, loneliness, want, and guilt-ridden fear, as he tried vainly to elude the shadow of his past and to overcome, through superhuman literary effort, his insatiable need for money. His first stopping place after leaving jail was Pittsburgh, where he rejoined his family and remained some eight or nine months, living at first in the modest Iron Front

Hotel managed by Mr. Roach but later in a cheaper hotel room which he shared with a young druggist named Jamison.[64] During this period of becoming painfully reacquainted with Margaret, now a child of twelve, Porter kept up his writing besides working on and off for the *Dispatch* to provide his own and her support; but he also continued his old ways of spending money faster than he made it on expensive clothes, poker, and whiskey. Thus, the pattern for the remaining years of his life— furious writing activity coupled with spendthrift indulgence— was never to change.

Before leaving Pittsburgh for New York in the spring of 1902, Porter published ten stories and had possibly five or six others accepted, which were published shortly afterward.[65] He was now turning them out at the rate of about two a month at $75 each—the sum paid him at first by *Ainslee's*—and drawing an average income of $150 a month, as he reported to Jennings in October.[66] But this amount was insufficient for his present needs; besides, he loathed Pittsburgh, deriding it as " 'the low-downedest hole on the surface of the earth.' "[67] He wanted to go to New York, and he was encouraged to do so by both the editors of the *Dispatch,* who could not pay what they thought his stories were worth, and those of *Ainslee's,* who were eager to pay him more. For by the end of 1901, stories already published in that magazine ("Money Maze," "Rouge et Noir," "Friends in San Rosario," and "The Passing of Black Eagle"), as well as others in other magazines, had begun to draw attention to the fresh new talent still concealed under a variety of pseudonyms. More- over, Porter was anxious to bury his identity in the nameless throngs of New York, though even there he would later confess to "the horrible fear that some ex-con will come up and say to me 'Hello, Bill; when did you get out of the O. P.?' "[68] As soon as possible, he therefore eagerly accepted the invitation and the $100 advance sent him months before by Gilman Hall, associate editor of *Ainslee's,* who was to become his best friend and benefactor in New York; and there at last Porter found his element.

"If ever in American literature the place and the man met," Smith sagely noted, "they met when O. Henry strolled for the first time along the streets of New York."[69] Within a short time he became an anonymous habitué of hole-in-corner hangouts and glittering restaurants. He mysteriously secluded himself in out-of-the-way hotels so that even publishers' representatives had trouble finding him. He prowled endlessly through New York streets to savor the varied color and texture of the city's life; but also, fortified by his two-bottle average daily intake, he turned out the stories that soon made everyone wonder who O. Henry was. Shortly after Witter Bynner tracked him down to purchase "Tobin's Palm" for $100 for *McClure's*, O. Henry's works were appearing with increasing frequency and often simultaneously in almost a dozen different magazines;[70] so that by the end of his first year in the city Porter had every reason to feel self-confident about his future. To date he had published more than twenty-five stories—among them such famous ones as "While the Auto Waits," "Roads of Destiny," and "A Retrieved Reformation"—yet he had barely tapped the abundant resources that New York had to offer him.[71]

His big break came, however, in the fall of 1903 when, having gained and lost a contract to supply the *Sunday World* with a story each week for $60, he signed a second contract with a new editor of the same paper for $100 a week. Since the *World*, with a circulation of nearly half a million, was the largest paper in America, Porter now enjoyed the greatest audience he had ever had, as well as double the income. He could begin to live more nearly in the manner he had always aspired to enjoy. Moving to roomier quarters, first on East 24th Street and later to 55 Irving Place (in the neighborhood of Gramercy Park), he found here among the reputed haunts of Washington Irving both a fitting berth and precisely the right atmosphere needed "to establish himself in what he called 'the business of caliphing,' and to indulge in the vagaries and extravagances appropriate to the generous handed role."[72] Within the confines of this area there were at one extreme such respectable establishments as Scheffel Hall, known throughout the city as a fine restaurant; the Westminster Hotel, where Dickens had stayed; and the Hotel America, frequented by Latin American exiles and delightfully caricatured in O. Henry's stories as El Refugio.[73] At the other extreme there were dives and honky tonks like McGlory's bawdy house, Tom Sharkey's saloon, and Tony Pastor's vaudeville theater.[74] Given Porter's talent for appreciating such kaleidoscopic scenery, it is not surprising that "from 1904 to 1907, O. Henry was Haroun in his golden prime."[75]

For all his lavish spending, however, Porter still shunned in the main the upper social levels where he was welcome, and he only gradually extended his friendship, though never his full confidence, to a small group of intimate acquaintances in the magazine world. Even those who had known him best repeatedly called to mind his extreme reserve, his cautious, even furtive reticence—except when tight—about women. Apart from Margaret and Athol's step-sister Nettie Roach, neither of whom he saw frequently, his relations with women above the shopgirl level remained stiff and awkward. An exception to this rule was his easygoing friendship until his death with Anne Partlan, a young writer whom he met occasionally; more typical associations were the brief platonic affair with Mabel Wagnalls, daughter of the publisher, which resulted in a charming little series of letters; and another correspondence romance shared with a lonely young woman named Ethel Patterson, which also came to nothing.[76] These brief, tentative gropings toward companionship accentuate the unfulfilled need, a longing in Porter's character and in all his relationships, causing one hometown acquaintance to remark that he "never knew a writer and a man so different. The only link between them was the wit that flashed both in the printed page and in the everyday speech."[77]

Never resolved, this ambivalence in Porter's nature manifested itself in a variety of seeming contradictions. Against the widespread public acclaim he so rapidly earned, there were his continuing private fear, self-imposed loneliness, and insecurity. In contrast to his avoidance of ordinary social functions, there was his constant solitary prowling about strange haunts, his mingling with whores and cancan dancers in Bowery clip joints like the Haymarket and with the crowds at burlesque shows, bowling alleys, and shooting galleries. Though he knew intimately and thoroughly enjoyed this seamier side of New York life, there were also his unfailing courtesy, kindness, generosity, and decency toward others, even the most downtrodden—his Christlike compassion for the suffering, as Anne Partlan called it, and his oft-noted refusal to tell dirty stories.

But the contradictions in Porter's character went deeper than these, as Gilman Hall noted in commenting on the "two antagonistic strains, aristocratic and common," revealed alternately when he had money or lacked it.[78] His lavish spending itself— those fabulous gratuities he scattered everywhere like an oriental potentate—was perhaps an outer sign of a deep-seated insecurity, coupled as it was with an irresponsibility toward debts that kept pace with his needs and were rarely repaid.[79] There were even contradictions, apparently, in his attitudes toward and relations with the exploited shopgirls, showgirls, and prostitutes whom he romantically immortalized in stories like "Past One at Rooney's," "The Memento," and "An Unfinished Story"—young women who, as one of them puts it, have to fight against men "all the way down the line from the manager who wants us to try his new motor-car to the bill-posters who want to call us by out front names . . . men leering and blathering at you across tables, trying to buy you with Würzburger or Extra Dry, according to their estimate of your price. . . . *When you know one man you know 'em all!*"[80] For on at least one occasion Porter is said to have confessed that he himself was Piggy, the suave, fat villain whose advances were rejected by Dulcie, the hungry shopgirl.[81]

Contrasts like these within the man and between the man and his work might be multiplied at length to support the view that "Porter lived in exile from the world, a self-imposed exile from which he never succeeded in escaping and which was the inevitable conclusion to an inner conflict dating back to the family situation of his boyhood."[82] Similarly, the contention that this inner conflict is reflected in his writings, which for all their multiplicity of sharply observed realistic detail are never fundamentally realistic in tone or texture, can be documented again and again. Almost invariably, his stories develop a literature of escape, a negation or refutation of life's grinding complexities and bitter defeats; whether in business, labor, social relations, marriage, or family life, they present human affairs not in the framework of their complex actuality—as Porter knew them to be—but in that of the heart's desire. They are the essence of popular romance. But to admit this critically is not necessarily to condemn. For at the heart of O. Henry's stories there is a quality of fulfillment which, as Carl Van Doren long ago observed

> is the supernatural providence of the world of fiction, and the changes which have come over the fashions in heroes and manners have not essentially altered it. Heracles, happening by, wrests Alcestis from the death that has been decreed; St. George appears just at the moment of despair and defends the English against the horrible Saracens; exactly at the right instant, in *The Church with an Overshot Wheel*, the stream of flour sifts

down through the gallery floor and reveals the lost Aglaia to her father. Deity, saint, coincidence—something must furnish the element of wonder and the desired miracle. One should not be misled by the fact that new names have been given to the mysterious agent. Named or nameless, it has existed and exists to accomplish in art the defeated aspirations of reality. It is O. Henry's most powerful aid, brilliant in his endings, everywhere pervasive. His strong virtue was the genius to select from the apparent plane of fact whatever might bear testimony to the presence in life of this fiery spirit of romance. By this he spoke to the public with something of the authority of a priest of their well-trusted providence.[83]

Assuredly, this priestly authority made O. Henry the spokesman of the 1900's, and it has kept his works alive and vibrant ever since in the popular consciousness throughout the world—despite the indifference and scorn of the literary critics. During the two-year period he served the *World* and scarcely missed a single weekly deadline, Porter produced for that newspaper alone 113 stories, which were syndicated all over the United States; moreover, twenty-five longer ones were published in monthly magazines like *Everybody's*, *McClure's*, and *Munsey's*. To keep up such a grueling pace, he developed a variety of tricky techniques which in varying combinations made up the streamlined "feature" package bearing the unmistakable O. Henry trademarks: the chatty, shortcut opening; the catchy, piquant descriptive phrasing; the confidential, reminiscent narrator; the chance meeting of old pals; and half a dozen or more versions of the surprise ending. Reading consecutively through the entire series of his *World* stories, one senses now and then the strain of composition, the effort to patch something or other together to meet the next week's deadline; but this quality would not have been so noticeable to his weekly readers. Rather, they marveled at his astonishing inventiveness of plot—always the same old sentimental themes of sacrificial devotion, recaptured dreams, integrity restored, and love triumphant; but they were ever in new combinations, settings, and situations.

By 1905, when Porter signed another contract with *Munsey's,* allowing that periodical a first refusal of all his future stories and calling for a rate of ten cents a word to him for all it published, the routine had begun to tell on him.[84] His pace was slowing down as the demand for his stories rose, and it was becoming more and more difficult for him to meet his deadlines. Yet he managed somehow to keep up, partly by juggling his story assets, stalling off one publisher's demands while satisfying another's more insistent ones; partly by developing an unbelievable speed of composition; and partly by purchasing plots from friends when the well ran dry. He kept a notebook for jotting down on the spot swift impressions and ideas for plots wherever in his wanderings they might occur to him; and on numerous occasions he was reported to have dashed off in an hour or so a whole story originating in a chance remark overheard or a fleeting glimpse obliquely captured; sometimes, in fact, he worked up two stories simultaneously while the impatient illustrator sat nearby waiting for his deadline copy. In just such a manner was one of the most famous of all his stories, "The Gift of the Magi," allegedly put together.[85] Whatever the method used to supply the needed copy, it is easy to see why a friend later exclaimed that "if Porter had written twenty-four hours a day with both hands he could not have turned out a tenth of the work sought by competing editors."[86] As a result of such demand, Porter was making more money than ever, averaging over $600 a month in 1905-06; yet he was as always chronically in debt. His need for money constantly outstripped his productive speed.[87]

By this time, too, he had undertaken a new venture destined to establish his permanent fame—the publication of his stories in book form. The idea of reissuing them this way had been in his mind for some time; but because short story collections as compared to novels still had little market value in the early 1900's, he put off the attempt until Witter Bynner suggested a plan of tying together his Central American stories by means of a single narrative thread to produce a simulated novel. Working in tandem, chiefly with scissors and paste pot, the two men thus turned out Porter's first book, *Cabbages and Kings,* published by McClure, Phillips and Company in November, 1904. The book was not an immediate financial success, but it drew favorable reviews and apparently sold reasonably well outside the United States, besides spearheading Porter's new career as a writer of books.[88]

When his second book, *The Four Million,* appeared in April, 1906, his world-wide fame was assured. A collection of twenty-five stories—most of them taken from the *World's* files and including top favorites like "The Gift of the Magi," "The

Furnished Room," "The Cop and the Anthem," and "An Unfinished Story"—this book broadcast to the far corners of the
earth Porter's message of the nameless "little people." As a refutation of Ward McAllister's chilly claim of significance for an
exclusive list of the "400," Porter's assertion that four million
New Yorkers were as well worth noticing in print touched a
magic democratic chord that not only made New York City his
own special province, but also appealed to everyone everywhere.
Like its predecessor, *The Four Million* did not draw an immediate avalanche of praise, but its appeal has been steady and
long lasting, as anyone can see by simply comparing the battered,
thumb-smudged copies of this volume with the dozen others of
an O. Henry set in any public library. There is perhaps no
way of estimating accurately how many millions of copies of the
The Four Million have been read and re-read all over the
world since 1906. But besides public acceptance at that time,
the book also received some favorable notice from serious literary
critics, who began comparing Porter to de Maupassant and other
eminent writers; so that now, although he allegedly shrugged
off this newly won kudos with a wave of the hand, he could
be certain that further volumes of his stories would be promptly
noticed.[89]

These books followed fairly regularly during his remaining
years and after his death. In 1907 and 1908 came *The Trimmed
Lamp* and *The Voice of the City,* bringing to seventy-five his
total of New York stories in book form; and during the same
years two more volumes were published, *Heart of the West* and
The Gentle Grafter, containing chiefly stories based on Porter's
experiences in Texas and in prison. Then, in 1909 two more
volumes of mixed contents appeared, *Roads of Destiny* and
Options; a third, *Strictly Business*—containing twenty-two more
New York stories, plus "A Municipal Report"—was published in
1910 shortly before his death. Still to come were the posthumous
volumes: in 1910, *Whirligigs,* with a dozen more New York
stories and a mixture of others, including "A Blackjack Bargainer"
and "The Ransom of Red Chief"; in 1911, *Sixes and Sevens,*
with fifteen more New York stories and a similar mixture of
others; in 1912, *Rolling Stones,* a mélange of unfinished stories
and other fugitive pieces dating from Porter's earliest writings;
and in 1917, *Waifs and Strays,* a further collection of the same
sort implied in the title. Nor was the list of volumes complete

even yet: for in 1920 a few more waifs and strays showed up in a limited edition entitled *O. Henryana,* which contained Porter's first story written for the *Sunday World,* "The Elusive Tenderloin"; and in 1936 came the quite important collection of his Houston *Post* sketches, edited by Mary S. Harrell and entitled *O. Henry Encore.*[90]

The Trimmed Lamp and *The Voice of the City* were greeted with the same enthusiasm inspired by *The Four Million,* since they brought together more of the same delightful vignettes of New York City life, which by now were receiving the plaudits of staid literary oracles like the *North American Review.* O. Henry, said the critic of this journal, had "breathed new life into the short story. . . . his mastery of the vernacular, his insight into the life of the disinherited . . . [and his] combination of technical excellence with whimsical, sparkling wit, abundant humor and a fertile invention [are] so rare that the reader is content without comparisons."[91] In contrast to this acclaim, however, the stories in *Heart of the West* and *The Gentle Grafter* were regarded as a distinct disappointment, partly because they were not concerned with "little old New York," as one critic put it, but chiefly because their basic intention, even their *genres,* were misunderstood. These stories were pompously condemned on the grounds of indelicacy, as being cheaply clever and grotesquely exaggerated: "His Texan cow punchers talk like intoxicated dictionaries, old-fashioned minstrels, and the advance agents of a wild west show. . . . At a time when such quality as he has shown is rare, Mr. Porter must take that talent a trifle more seriously."[92]

Toward the end of 1907, however, there was not much hilarity left in Porter's soul. Though at the peak of his success and though his stories were in great demand, he was world-weary and on the verge of a crack-up. To avoid importunate publishers, he had moved several times, settling finally in the Caledonia Hotel, where he practically barricaded himself against all intrusions. Because of flagging energies his output had noticeably fallen off; for he published only eleven new stories in 1907 as against nineteen in 1906 and 120 in the two years before that. Moreover, he had drifted into a second marriage, apparently without considering how temperamentally unsuited he would be as a husband.

As in almost any of his own improbably sentimental stories,

Porter's courtship of Sara Lindsay Coleman had grown out of the chance discovery her mother made on a visit to Greensboro in 1905 that the famous New York writer O. Henry was the same hometown boy, Will Porter, who had played with her twenty-five years before. Sara, now a spinster of thirty-seven with literary inclinations of her own and with several published stories in the *Delineator,* admired O. Henry's work enough to write him and ask if he was the boy "who once liked a small girl in a green-sprigged muslin dress," mentioning by the way that she "loved his story 'Madame Bo-Peep of the Ranches.' "[93] Porter, who gaily confirmed his identity, kept up the correspondence thereafter, gradually warming up to the suitor's role throughout the next two years, advising her and encouraging her literary efforts, and finally urging her to come and visit him. She did so in the summer of 1907; and, when they met on his birthday, Porter proposed to her and was accepted. They were married in November, but not before Porter had manfully overcome the agonizing problem of confessing his past and giving Sara the opportunity to back out.

From almost any viewpoint the marriage was doomed to failure. Not only was it difficult for them to readjust to each other's fixed habits; Margaret also joined the family, and the strain was intensified by the increased demands now being made on Porter's diminishing creative energy and poor health. Since his need for money was greater than ever and since writing stories was the only way to obtain it, he drove himself remorselessly, producing twenty-nine new ones in 1908 for an income of about $14,000. But the effort was torture and the income still insufficient for his lavish way of living. In addition to a Long Island cottage requiring two servants, he rented a second apartment in New York where he could write undisturbed; and, when this arrangement failed, he rented still another luxurious one in Washington Place in the fall of 1908. But the strains of his marriage deepened as his health and energy failed; so that by the summer of 1909 these efforts to maintain a normal family life were abandoned. Sara returned to Asheville for a long visit, Margaret was sent to another school in New Jersey, and Porter reverted to his old bachelor habits.[94]

As his health declined during these final months, Porter grew morbidly dissatisfied with his stories; they now seemed purposeless, their surprise endings "nothing but a trick" that he was tired of fooling with. He wanted to do more serious work, and he actually planned a whole series of stories intended to draw a contrast between the Old South and the New—"to show up the professional Southerner who was still trying to blame all of his troubles on the Civil War," as against the new Southerner who was too busy making good to worry about lost causes. His idea was outlined in sufficient detail to gain a contract from *Collier's*, but the series was never written—nor was the long serious novel which Porter planned and which he used to convince his publishers, Doubleday, Page and Company, that he deserved generous cash advances.[95] While purportedly working on the novel, he was actually collaborating with Franklin P. Adams in composing the musical comedy *Lo!*, based on his recent story "He Also Serves," one of the last few he published in 1908. Though most of his effort the following year went into the play, it folded during the road tryouts before reaching New York. But it attracted the attention of another theatrical producer, George Tyler, who tried to interest Porter in writing a dramatization of his early tale "A Retrieved Reformation."

Now toward the end of 1909, his health shattered, and still desperately in need of money, Porter passed up the chance of a lifetime. He had finally accepted his friend Harry Steger's advice to take a prolonged rest cure and had gone to visit Sara in Asheville, where he stayed for the next five or six months, still deluding himself that the "neurasthenia" which had baffled his New York physicians for over a year could be cured with fresh air and hill climbing, as related in his amusing posthumous story "Let Me Feel Your Pulse."[97] But while there, instead of writing the play Tyler wanted, he insisted on doing another based on his story "The World and the Door"; and when Tyler, impatient over the delay, offered him $500 for the dramatic rights to "A Retrieved Reformation," Porter sold them for that sum. The story was turned over to another writer, Paul Armstrong, who emerged after a week's concentrated effort with *Alias Jimmy Valentine*, one of the smash hits of the era, which brought Armstrong over $100,000 in royalties by the end of its first run.[98] Having missed that boat, Porter still tried to interest Tyler in backing his proposal to finance a play based on "The World and the Door"; and he managed, before returning to New York in March, 1910, to extract from him advances of over $1,200, virtually a gift on Tyler's part, for the play was never written.[99]

When Porter went back to the Caledonia, he was finished and doubtless knew it; but he kept up the brave pretense that his creative faculties were still unimpaired. He could no longer summon up enough energy in a week to finish a short story which several years before he could have tossed off in a few hours; yet he did not want to die, he told Anne Partlan, because he was "swamped with obligations" that had to be fulfilled. Virtually an invalid during these last few weeks (his "neck stood in his collar like a stick in a pond, his face mercilessly lined, his lisp a broken whisper murmured with an effort," said H. M. Lyons, the staff member of *Hampton's Magazine* who completed "The Snow Man," one of the last stories Porter tried to write before his death[100]), he refused all company and rarely emerged from his room. He kept himself alive with whiskey until his collapse on the evening of June 3. Among the last to see him still conscious were Anne Partlan, whom he summoned by telephone, and her physician, Dr. Charles Russell Hancock, who took him to the Polyclinic Hospital. Sharp of wit to the end (for he is said to have told the attendant who inquired his name: "Call me Dennis. My name will be Dennis in the morning."), though suffering from an advanced stage of cirrhosis of the liver and diabetes, he died there on the morning of Sunday, June 5. After a funeral service in the Little Church Around the Corner, he was taken to Asheville for burial.

Porter's end, like his beginning, was touched with pathos and irony. "He had no property, or keepsakes, or anything," Doctor Hancock recalled; and he had apparently made no preparations to have his wife come to him in time. Owing thousands of dollars advanced to him by the Roaches, by publishers, and by numerous friends, he died unknown and unrecognized—and possibly unmourned by all but a handful of the literary folk who attended his funeral service. By a final quirk of fate that he would have appreciated, even that was hastily pushed along to make way for a wedding thoughtlessly scheduled for the same hour. Yet Porter had given pleasure to millions through his stories, and he had made the name "O. Henry" an indelible symbol in American life.[101]

CHAPTER 2

O. Henry's Southern Literary Heritage

THE FACT THAT PORTER seriously intended writing a series of stories on the contemporary South, and even worked out a detailed outline for them, is a clear indication of his life-long attachment to the spirit of his native region. Had he lived to carry out his plan, a significant new chapter might possibly have been added both to the annals of Southern literature and to his own literary career; for few writers of his generation were better equipped than he to capture the essential traits of Southern life and character. Like the old Negro hack driver in "A Municipal Report," "He knew; *he knew;* HE KNEW."

Between the publication of "Vereton Villa" in 1896 and "Let Me Feel Your Pulse" in 1910, Porter published about twenty-eight other short stories which are either laid in a Southern setting (exclusive of Texas and the Southwest) or concerned with the activities and inclinations of Southern characters as opposed to those of characters from other backgrounds. Numerically, these stories add up to less than one-tenth of Porter's total output, but they fully establish his claim to a Southern literary heritage. Some of them connect him with the ante-bellum Southern tall-tale humor tradition; others, with the post-Civil War Southern local-color school; and all of them display the unmistakable characteristics of Southern attitudes, manners, and speech. Close study of Porter's Southern stories with reference to these three points reveals that his methods in them produce a subtle blend of two basic strains in Southern fiction—the frontier strain and the local-color strain; and this blend can be further seen as a dominant characteristic in nearly all the rest of Porter's fiction, particularly in those stories dealing with Texas outlaws and with swindlers, embezzlers, and fugitives from justice. Though few in number, these Southern stories offer an important key to the understanding of his work as a whole.

The basic features of Southern frontier humorous fiction, as shown by numerous authorities,[1] emerged from the fluid, open, unregulated social conditions of the old South, as opposed to the more settled, organized patterns of life established in New England towns and villages. The frontier was the natural habitat of the adventurer and the rogue, whose characteristics—like those of Hooper's Simon Suggs—were "nomadism, insensibility to danger, shrewdness, nonchalance, gaiety."[2] From the exploits of frontier heroes possessing these qualities—Mike Fink's bottomless capacity for whiskey and Davy Crockett's unerring aim—grew the oral literature of the frontier, a richly humorous body of folklore, whose comic appeal was based on physical prowess, amoral attitudes, and relaxed ethical motivation.

But the form of the frontier tall tale was as important as its content, if not more so; for it depended on the skillful characterization of a narrator, or *raconteur* who was capable of holding an audience spellbound as he spun his fantastic yarns and of employing a racy, untutored vernacular peculiar to his own background and locale. Typically, these yarns told of comic experiences encountered while traveling, attending to business, enjoying a wedding or a frolic, or—most often—while hunting. To lend authenticity to them, and thus enhance their comic flavor, their authors generally set them forth in a simulated or "mock" oral framework. Opening with a brief descriptive passage to set up the scene and situation—usually a fireside gathering after the day's hunt—the story introduces the narrator, who, after a few more descriptive lines about his outward appearance, voice, and gestures, drifts naturally into the telling of his tale, which then moves along swiftly through its linked scenes to an explosive conclusion. A brief passage might also be tacked on at the end to describe the effect of the yarn on the assembled listeners.

This age-old device proved its effectiveness through the hundreds of variations with which it could be manipulated and developed, its seeming artlessness giving it dramatic force and the illusion of reality in the person of the narrator, and its comic appeal resting upon several types of incongruity between the narrator and his yarn and the circumstances under which he tells it. Literally hundreds of these yarns, written by Southerners before the Civil War, appeared in newspapers and were reprinted in a popular New York sporting journal, *The Spirit of the Times*, which was widely read in the South between 1830 and 1860.[3] Thus, at the heart of the humorous tall tale, whether written by the old Southern frontier yarnspinners or later by O. Henry, there is a funny narrator plus incongruity—the juxtaposition of unexpected, inharmonious elements built into the structure of the story.[4] As his technique developed, O. Henry could do this kind of thing with great finesse, yet preserve its essential spirit of rollicking gaiety by toning down its vulgar explosiveness, as in "The Rose of Dixie" or "Hostages to Momus."

In doing so, however, he moved in the direction of local-color regionalism, taking his cue from a host of later Southern writers who exploited the manifold picturesqueness of the post-Civil War South in a variety of ways. The local-color movement, though a national literary phenomenon shared as well by Eastern and Western writers, was ideally suited to the basic aims of the Reconstruction era; and, while Porter was growing to manhood in the 1870's and 1880's, it served as a means of restoring the South to respectable literary company on the national scene. Continuing in force till the end of the century, it produced a flood of stories from the pens of such writers as G. W. Cable, J. C. Harris, Mary N. Murfree, Constance F. Woolson, Thomas N. Page, Sherwood Bonner, Kate Chopin, Grace King, and many others. The parallels between their stories and many of O. Henry's are too numerous and too obvious to leave the relationship between them in doubt.

Though varying considerably in their work from writer to writer, the local colorists tacitly adopted certain norms, dictated by the prevailing taste of the age; and they followed certain common practices in their portrayal of regional life. Judged by the standards of their time, most of them were contributing, sometimes daringly, to an emerging concept of realism, though by present standards a realism decidedly limited. In representing the life peculiar to their respective regions, their fidelity to the actual scene can be noted first in their treatment of setting, rendered in more or less literal photographic detail; second, in their effort to transcribe in dialogue form the actual demotic speech of the region, despite its jarring impurities of grammar and idiom; third, and much less frequently, in their attempts to depict a logical cause-and-effect relationship between the backgrounds and the behavior of their characters.[5]

The limits beyond which most local colorists would not venture were set by the taboos of their time, and O. Henry along with the rest willingly adhered to these restrictions. (He resented being compared to de Maupassant, for example, and often boasted that his works contained nothing unclean.[6]) Many of them tended to focus on the past rather than the present in order to idealize human behavior by casting over it a misty, nostalgic glow, as Thomas Nelson Page did in glorifying the age of slavery. Most of them studiously avoided the unpleasant and the sordid, preferring to go along with the popular demand for stories "that end well," even when a note of tragedy was involved—a practice visible in the vast majority of O. Henry's stories. Practically all of them likewise ignored the problem of sexuality in either its psychological or physiological manifestations, regardless of the social levels and relationships presented in their stories. The local colorists, accordingly, tended "to make oddities seem picturesque, to make the primitive seem romantic; . . . they specialized in cultural islands where peculiarities had survived, or they depicted a past age during which local individuality had flourished. . . . Significantly, a large proportion of local-color fiction concerns itself with the poor, yet it must quickly be said that poverty is generally accepted as a fact of life, sometimes with a recognition of its hardships, sometimes with a sentimental view of its compensations; the note of protest is exceptional."[7]

How well O. Henry's Southern stories fit into the foregoing general patterns may be seen by examining in some detail their dominant characteristics and the resulting sub-classes which these characteristics suggest. For convenience's sake, the twenty-eight stories may be divided into four groups: (a) tall tales; (b) local-color romances; (c) romantic adventure tales with incidental local-color touches; (d) blended local-color tall tales. Such a classification is, of course, arbitrary; but its relevance to O. Henry's Southern stories may be demonstrated in the following terms: the eight stories in group (a) are labeled tall tales because, though laid in the South, their chief interest resides in the interplay of narrator and plot, a series of wildly improbable adventures that might have occurred anywhere; on the other hand, the six stories in group (b) are distinctively local-color romances, since the close relationship in them between setting and character motivation is clearly intended to determine the development and outcome of the plot. The other two groups,

(c) and (d), are further distinguished by the presence or absence of definite tall-tale characteristics in the stories; for all fourteen show at least some traces of local-color influence.

I *The Tall Tales*

Significantly, six of the eight stories listed here as tall tales appear in a single volume, *The Gentle Grafter,* a collection of fourteen stories centering about the activities of swindlers and con-men, which O. Henry is said to have picked up from his cronies in the Ohio Penitentiary. *The Gentle Grafter* is of interest to students of O. Henry for several reasons: first, it is the only volume in the O. Henry canon containing a majority of stories which were not previously published or later reprinted in magazines, Porter having written them specifically for this collection during his final spurt of productivity in 1908. Second, it is the only volume in which a central character dominates all but three of the stories in it. Strictly speaking, all fourteen stories in the collection are tall tales of the picaresque variety; but only six of them are laid in the South. Of these six, five are concerned with the exploits of the narrator, Jeff Peters, who is O. Henry's most fully rounded character.[8]

Jeff Peters, the Gentle Grafter, is an amusing rogue whose doctrine is "a kind of mulct 'em in parvo" (3) and whose lineage goes back in the tradition of picaresque fiction to Lazarillo de Tormes and to Robin Hood. But more in the manner of Harris' Sut Lovingood, Jeff carries the narrative forward, chiefly in dialogue form; and much of the humor in any of his yarns emerges from his free-wheeling colloquial speech, full of outrageous puns and malapropisms, usually couched in a pseudo-erudite style. The rest of the humor is lodged in the absurd predicaments and petty grafting schemes which he tells of having shared with his partner, Andy Tucker. Though all of these stories could have come straight out of the old *Spirit of the Times,* most bear the unmistakable trademark of O. Henry's surprise ending.

In "Jeff Peters as a Personal Magnet," Jeff tells of his "earlier days when he sold liniments and cough cures on street corners" and got picked up (despite a $5.00 bribe) by the constable of Fisherville, Arkansas, while disposing of "Resurrection Bitters" at fifty cents a bottle without a city license. In the mayor's office next day he met his future partner, Andy, also low in funds and in search of easy graft; and the two managed, through a complicated series of moves undisclosed until the end, to outwit the authorities and make off with $250, the capital with which they went into business together. Later, in "A Midsummer Masquerade," while resting from their swindling labors, they vacation at a mountain resort in Tennessee (probably Gatlinburg), posing as visiting dignitaries at the request of the proprietor of the Woodchuck Inn—also a swindler—because he did not want to disappoint a houseful of normal school teachers lured there with the expectation of meeting the Duke of Marlborough and Peary, the polar explorer. As Andy comments at the outset: "'I want to loaf and indict my soul, as Walt Whittier says'" (89).

Often the best wit of an O. Henry yarn comes in the first page or so, as he warms up to his plot by dropping some ironic wisecrack with a topical allusion related to his main theme. In "Shearing the Wolf," for example, Jeff begins as usual by ruminating about the ethics of the swindler's profession and about the difference between his standards and his partner's: "I didn't approve of all of Andy's schemes for levying contributions from the public, and he thought I allowed my conscience to interfere too often for the good of the firm. We had high arguments sometimes. Once one word led to another till he said I reminded him of Rockefeller." Jeff accepted the taunt but, turning the other cheek, reminded Andy that he had yet "to shake hands with a subpoena server" (99). And so he launched into another tale of how he and Andy fleeced a hypocritical small-town Kentucky merchant who was bent on exposing for his own profit a mail-order, counterfeiting scheme. In "The Man Higher Up" O. Henry varies this opening technique by setting himself up as his own narrator; he explains in the first page how much he enjoyed Jeff's winter visits to New York during his off-season, his range of swindling activities then being from Spokane to Tampa. Then he lets Jeff take over by classifying three kinds of graft, his own and two illegitimate sorts:

> "'There are two kinds of grafts,' said Jeff, 'that ought to be wiped out by law. I mean Wall Street speculation and burglary.'
> "'Nearly everybody will agree with you as to one of them,' said I with a laugh.
> 'Well, burglary ought to be wiped out, too,' said Jeff, and I wondered whether the laugh had been redundant." (p. 138)

Again, in "The Ethics of Pig" Jeff relates "his latest Autolycan adventure" (22), which occurred the preceding summer during his temporary association with a hog stealer, Rufe Tatum, whom he employed to act as decoy in a shell game he was operating at a county fair in Kentucky, but who mulcted him instead to the tune of $800, proving his original point concerning the difficulty of finding a reliable partner in graft.

Taken singly, the Jeff Peters yarns are mildly amusing, but over a long haul their thinness of invention grows as tedious as a string of Mack Sennett comedies. In "Hostages to Momus," however, one of several in *The Gentle Grafter* that O. Henry had published earlier, he reached the peak of the fantastic in recounting a ludicrous kidnaping, the idea for which he is said to have derived from Twain's *Adventures of Tom Sawyer*.[9] Here the protagonist is another bumbling swindler, Parleyvoo Pickens, who begins by telling how he and his buddy, Caligula Polk "of Muskogee in the Creek Nation" (198)—having been run out of Mexico and later New Orleans for running a crooked lottery—found their way to Mountain Valley, Georgia, where they conceived the idea, after sampling a wretched breakfast of hog and hominy, of kidnaping the town banker, Colonel Jackson T. Rockingham, president of the Sunrise and Edenville Tap Railroad, and of holding him for a ransom of $10,000. Their venture is undertaken, but it is completely frustrated by their expensive methods of entertaining the kidnapee with rich foods—and by the fact that the president's profitless railroad has been mortgaged eight times, his gullied land sold and re-sold for taxes, and that neither he nor anyone else in the community has anything to eat but hog and hominy. The yarn is utterly ridiculous, yet a fine example of the ante-bellum tall tale. The sheer absurdity of the situation; its pure fantasy, exaggerations, satire, wise-cracking; its contrast between poverty-stricken, eroded land and miserable diet on one hand and the pretension of social status and appreciation of a gourmet's delicacies on the other—all evoke a tissue of incongruities straight out of the frontier humor tradition.

A still better example—perhaps the best, as Booth Tarkington insisted[10]— is "The Ransom of Red Chief," another kidnaping tale cut on a pattern similar to O. Henry's many other con-man yarns, but with no wastage of words or cute posturings. Sam, the narrator, begins the story: "'It looked like a good thing: but wait till I tell you. We were down South, in Alabama—Bill Driscoll and myself—when this kidnaping idea struck us. It was, as Bill afterward expressed it, 'during a moment of temporary mental apparition;' but we didn't find that out till later'" (100).

The nearly homonymous "apparition" sets the comic tone precisely and is supported by similar miscues scattered throughout the tale whenever Bill is quoted by his more learned partner who tosses off terms like "Undeleterious" and "philoprogenitiveness," thus balancing off the malapropisms with an amusing linguistic contrast. But the beauty of this story inheres in its combination of elements neatly fitted together: the absurd situation of two grown men reduced to exhaustion and desperation by their victim; the boy's audacity and exuberant high spirits in contrast to their weary discomfiture; the dryness of his father's "counter proposition," an offer to take Johnny off the kidnaper's hands for $250 in cash; the narrator's serious, dead-pan tone throughout—these together with the sparkling word play combine to make a delightful yarn, understandably a great popular favorite still among high school anthologists.

By comparison, "Phoebe," published the same year, is poor stuff despite a profusion of fantastic adventures stuffed into the same "mock oral" mold.[11] The opening scene, laid in a Congo Square bistro in New Orleans, introduces the yarnspinner as a surprisingly experienced young ship captain named Patricio Malone—"a Hiberno-Iberian creole who had gone to and fro in the earth and walked up and down in it"—and starts him off on the subject of luck, telling a tiresome string of mishaps suffered by a sailor called Bad-luck Kearny. Every activity Kearny got into turned sour, he was convinced, because of the evil influence of *Phoebe*, a small red satellite of the planet Saturn. But the reader is worn out long before reaching the end of Kearny's troubles while he is on a filibustering expedition in Central America—troubles climaxed by his marriage to a huge domineering woman named Phoebe. Though the form of the tall tale is present in this story, its spirit of rollicking humor misfires.

II   *The Local-Color Stories*

Something of the same unevenness is noticeable in the six local-color stories of the South chosen here as models of O. Henry's mastery of this *genre*; yet all six offer striking examples of his ability to combine and render in convincingly realistic dialogue and narrative the remembered experiences from his North Carolina background, his own personal history, and his first-hand observations of the various types and classes of people he had known. Several of them, moreover, are generally recognized as being among his finest stories. These six are "A Blackjack Bargainer," "The Duplicity of Hargraves," "The Guardian of the Accolade," "The Emancipation of Billy," "Blind Man's Holiday," and "A Municipal Report."[12] All but the last of these stories were among O. Henry's earliest efforts, most having been written during his prison days and published shortly afterward.

Aside from the authenticity of dialect, perhaps the outstanding characteristic shared almost equally by these stories is their feeling of place—the rightness of the setting and the people in it. With a few broad strokes O. Henry establishes the linkages between them; so that however implausible the plot, the skeptical reader is disarmed and taken in by the illusion, at least temporarily. "A Blackjack Bargainer," for example, develops a rather specious plot based on the hackneyed theme of a wastrel's noble self-sacrifice to preserve a last shred of family honor. It rests on hackneyed "Old South" characterization, family feuds, chivalric codes, and the like; and the problem of the disreputable lawyer Yancey Goree, who drinks and gambles away his entire family estate and then sells even the rights to the long-standing feud between his family and the Coltranes, is absurd. Yet O. Henry manages to arouse interest and to suppress disbelief by injecting into the story the social aspirations of ignorant but *nouveau riche* hill folk, the Pike Garveys, and thus creating an ironical class conflict which the reader is anxious to see worked out. The sentimental denouement may be hard to swallow today, but the motivation of the three leading characters is understandable in terms of their respective backgrounds.

In "The Duplicity of Hargraves" the close relationship between character and background again produces a satisfying variety of local-color romance, but in it the immediate setting is less important than the reflected one. The story is laid in Washington, where the impoverished "Major Pendleton Talbot, of Mobile, sir, and his daughter, Miss Lydia" have come to stay in a modest boardinghouse while he finishes writing his book, "Anecdotes and Reminiscenses of the Alabama Army, Bench, and Bar,"[13] the anticipated sales of which are their only hope for survival. But the tall, courtly, old-fashioned Major lives entirely in the past, leaving the petty present-day datails of board and laundry bills to his daughter; and that past—"the splendid, almost royal, days of the old planters" with their thousands of slaves and bales of cotton, their fox hunts, 'possum suppers, hoedowns, jubilees, and all the rest[14]—is the real subject of the story, though with a typical O. Henry twist. The only person interested in the Major's garrulous reminiscences is a young character actor, Hargraves, who listens to them by the hour, studying the Major closely in order to reproduce in a stage play all the lost glory he symbolizes. When the Major chances to see himself thus represented, even to the least detail of his mint-julep ritual, he is outraged; but the play is a great success, bringing fortune to Hargraves and enabling him through the duplicity of another role to thwart the Major's animosity and his poverty by playing the part of a long-forgotten ex-slave, Cindy's Mose, who comes to Washington just in time to square an old debt. With extraordinary deftness, especially in his management of Negro dialect in the climactic scene, O. Henry weaves together past and present, background and character motivation; and all are rendered in a finely restrained tone of mingled irony and pathos.

Light irony is perhaps the distinguishing quality that rescues O. Henry's portrayal of "Old South" values from the sticky sentimentality found in many of the earlier groups of Southern local-color stories. Suffused throughout the texture of his better tales, this irony reveals both a genuine admiration for and a critical re-appraisal of a vanished era. It functions again as an undercutting instrument in "The Guardian of the Accolade" and in "The Emancipation of Billy," both of which are clearly based on recollections of Greensboro, Porter's bibulous father, and the "old timers" who hung around his Uncle Clark's drugstore. Both stories recapture a glimpse of the past—tenderly, but with a touch of foolery. The first centers upon faithful old Uncle Bushrod, and his determination to preserve unspotted the family escutcheon of his boss, Robert Weymouth, president of the local bank, by making him hand over, before boarding the train, a suitcase which the old Negro had seen him stuffing in the bank vault. When Weymouth reaches his destination, a fishing rendezvous, he confesses with some chagrin the loss of the suitcase—

which had contained " 'two quarts of the finest old silk-velvet Bourbon . . . you ever wet your lips with' " (39).

Excellent description of the setting and skillfully contrived dialogue passages provide the realistic touch in both these stories; but a different facet of the Old South-New South contrast is revealed in "The Emancipation of Billy." In the person of aged "Governor" Pemberton, grand old Civil War hero, and his daily progress from a musty mansion up Lee Avenue past the First National Bank and the Palace Hotel to the drugstore where Mr. Appleby sets up drinks for the Old Guard, O. Henry symbolizes the pathetic, decadent, nostalgic Old South. The energetic "New South" is embodied in Pemberton's son "Billy," a successful lawyer in his forties who has gained a national reputation by winning cases before the United States Supreme Court, but who, much to his discomfiture, remains in the shadow of his pompous father. He is "Billied" and "sonned" by the older citizens of Elmville until a flamboyant event sets him free. Once more, though climax and denouement are far-fetched, dialogue and description save the day for local-color realism.

In "Blind Man's Holiday" and in "A Municipal Report" O. Henry shifted his focus from the village and small town to the Southern city. His use of a New Orleans setting in the earlier story offers a preview of his future treatment of the New York scene; while the Nashville portrayed in the later one calls to mind the 150 or more Bagdad stories O. Henry had already published when he wrote it. Between the two stories lies a noticeable contrast in tone and technique. As examples of his local-color writing, however, they are alike in one respect: the interest centers in both not so much on the problem of environmental effect on character but rather upon that of psychological tension, upon conflicts of loyalty, honor, duty, and the like, which the leading characters must resolve for themselves irrespective of background influences. In neither did O. Henry attempt to probe very far beneath the surface but resorted to trickery of one sort or another to resolve his crises—an off-stage murder in "A Municipal Report," and a *deus ex machina* in the person of a kindly priest in "Blind Man's Holiday." Nevertheless, he successfully evokes the local scene in both stories.

"Blind Man's Holiday" is a hopelessly idealized hodge-podge based on the hackneyed theme of noble self-sacrifice and strung out through a series of woodenly unconvincing scenes culminating in a didactic harangue that is quite untypical of O. Henry's later work. At issue is the Hamlet-like indecisiveness of Lorison, a drifting young artist, self-exiled for a year in the old French Quarter, who has fallen in love with a girl about whom he knows nothing except her name, Norah Greenway, and the fact that she lives with her brother. Wavering between a delicate sense of honor and pride, he hesitates to declare his love because of guilt feelings over a shadowed past (an obvious parallel with O. Henry's own painful history), but he blurts out a proposal after Norah reveals an equally spotted one. Their hasty marriage, performed by an Irish priest, brings no immediate consummation, however, as Lorison's integrity must be further tested by his wife's plea for one more day of freedom. Assenting but puzzled, he roams the streets until an encounter with a *femme de nuit* under arrest (quite the best scene in the story) drives him into a frenzy of uncertainty over Norah's chastity. In desperation he returns to Father Rogan, who provides reassurance at last by taking him on a guided tour, first to Norah's boardinghouse, to see her brother, a sweet, frail orphan of eight or nine; then to a kind of all-night sweatshop, where the innocent Norah, his sole support, is seen "toiling, toiling" at her sewing machine. Thus, Lorison's blindness is cured! Saturated with bathos of the "true romance" variety, the story may yet interest today's reader as a period piece—as a study in outmoded taste as well as in O. Henry's groping experimentation with fictional autobiography.

In sharp contrast, self-assurance can be felt in every line of "A Municipal Report," which is perhaps justly famed as one of O. Henry's finest efforts, but it hardly deserves any longer the extraordinary praise given it forty or fifty years ago. For in it also economy is sacrificed in the attempt to build up by means of several posturing tricks the narrator's character as an ironic foil for the three principals within the story: Caesar, the faithful old Negro cabby; Major Caswell, the rat; and the starving authoress, Azalea Adair. Following the opening verse by Kipling and the quotation from Norris, for example, there are two paragraphs of wise-cracking about cities to introduce the idea of rashness in predicting that no romance is possible in any given one; then the Rand-McNally thumbnail description of Nashville; then the narrator's further wise-cracking about Nashville's limitations as he checks in at the hotel, eats dinner, and steps out to look over this somnolent little city, where nothing goes on after sundown; and finally, his interception by Caswell, the professional Southern bore, on his return to the hotel. So the story runs on for six pages or so—one-third its full length— with further passages of Chamber-of-Commerce prose on Nashville dropped in here and there before the narrator gets round to revealing his mission in the humdrum little city as an agent of a Northern literary magazine with a contract for Miss Adair. From this point the story does fulfill O. Henry's stated purpose; it also moves swiftly toward its climax and its neatly muted denouement to refute Norris' thoughtless supposition. But in it, as elsewhere, O. Henry's forte is seen chiefly in his management of picturesque dialect and sharp descriptive detail, not in the analysis of complex character in action.

III *Romantic Adventures with Incidental Local Color*

Fundamentally, there is little difference between the stories in the foregoing group and the eight to be considered next except for the noticeably slighter use made in them of regional or local background as an environmental conditioning factor in the development of character and action. All are similar in their dependency upon chance agencies rather than upon logical cause-and-effect happenings to aid in the unraveling of the plot, or upon a sleight-of-hand contrivance to achieve their intended surprise endings. All likewise stress romantic adventure, involving idealized characters of a two-dimensional sort with only superficially distinguishing features; many of their characters might be redistributed among them with relatively little sacrifice of identity. One's interest in reading these stories is fixed therefore primarily on the working out of the plot, which does, of course, reveal the inventiveness for which O. Henry is famous; for plot development in these seven stories varies considerably. In the order of their original publication dates the stories are "Whistling Dick's Christmas Stocking" (1899), the first story published in a national magazine under his pen-name; "Bulger's Friend" (1901); "The Renaissance at Charleroi" (1902); "A Retrieved Reformation" (1903); "October and June" (1903); "The Church with the Overshot Wheel" (1904); "The Door of Unrest" (1904); and "Thimble, Thimble" (1908).[15]

Localized background details function slightly as a means of initiating and concluding the action in "Whistling Dick's Christmas Stocking": the professional hobo's emergence from a boxcar in the midtown, riverfront district of New Orleans; his encounter with the friendly German policeman, Fritz, who moves him on; and his progress down the levee past the French Market toward the Chalmette sugar plantations—all lend authentic local color to the scene. But once Dick reaches the Bellemeade plantation, becomes involved in "Boston Harry's" gang, and saves the unnamed planter's family from armed robbery, the setting has become unimportant. Only the bright, buoyant sounds of Dick's departing whistle, "clear as the cleanest notes of the piccolo," as he hits the road again the following morning, have genuine artistic significance. The same is true of "The Renaissance at Charleroi," a weirdly romantic love story woven of fierce Creole passions reminiscent of Poe and G. W. Cable, but based on the trite plot idea of the vanished brother's miraculous return to reunite two loving hearts. Though heavily freighted with specific details of speech, place names, furnishings, dress, mannerisms— all of which help to evoke an appropriately gallicized south-Louisiana atmosphere—the story could be as effectively rendered with any other combination of Arabian Nights decor.

In contrast to these two, however, the other stories depend even less on localized setting to achieve their effects. "Bulger's Friend," a thin little tale about a miserly Salvation Army convert, is set in an unnamed Southern community. "A Retrieved Reformation," possibly the most profitable of all O. Henry's tales so far as monetary returns from its many dramatized versions are concerned, could have been laid anywhere else in the United States as well as in the little town of Elmore, Arkansas. Actually a rather slight piece of romantic fiction, the story possesses two sure-fire qualities that give it dramatic punch: O. Henry's vividly realistic representation of the burglar's professional equipment, methods, attitudes, and milieu; and the breathless scene of the reformed Jimmy Valentine's cracking open the bank vault in time to rescue the trapped child and thus secure his reprieve from the detective who has been tailing him. That no detective in his right mind would ever behave as Ben Price does in this story is of no consequence to the myriad readers, moviegoers, and television viewers who have taken Jimmy and his creator into their hearts. Similarly, in "The Church with the Overshot

Wheel" the whole interest centers (as Carl Van Doren pointed out long ago) on the miraculous reunion of the kindly old miller and his long-lost Aglaia. The facts that the converted mill that serves as a church happens to be situated in the Cumberland Mountains and that Aglaia grew up in a little town near Atlanta are of no significance to the outcome; for her story is timeless and without geographic limits.

Setting is still less significant in "The Door of Unrest" and in "October and June," but these stories are very different from each other and from those just mentioned. "The Door of Unrest," in fact, is almost unique among O. Henry's many tales, for it is a variation of the Wandering Jew theme as reported through the experience of a small-town newspaper editor vaguely situated somewhere in the South. It is the new editor's encounter with a disheveled old crank who claims personal acquaintance with historic figures as far back in time as Caesar Augustus and beyond, but whose memories of them are uttered in a rich Irish brogue, that provides the interest; this, plus O. Henry's clever word play, which leads to the editor's discovery that his hoary New Testament babbler, Michob Ader, is only the town's drunken old shoemaker, Mike O'Bader, whose periodic affliction of garrulity is the result of a trauma suffered thirty years before when he abandoned his prostitute daughter to the vengeance of an angry mob. Much slighter in substance, "October and June" is merely an expanded anecdotal variation on the ancient theme of marriage between youth and age; it exists solely for the surprise reversal disclosing in the last line that the youthful partner is not the woman as expected, but a nineteen-year-old captain of the Chattanooga cadets.

Clever trickery in the manipulation of details revealed and withheld early became one of O. Henry's best-known devices. His management of it in "October and June" points forward to the more elaborate legerdemain he performed in "Thimble, Thimble," a story frankly acknowledged as an outright imitation of Frank Stockton's sensational "The Lady—or the Tiger?" Though necessarily overshadowed by its more famous model, O. Henry's yarn produced a minor sensation of its own when *Hampton's* magazine held a contest and awarded prizes for the best solutions sent in to the problem raised but not answered by the story.[16] Like the stories of Jimmy Valentine and Hargraves, "Thimble, Thimble" lends itself readily to dramatization and is one of ten stories by O. Henry published as one-act plays in 1934; but it is also analogous to "The Rose of Dixie" in its ironical presentation of "a Southerner's idea of a Northerner's idea of the South," one of Porter's favorite ploys.

Although the setting of "Thimble, Thimble" is a New York business office, the substance and flavor of the story derive about equally from O. Henry's allegiance to his native region and from his "New South" philosophy which honored the ancient traditions of the South but sought to merge them within the broader traditions of the nation. Thus, the issue of the story turns on the question: given two young Americans of common ancestry, equal abilities, opportunities, and personal qualities, but reared in the atmosphere of the Chesapeake on the one hand and in that of Massachusetts Bay on the other, how can one distinguish between them? O. Henry, the old hoaxer, laughingly stands in the wings waiting to baffle the reader as thoroughly as poor old Uncle Jake, who cannot tell the difference between his "young Marster," Blandford Carteret, and Blandford's Yankee cousin, John Carteret. But the underlying idea supporting the comic scene played out on his little stage between the young Carterets, Uncle Jake, and the mercenary *ficelle*, Olivia De Ormond, is a serious one; and without the intimate feeling for the South that O. Henry subtly revealed in the story, much of its effectiveness would be lost.[17]

IV *Local-Color Tall Tales*

The six stories in this last collection of tales reflecting O. Henry's close observation of customs and manners in the South differ from those of the preceding group in two respects: they disclose a somewhat heavier concentration of local-color features; and, in achieving their intended effects, they rely mainly upon tall-tale elements, either farcical or satiric. Strictly speaking, they are neither tall tales nor local-color stories exclusively but rather, at their best, a skillful blend of the two types. They are at their best, moreover, in their later form when O. Henry, having become seasoned through the writing of over two hundred stories, could mix his ingredients with a degree of sophistication and finesse that was lacking at the outset of his career. Three of these stories were among the earliest he wrote, possibly while still in prison or during his sojourn in Pittsburgh. All published in 1903, their titles are "Cherchez La Femme," "The Whirligig of Life," and "Out of Nazareth." The later group, written and published during the last two years of his life, are "The Rose of Dixie" (1908), "Best Seller" (1909), and "Let Me Feel Your Pulse" (1910). Geographically, the Southern settings for these six stories range from Louisiana to Virginia and are functionally significant in all but the last one.[18]

"Cherchez La Femme" is in the local-color vein reminiscent of Cable's writing, which O. Henry must have studiously examined; for he captures here much the same flavor in setting, characterization, dialogue, and tone as may be found in *Old Creole Days*. The story opens with two newspaper reporters (Robbins of the *Picayune* and Dumas of *L'Abeille*) drinking absinthe together "in the little Creole-haunted cafe of Madame Tibault, in Dumaine Street."[19] While scanning the morning's news, one of them spots a reference to a forthcoming auction which leads to their recollection of the mysterious disappearance two years before of the Madame's $20,000 that had been entrusted for safekeeping to a certain M'sieur Morin, deceased. From this point the action develops into a wild and rather expensive goose chase as the two men undertake to discover the hidden treasure, for Dumas insists that the proverb *"cherchez la femme"* would explain both its original loss and present whereabouts. They find it eventually in the form of United States four per cent gold bonds which Madame Tibault had used to paper over a crack in the wall of her own back parlor, ignorantly supposing them to be pretty commercial calendars given her by Morin. Aside from the Madame's fractured French-English ("M'sieur Morin, he leave those li'l peezes papier in those table, and say ver' much 'bout money thass hard for me to ond'stan. *Mais* I never see those money again"),[20] the story is unimpressive. The other two stories are scarcely less so; for even the plots in both "The Whirligig of Life" and "Out of Nazareth" lack spontaneity and inventiveness, as well as the element of surprise expected of O. Henry.

The only feature that saves "The Whirligig of Life" from total impoverishment is O. Henry's sensitive control of picturesque hill-country speech, which makes the characters portrayed by it moderately interesting, even though their actions are manifestly contrived and unbelievable. As Benaja Widdap, the ignorant justice of the peace in a sleepy little east Tennessee mountain settlement, takes the necessary legal steps to grant a divorce to Ransie and Ariela Bilbro for a five-dollar fee; gets robbed of the five dollars so that Ariela can be paid the alimony she demands; and finally regains the same five-dollar bill when he remarries the reconciled couple, the reader can too easily see through the basic contrivance of the plot. But this thinness may be over-looked because the story is presented almost entirely through the dialogue of the three characters whose accusations, admonitions, and reconsiderations are uttered in seemingly natural, unretouched language which is, of course, comically appealing. "Out of Nazareth," however, lacks even this modest compensation; and it rightfully belongs where it is collected, among the poorest of O. Henry's *Waifs and Strays.* A dull, uninspired piece of fiction, the story fails in its attempt to fuse the tall-tale fantasy of an elaborate real-estate swindle in the Georgia hills with the sentimental appeal of aged innocence requited; for the characters, as well as their speech and actions, are implausibly conventionalized.

One turns with relief, therefore, to "The Rose of Dixie" and its uproarious satire of "Old South" stuffiness in the person of Colonel Aquila Telfair, scion of a grand old family, who undertakes to edit a high-minded Southern literary journal in Toombs City, Georgia. Promptly surrounding himself with a staff of impeccably *Confederate* assistants—"a whole crate of Georgia peaches"—the Colonel adamantly refuses to sully his journal with any writings produced by Northerners; for everything in it must conform to the watchword: " 'Of, For, and By the South.' "[21] He wavers slightly when a fast-talking New York sales promotion agent, T. T. Thacker, tries to persuade him to junk a portion of the Southern dead wood scheduled for the next issue and to substitute in its place some popular literary fare from elsewhere so that circulation can be boosted. But in the end the Colonel fills the space tentatively agreed on with an article entitled "Second Message to Congress / Written for / THE ROSE OF DIXIE / BY / A Member of the Well-known / BULLOCH FAMILY OF GEORGIA / T. Roosevelt." Thus, "The Rose of Dixie," though lacking O. Henry's usual romantic appeal of virtue rewarded, love requited, or innocence preserved, still bears his trade-mark, the surprise ending. But better than this is the delightful spoofing that goes on all through the interview between Telfair and Thacker, both of whom are brilliantly conceived: the one with his stiff, self-righteous Southern intransigence; the other with his brash Yankee practicality. The story is not only a splendid take-off of ante-bellum Southern magazines, all the funnier for being at once truthful and yet kindly; but, since the build-up of Thacker is equally barbed, its satire cuts both ways—against over-principled Southern states rightsism, poor but proud; and against unprincipled Northern commercialism, indifferent toward any ideal but that of making a "fast buck."

Light literary satire also carries the reader through "Best Seller," characterized by one critic as a story that "champions the 'Prisoner of Zenda' type of tale, with a commonplace parallel of its seeming improbabilities."[22] The story accomplishes a little more than this, however; for O. Henry's ironic tone throughout subtly parodies both the overdone romantic best seller of the period with its ridiculously contrived escapades between American businessmen and European princesses, as well as his own brand of more commonplace realistic romance. John A. Pescud, the protagonist, who flings down in disgust a novel entitled *The Rose Lady of Trevelyan* because it is so far-fetched, and yet promptly reveals to the narrator his own romantic pursuit of the girl he married (without being aware of its romantic elements), thus plays a dual role: he serves the author as a mouthpiece for ridiculing badly written fiction and as a symbol of ordinary middle-class American life. The idea implicit here is that, although "life has no geographical metes and bounds," to give it valid fictional meaning requires both imagination and finesse. O. Henry is not wholly successful, as the story is marred by too many of his incorrigible pranks and posturings; yet it does show to advantage his mastery of five different varieties of dialogue.

Of all the stories O. Henry ever wrote, he came closest to total success in the art of fusing comedy and pathos, fittingly enough, in the last one he completed during his lifetime: "Let Me Feel Your Pulse."[23] Facing certain death and fully aware that no medicines, nostrums, or panaceas were likely to cure his shattered health, he brought to bear all his talents in fashioning a delightfully ironic little allegory based on his own painful search for relief—his futile interviews with doctors in New York; his extended rest cure in Asheville—but embracing in its sensitive grasp broader implications touching all human endeavor. "So I went to a doctor," his narrator begins. And for the next fifteen pages O. Henry's jocularity bubbles through his account of ordeals endured at doctors' hands as he gets bumped, probed, stuck, prescribed for. At last in the Blue Ridge Mountains he meets old Doctor Tatum, who tells him: "Somewhere in these mountains . . . there's a plant growing—a flowering plant that'll cure you, and it's about the only thing that will. It's of a kind that's as old as the world; but of late it's powerful scarce and hard to find. You and I will have to hunt it up" (170). Almost imperceptibly O. Henry has taken the reader into the realm of fantasy to show him that the only cure he knew for human ills lies in the imagination; for the magic plant they sought together was amaryllis, symbol of love and poetic release since the days of Theocritus.

This story ends with a question that delicately implies all that O. Henry had discovered about himself and the world, and about his relationship to the world as an artist: "What rest more remedial than to sit with Amaryllis in the shade, and, with a sixth sense, read the wordless Theocritan idyl of the gold-bannered blue mountains marching orderly into the dormitories of the night?" (173). All who are familiar with Milton's *Lycidas* will recall that the next few lines following that familiar allusion speak of Fame as the "spur that the clear spirit doth raise . . . To scorn delights, and live laborious days," as well as of "the blind Fury with the abhorred shears [that comes] and slits the thin-spun life."[24] Death was much on O. Henry's mind at this time, but his swan song uttered a clear, pure note.

It is quite conceivable that had O. Henry never seen the South, he would have written as many stories and become just as famous as he did. But it is doubtful that his work would have possessed the same combination of qualities that have set his writings apart from all others of his period and made his name a by-word in the field of popular short fiction. For the most prominent of those qualities—his playfulness and fondness for the exotic, the exaggerated, and the picturesque; his awareness of the distinctive differences between Northern and Southern aims; and especially his sympathetic feeling for changing Southern attitudes—are all products of a Southern literary heritage. Even without his frank avowal of loyalty to Southern ideals, as in "A Municipal Report," the debt he owed to this heritage would be visible in both his tall tales and his local-color romances.

CHAPTER *3*

O. Henry's Western Apprenticeship

IF THE OLD SOUTH was the nursery of O. Henry's art, the West was its prep school. The literary traditions, folkways, interests, and attitudes that he carried with him to Texas as a youth of twenty took their eventual forms of expression largely from the further conditioning he underwent during his fourteen years of literary apprenticeship on the ranch, in Austin, and on the Houston *Post*. Like Hawthorne's twelve years of solitude in Salem before the publication of his *Twice Told Tales*, O. Henry's fourteen years in Texas were also—in a double sense—a period of trial and error during which his genius worked toward the forms best suited to his talents and his interests. Inevitably, his surroundings played an important part in this shaping process; for, much as O. Henry loved books and the chameleon-like qualities of words, he loved even more to observe the flow of life around him—to note its unity in variety—and whenever possible, to capture its color and flavor. The West, particularly Texas, gave him both the raw materials and the incentive with which to work through the arduous task of developing an individual art form and a style of his own. And this debt, at least, he repaid by writing between eighty and one hundred short stories and sketches based on his Western experiences, most of them written and published before he became firmly established on the New York *Sunday World* in December, 1903.

The shaping process began with the early letters O. Henry wrote to friends back in Greensboro in the 1880's; in them he described his new surroundings and activities and contrasted these things with remembered conditions at home. The few surviving letters from this period disclose three qualities that foreshadow the writer to come: an eye for specific detail, a feeling for the suggestive power of words, and a sense of the effect, chiefly risible, which the proper combination of words can produce on the reader. In November he informs Mrs. Hall that the breeze vainly looked for the summer before "is with us now, as cold as Callum Bros. suppose their soda water to be"; and he describes a certain ranch hand as one who "wears a red sash and swears so fluently that he has been mistaken often for a member of the Texas legislature."[1] Warning his friend Dr. Beale to dissuade others from coming to live in Texas, he describes the ranch country as "a silent but eloquent refutation of Bob Ingersoll's theory; a man here gets prematurely insane, melancholy and unreliable and finally dies of lead poisoning."[2] The *double entendre,* slipped in quietly, he knows will be appreciated, along with other effects, by an alert audience of one. To amuse an Austin friend gone to Colorado, for example, he parodies the style of the local newspaper by describing the horrendous results of a river flood; then he builds up the description to a ludicrous climax in an anecdote about a New York banker at the scene whose efforts to take up a collection for the forlorn sufferers produced "one dollar and five horn buttons. The dollar he had given himself. He learned on inquiry that . . . all they had lost by the flood was a few fishing poles."[3] In another letter to the same friend he contrives a mock-serious paragraph on the problem of suicide by leaping into the Colorado River ("What shall we find in your depths? Rest? Peace?— catfish? . . . oblivion or another world? Who can tell? A man once dived into your depths and brought up a horse collar and a hoop skirt"); and he concludes his speculations with a triple pun—"sue a side-partner," "sewer sighed," "pursue a side issue."[4]

Many such examples from O. Henry's earliest extant writings bear witness to the artist in embryo. An impish spirit, eagerly seeking out the ludicrous incongruities and the unexpected occurrences everywhere awaiting an observing eye and ear, fulfills itself in these youthful *jeux d'esprit* through the medium of his shaping talent. Everything becomes grist for his mill, demanding expression. When he took up *The Rolling Stone* and later served as the Houston "Postman," quips and squibs and little yarns, comic verses, parodies, burlesques, and touching little tales on "life's little ironies" poured in profusion from his pen. All these were but a step from the more finished pieces he would soon be writing in prison as he turned to account his memories of Texas, New Orleans, and Central America. Of the nearly one hundred items based on these experiences, well over two-thirds were published before 1904.

I *Early Short Fiction*—The Rolling Stone

A complete file of *The Rolling Stone* has never been republished, but enough of its contents are available in print to bear out Langford's comment that during its short career "its high-spirited gaiety camouflaged completely the editor's financial worries, as well as his difficulties at home and in the bank" (253). In the twelfth volume of O. Henry's collected works, published in 1912 under the title *Rolling Stones*, his friend Henry Steger gathered together a number of representative pieces from the little weekly, prefacing them with a short appreciative introduction explaining the nature and variety of its contents.[5] Here can be seen, besides several short stories, facsimiles of O. Henry's amusing prospectus—promising "to fill its pages with matter that will make a heart-rending appeal to every lover of good literature, and every person who has a taste for reading print; and a dollar and a half for a year's subscription" (x)—as well as reproductions of cartoons and sample pages, especially of those containing "The Plunkville Patriot," the paper's most characteristic feature.[6]

One of the first critics to recognize the latent artistry in these youthful effusions was the late Professor Hyder E. Rollins of Harvard, who in 1914 wrote a series of critical analyses of O. Henry's artistic merits and shortcomings and traced both to their origins in *The Rolling Stone*.[7] Though unimpressed with "The Plunkville Patriot," he found O. Henry's burlesque interviews and satires "extremely funny. They represent the true O. Henry, both in method and in manner, as well as do his last productions."[8] Rollins believed that if *The Rolling Stone* were still running in 1914 under Porter's editing and someone else's sound financial management, it would be rivaling *Life* and *Judge*, a view he reiterated in stressing the "delightful quality" of its short stories, in which one could detect "the touches and mannerisms that made O. Henry great."[9] A later critic scoffed: "The mannerisms, yes, but hardly the touches. In that early work there were originality and promise, but at best it was the work of a talented prentice hand; and Porter had to go far and learn

much before he began to master the mechanics of his craft,
above all the art of compression."[10]

It seems idle, however, to split hairs over "touches and mannerisms," as both are abundantly evident in the short stories as
well as in the briefer thrusts and parries the young editor carried
on while poking fun at a variety of targets—for example, a
spoofing news reporter's interview with President Cleveland;
the German citizenry in Austin; the "new woman" with her
freakish fashions and breezy manners—enough, at any rate, to
support Langford's observation that "the spectacle of life in and
around Austin . . . received most of Porter's attention, and although the quality of his humor varies considerably, the occasions
for it seem to have been endless" (254). Similarly, although the
short stories do betray a prentice hand and not a master's, there
is no lack of either compression or witty touches in such pieces
as "Aristocracy Versus Hash," a burlesque on genteel Austin
boardinghouse keepers; "The Prisoner of Zembla," a parody of
chivalric romance; "Fickle Fortune or How Gladys Hustled,"
another parody of the Hairbreadth-Harry type of adventure
romance; or "Tictoq" and "Tracked to Doom," a pair of burlesque
crime stories.[11]

But by far the most impressive of these early writings is "Bexar
Scrip No. 2692," a remarkably tense story of mystery, chicanery,
and revenge in which O. Henry cleverly combined the setting
of the General Land Office he knew so well with "a well-known
tradition in Austin and vicinity that there is a buried treasure
of great value somewhere on the banks of Shoal Creek, about
a mile west of the city."[12] The story tells of a brutal murder
committed by a crooked land agent named Sharp who, while
trying to remove from the Land Office files certain legal papers
establishing a claim to some land, was discovered by the son
of the claimant. Upon the disappearance of the young victim,
Harris, and the papers, Sharp secured the land; and his guilty act
was revealed only twenty years later after his own death when
some young treasure seekers discovered Harris' remains with
the buried evidence. In this story were fused the results of personal experience, observation, and imagination (Will Porter
himself had actually been one of the young men in search of
buried treasure, which became a kind of compulsive theme in
his later stories);[13] and, if one could not detect the future O.
Henry in it, he was not to be found at all.

II *Early Short Fiction—The Houston* Post

When O. Henry took up his duties on the Houston *Post* in 1895, he began for the first time in his life to draw regular pay for doing the kind of work he was both inclined and best fitted to do. Even under favorable circumstances and with no cloud of recent unresolved court action hanging over him, the results of his efforts during the next six months would have been remarkable: a total of fifty-nine short stories and sketches, besides numerous other pieces of writing. All these remained entirely unknown for over twenty years after his death, and a complete file of these pieces is still unavailable in print.[14]

Like the materials in *The Rolling Stone,* O. Henry's *Post* stories and sketches were based on personal experiences which he had either participated in, observed—or discovered in the writings of Longfellow, Mark Twain, Stephen Crane, Rudyard Kipling, and other authors.[15] Besides a daily column of anecdotes about prominent persons and events, numerous sketches described downtown shoppers, Christmas and New Years' scenes, horse-race and circus crowds, city night life, and miscellaneous odd characters about town. Equally varied in their appeal to popular tastes, his stories covered a range of topics from the comic to the sentimental and pathetic: sick newsboys, heroic tramps, slick gamblers, disguised lovers, embarrassed husbands and wives, lonely artists, mirages, and buried treasure. He also transformed the results of his readings into new forms intended to instruct or amuse, as in the example of his serious critical essay on "Newspaper Poets," or that of his burlesque mimicry of well-known fiction, such as "Vereton Villa," mentioned in the preceding chapter;[16] "The Legend of San Jacinto" and "Binkley's Practical School of Journalism," which parody the kind of spoofing found in Twain's *Roughing It;*[17] and "The Blue Blotch of Cowardice," a take-off of Crane's celebrated *Red Badge of Courage.*[18] "Vereton Villa," a satire of both Harriet Beecher Stowe and the carpetbaggers of the Reconstruction era, is one of O. Henry's funniest parodies.

Purportedly a "tale of the South" written by a Boston schoolmarm who has never seen the South but imagines accurately what its life and people are like, this story recounts, in the first person, the harrowing experiences of Miss Penelope Cook, who goes to live and teach on a Texas plantation in order to save enough money to marry Cyrus Potts, a struggling professor of chemistry. As she approaches the mansion in an ambulance driven by a sobbing old Negro, a mule bursts out of the front door; it is propelled by the aristocratic, be-diamonded, broom-wielding Mrs. De Vere, who graciously invites Penelope in and presently offers her a chaw of tobacco. In the magnificently furnished parlor Penelope notes certain evidence of Southern sloth: a wheelbarrow of dried mortar in one corner, a pair of pants hanging from the chandelier, and several chickens roosting on the piano. Aubrey De Vere, the towering god-like young son, wearing "a dress suit of the latest cut," greets her with patrician courtesy "in a deep musical baritone"; but she notes that he is shirtless and barefooted, his mouth streaked with tobacco juice. At the mention of Jefferson Davis, whom Penelope calls a traitor, he seizes one of the chickens, wrings its neck, and flings its carcass on the Brussels carpet and its head into her face; then he humbly begs her pardon on one knee, recalling that "twenty-eight years ago today my father was killed at the battle of Shiloh." And so the fantastic contretemps pile up, steadily revealed, however, in a dry, matter-of-fact tone. At a truly Southern supper consisting of everything imaginable from opossum and sweet potatoes to catfish and squash, Aubrey buries his carving knife to the hilt in the old Negro for spilling gravy on the tablecloth; later he demonstrates the accuracy of both his musical knowledge and his aim by showing Penelope that the A natural note she had struck in a run of diminished sevenths should have been A sharp; and the neighboring black key is designated for her by a stream of tobacco juice from across the room. Later still he proves the depth of his jealous passion and subsequent remorse when, his ardent love-making repulsed, he pitches Penelope through the window and sets fire to her, then rescues her and goes all the way to Boston to fetch Cyrus. And as the affianced pair bid good-bye to the South, he finally blows himself up with a keg of dynamite, leaving Penelope a memento for her married life—his great toe, which she keeps in a bottle of alcohol on her writing desk. She vows never to return to the South, however, because the Southern people are too impulsive. If we grant a certain youthful exuberance in "Vereton Villa" leading Porter into crudities of expression offensive to genteel tastes, his boisterous spoofing in this early story was squarely within the frontier tall-tale tradition.

More significant than the parodies, however, are O. Henry's themes, situations, and methods in the numerous *Post* stories embodying original composition; for these show the artist at work experimenting with techniques and developing an individual style. As M. S. Harrell indicates: "The word-usage, sentence-structure, mythological allusions, plot-manipulation, character types, and central ideas that characterize O. Henry's short stories generally, are also plainly recognizable in these selections."[19] In one story based on his favorite *Arabian Nights* legends, for example, the whole effect turns on the punning of "too gross" and "two gross";[20] in another, on the fitting together of the two halves of a concert ticket;[21] and again and again, the outcome is a shocking discovery that upsets the complacency of the characters involved.[22]

From the viewpoint of plot-manipulation alone, perhaps the most interesting of these stories is "Simmons' Saturday Night," an elaborately worked-out variation on the old theme of the "biter bit," which introduces a harmless-looking Texas greenhorn to a snappily dressed Houston dandy posing as a railway paymaster. Quickly sizing up the yokel as an easy victim, the dandy offers to show him the sights, takes him first to a nightclub to soften him up, and then to a gambling house. "The old story of the hawk and the pigeon has been told so often that the details are apt to weary,"[23] says the narrator; and from here on the rising tension of the poker game is so neatly built up to its climax with slight touches arousing pity for the poor pigeon that, when the *coup de grace* falls in a reversal of roles, the unwary reader is totally unprepared to find Simmons transformed into Diamond Joe, a slick New York gambler traveling incognito to earn his expenses en route. All the elements of the carefully plotted O. Henry tale are in evidence along with the disguise motif, the spare but meaningful descriptive detail, and the use of realistic dialogue for enhanced dramatic effect. The many swindling yarns to be told later with slightly more humor and finesse by O. Henry's Jeff Peters seem clearly foreshadowed in this story.

Indeed, perhaps the most significant fact about many of these Houston *Post* stories is the part they played as models for O. Henry's later ones; for various instructive parallels can be drawn between them and the well-known stories written for New

York magazines. The slight sketch entitled "A Houston Romance,"[24] for example, is almost a verbatim replica of "The Robe of Peace," a far-fetched tale of a fashionable young American who disappears and is later discovered by friends in a Swiss monastery, thoroughly contented to stay there forever with his friar's garb because it does not bag at the knees.[25] Whereas the earlier version is only three pages long and sketchily developed, the later one, twice as long and with New York names substituted for Houston ones, shows by comparison how O. Henry worked to strengthen his illusion and build up his climax. Similarly, a four-page story entitled "An Unknown Romance,"[26] developing the theme of disparity between wealth and poverty through the device of mistaken identity, reappears in varied forms in at least half a dozen later stories. In the early version two wealthy young Americans fall in love while vacationing in the Alps, but, mistaking each other's peasant garb for the real thing, they give up the idea in favor of marriages of convenience arranged by their families, only to find that they are destined for each other.[27] Variations of the identical situation are worked out in "A Night in New Arabia"[28] and "Lost on Dress Parade,"[29] and with roles reversed in "Transients in Arcadia"[30] and "The Caliph and the Cad,"[31] and again with a double reversal in "While the Auto Waits,"[32] one of O. Henry's most famous stories.

Actually, the disguise or impostor motif, coupled with the idea that destiny or fate imposes inescapable roles on the individual, is a dominant theme that recurs in many forms throughout all of O. Henry's writing; and its treatment, both serious and comic, can be seen in the majority of his earliest stories. The fatalistic notion that "we are all marionettes that dance and cry, scarce at our own wills," expressed in one of the *Post* stories,[33] is implicit in most of the others regardless of the social levels of his characters or the kinds of situation he places them in. Like the helpless young lovers, the opium-eating bum who imagines himself to be a wealthy scholar;[34] the sodden tramp who responds to a kind word with kingly grace;[35] or the thoughtless mother who locks up her little children at home while she runs to tell her neighbor of a nightmare in which she as a child had destroyed herself with fire[36]—all these and still others convey the fundamental idea that the individual with or without a mask must play the part cut out for him, and that no matter what choices he is offered or what roads he takes, he is inevitably destined for the same predetermined end.

Whether such emphasis bears out Langford's interpretation that in 1896 O. Henry already "understood himself well enough to express in terms of fatalism his inadequacy in dealing with the actualities of life" (94) is open to debate. What is certain, however, is that he reworked these same themes and situations again and again in later stories, giving them a finer finish, a higher polish, in order to make his mirrored illusory world of fiction a more enchanting one. Can this artistic growth be blandly lumped in as part of his inadequacy?

III   *The Western Stories*

O. Henry's professional career as a successful writer of short stories can be most conveniently divided into two periods—before and after the beginning of 1904. This breaking point is significant for several reasons: first, from the time of his release from prison in 1901 until the signing of his contract with the New York *Sunday World* in the fall of 1903, he was striving for recognition; and, still uncertain of a steady income, he gladly accepted any reasonable price for his stories. After 1903 he quickly gained both recognition and increasingly larger fees, for more and more editors, competing for his services, bid up the prices they were willing to pay for the drawing power of his name. Second, before his regular weekly appearance in the *Sunday World,* his stories varied considerably in length, structure, and content, as they had during his brief tenure on the Houston *Post;* after his association with the *World* began, they gradually jelled into the compact form that has come to be known as *the* O. Henry story—tight, crisp, breezy—at its best an inimitable bit of literary fluff—focused chiefly on the New York scene, though he continued writing, off and on, stories about other places as well. Third, about two-thirds of all the stories he published in national magazines before 1904 deal with Western and Latin American scenes and characters; afterwards he published relatively few of these in proportion to the vast number of his stories about New York City.

O. Henry's Western stories, excluding those published in the Houston *Post* and the *Rolling Stone,* number about eighty in all. For purposes of discussion these may be further subdivided into three groups, the largest of which consists of thirty-nine stories with Texas settings. The smallest group, though similar to these in many respects, consists of seventeen stories with settings in other Western states; and the third group, numbering twenty-four stories, are those with settings in Latin American countries. About half of all these Western stories were published in the three-year period prior to 1904, publication of the other half being scattered over the remaining six years of O. Henry's life. While these figures show that the West, like the South, never faded from his consciousness (indeed, five of his Western stories were not published until shortly after his death), a closer look at individual titles also reveals that, notwithstanding their original publication dates, many of his Western stories were written long before they first found a publisher. In the main, therefore, they belong to the earlier of the two periods indicated.

IV *Texas*

"In Texas you may travel a thousand miles in a straight line. If your course is a crooked one, it is likely that both the distance and your rate of speed may be vastly increased."[37] Thus typically, O. Henry begins one of his Texas stories; he fixes in two short sentences the feeling of spaciousness and the suggestion of fraud and violence to be dramatized presently on this huge stage, where a whole parcel of New Jerseys and Rhode Islands "could have been stowed away and lost in its chaparral."[38] However implausible the plots, the settings in many of his Western stories are often their most distinguishing feature; they are usually depicted with a bare minimum of detail, yet so realistically that both the physical arrangements and the atmosphere of the place are brought sharply into focus. This characteristic is especially true of the nearly forty stories laid in Texas, most of which deal with the southwestern or chaparral region, a vast domain of sheep and cattle ranches extending southward from the vicinity of San Antonio and the Frio River to the Nueces and beyond, through the thinly populated "no-man's land" of the outlaws lying between the Nueces and the Rio Grande.[39]

In this huge, open, rolling area, covered with mesquite and low-lying evergreen oaks, the qualities that O. Henry brings to light first are the beauty of the natural scenery, despite its general aridity and endless vistas of unrelieved monotone; and, second, the simplicity and freedom of movement inspired by life in such a country. "They swept out of the little town and down the level road toward the South. Soon the road dwindled and disappeared, and they struck across a world carpeted with an endless reach of curly mesquite grass. The wheels made no sound. The tireless ponies bounded ahead at an unbroken gallop. The temperate wind, made fragrant by thousands of acres of blue and yellow flowers, roared gloriously in their ears. The motion was aerial, ecstatic, with a thrilling sense of perpetuity in its effect."[40] Again and again, O. Henry sends off a pair of characters on horseback, riding for miles "in silence save for the soft drum of the ponies' hoofs on the matted mesquite grass, and the rattle of the chaparral against their wooden stirrups";[41] or in a buckboard speeding "upon velvet wheels across an exhilarant savanna ... and ... the uncharted billows of the grass itself ... [where] each tiny distant mott of trees was a signboard, each convolution of the low hills a voucher of course and distance."[42]

Their destination is usually an unpretentious ranch house like the Rancho Cibolo, "composed of four large rooms, with plastered adobe walls, and a two-room wooden ell ... set in a grove of immense live-oaks and water-elms near a lake";[43] or it is like Rush Kinney's two-room affair, resting "upon the summit of a lenient slope" amid a broad prairie, "diversified by arroyos and murky patches of brush and pear," in an atmosphere "heady with ozone and made memorably sweet by leagues of wild flowerets," its silence disturbed only by the occasional drumming rush of frightened sheep in the corrals, the shrill yapping of coyotes in the distance, the twittering of whippoorwills, and "the clear torrent of the mockingbirds' notes that fell from a dozen neighboring shrubs and trees."[44]

The peacefulness, orderliness, and simplicity of living conditions in these surroundings are enhanced by the contrasts between them and the ramshackle little towns like Nopal, which "seemed to have been hastily constructed of undressed lumber and flapping canvas";[45] or like Paloma, where the Southern Pacific train stopped "at noon for the engine to drink and for the passengers both to drink and to dine. There was a new yellow-pine hotel, also a wool warehouse, and perhaps three dozen box residences. The rest was composed of tents, cow ponies, 'Black-waxy' mud, and mesquite-trees, all bound round by a horizon."[46] To such grim little settlements came the ranch-hands with their chuck wagons to pick up supplies, patronize the saloons, gamble, and indulge in other primitive forms of recreation. If lucky, some might even get up to see the fairs and the races at San Antonio, "the hub of the wheel of Fortune . . . [where] cattlemen played at crack-loo on the side-walks with double-eagles, and gentlemen backed their conception of the fortuitous card with stacks limited in height only by the interference of gravity."[47]

Whether at work or play, men living under such conditions were active; their life in general was vigorous and rugged, if slow-moving at times in the hundred-degree summer heat along the Mexican border. When the branding season came, the *vaqueros* were up before dawn, mustered in forces of up to twenty-five men "ready to start for the San Carlos range, where the work was to begin. By six o'clock the horses were all saddled, the grub wagon ready, and the cow-punchers were swinging themselves upon their mounts."[48] When idle, "they pounded one another hurtfully and affectionately; they heaped upon one another's heads friendly curses and obloquy";[49] they played boyish pranks such as staging mock-marriages among themselves; or with their six-shooters they pumped holes into the high silk hat of an occasional visiting dignitary soliciting votes at their camps.[50]

The same primitive conditions that made for high jinks of this sort, however, also gave rise to widespread violence and ferocity, theft and fraud in a land where "the law was mainly a letter." Outlaw bands roamed the open country along the border, from time to time running off "some very good companies of horses from the ranges, and a few bunches of fine cattle which they got safely across the Rio Grande and disposed of to fair advantage. Often the band would ride into the little villages and Mexican settlements, terrorizing the inhabitants and plundering for the provisions and ammunition they needed."[51] At any moment the quiet of a sleepy town like Quicksand might be shattered by the exuberant sharp-shooting of a drunken Calliope Catesby; then "glass fell like hail; dogs vamosed; chickens flew, squawking; feminine voices shrieked concernedly to youngsters at large."[52] Doubtless more often the forces of law and order had to deal with the depredations of wild men on the loose like the Trimble gang—"ten of 'em—the worst outfit of desperadoes and horse-thieves in Texas, coming up the street shooting right and left . . . straight for the Gray Mule," a saloon which they proceeded to tear apart, "drinking what they wanted and smashing what they didn't."[53] But oftener still, very likely, the authorities were obliged to settle the bitter conflicts between evicted settlers and land sharks which "entailed incalculable trouble, endless litigation, a period of riotous land-grabbing, and no little bloodshed."[54]

Such, in brief, was the colorful background against which O. Henry built his many romantic episodes of life in the Texas he knew. Whether he writes about town or open country, the few details he unerringly selected in each story bring the scene to life and also appeal strongly to the senses of sight, sound, smell, and taste: the guitar's tinkling accompaniment to a señorita's sad ballad in "A Fog in Santone"; the acrid fumes rising from a sheep-dipping vat in "Law and Order"; the dull thumps of hobbled ponies moving about for fresh grass in "Jimmy Hayes and Muriel"; brown cottontails frolicking through a ranchyard while a covey of white-topknotted blue quail run past, in single file, twenty yards away in "The Last of the Troubadors"; a party of ranchers' wives and daughters gaily setting off for a ten-mile jaunt in a buckboard "with their Easter hats and frocks carefully wrapped and bundled against the dust";[55] the crash and whine of gold coins being rapidly counted by the nimble fingers of a bank examiner in "Friends in San Rosario"; the crowds of gaping cattlemen thronging the Capitol during a legislative session in "Art and the Bronco"; little black heads of Mexican children peering at a neighbor's strawberry patch through "a crazy picket fence overgrown with morning glory and wild gourd vine"[56]—the list could be endlessly extended since virtually every story yields up its handful of vivid details.

Turning from background to foreground, however, one quickly sees that O. Henry was less interested in presenting real-life situations than in creating a realistic stage for his puppets. One can believe in his Western environment because it is firmly established—three dimensional. One cannot believe in the reality of most of his principal characters because they are mere pawns in human form, lacking the complexity of motives governing the lives of even simple human beings, lacking inner conflict and the power to act in ways consistent with their alleged make-up, lacking individuality. Yet, in another sense they are consistent in that their actions conform to O. Henry's own limited view of the human predicament. Chance governs their lives in much the same way as he believed that the actions of real human beings were managed by a master puppeteer jerking the strings. One's interest centers, accordingly, on the dance they dance— its antic gyrations, leaps, and caracoles—not on what they are.

Inevitably, this sort of approach to life results in a thinness of thematic content. In O. Henry's Western stories, as in his others, there is little depth or complexity of meaning, as the actions and interactions of his characters remain largely on the surface of things. Usually a few basic passions are involved—love, hate, fear, greed—and the conflicts between them end in marriage or death, satisfaction or sorrow, which the reader must accept on faith, since little or no analysis of motives has been attempted. The characters, the great majority of whom are men, fall into a number of recognizable, conventionalized types—good guys and bad guys—but there is such a great variety of these types, and such interesting variations are worked out among some of them, that the reader is easily beguiled into overlooking their lack of individuality. For his Texas stories alone, O. Henry created over 250 characters with speaking parts, representing more than forty distinct types drawn from town, village, and open range.[57] Besides the predominating cowboys and outlaws— the most colorful of the lot—they include sheepmen, rangers, cattle kings, station agents, burglars, doctors, bankers, clerks, farmers, hoboes, cooks, and assorted wives and daughters of some of these and of still other types. Thus, by picking and choosing from this motley society a few types for each story and by varying slightly the relationships among them, O. Henry can mesmerize his readers with successive plot situations which compensate in varied entertainment for what they fail to provide by way of insight into the springs of human nature.

As might be expected, the prevailing situation is a variant of the boy-meets-girl problem, involving either rivalry between two or more men for possession of the woman, or barriers between a man and woman which, until removed in the story, prevent a harmonious resolution of the problem. Nearly half of O. Henry's Texas stories develop one or the other aspect of this situation. The barrier may be one of pride, as in "Hearts and Crosses," "The Princess and the Puma," and "The Indian Summer of Dry Valley Johnson"; or it may be one of misunderstanding, the

result of mistaken identity, as in "The Marquis and Miss Sally";
or a mixture of both, as in "Madame Bo-Peep of the Ranches."
Essentially, the only difference between Santa McAllister, the
proud cattle king's daughter in "Hearts and Crosses" and Pan-
chita O'Brien, the little Mexican heroine of "The Indian Summer,"
is a difference of wealth and social status; for both are strong-
willed women who know how to get their man by yielding to
him at the appropriate moment. And so are Josepha O'Donnell,
the sharp-shooting "princess," and Madame Bo-Peep—all sisters
under the skin.

Similarly, in developing the male-rivalry situation O. Henry
follows oftener than not a predictable pattern in which the
surprise at the end grows less entertaining, as one reads on, than
do his methods of setting it up. In "The Red Roses of Tonia,"
for example, the plot hinges on a race to bring a new Easter
bonnet with red roses on it to an impatient ranch girl; in "Buried
Treasure" it is a matter of stumbling upon the girl hidden away
in the mountains by an obstinate father; in "The Pimiento
Pancakes" strategy wins the day for a scorned sheepman, who
outwits his rival by making the girl think he is insane. Occasionally the contest is a draw, as in "A Poor Rule," in which
all four rivals are sacrificed by the heroine for a career as a
concert singer; or as in "The Sphinx Apple," in which the heroine
falls asleep while listening to *her* four admirers' competitive
efforts to tell a story. Or again it may be coupled with a revenge
motif, harmless as in "The Moment of Victory," when undersized
but gamy little war-hero Willie Robbins tells off the girl who
had rejected him; or violent, as in "A Chaparral Christmas Gift,"
when the rejected suitor turns desperado, nearly murders his
rival, and is later shot to death by another man. But whether
grim or light-hearted, the denouement is usually less rewarding
than the path leading toward it.

The reformation or rehabilitation motif is another fruitful
source for plots in O. Henry's Western stories, as in all his others;
and in the main he was more successful in dealing with it than
with the battle of the sexes. Possibly because of a strong autobiographical element, "Hygeia at the Solito" is one of the best
of this group. The story concerns a spunky little New York
hoodlum, "Cricket" McGuire, whose rehabilitation begins when
Curtis Raidler, a burly cattleman, discovers him sitting, sick
and disconsolate, on the railroad platform in San Antonio.

Raidler carries him off to his ranch, and the whole story from there on is a fierce contest between the tough little ex-pugilist and his equally tough but kindly host who is determined to make a man of him. "The Higher Abdication" follows much the same formula, though in this story Curly, the broken-down tramp, is whipped into shape through hard knocks and ostracism so that in the end he may be served up as the long-lost son whose miraculous reappearance can unsnarl a frustrated love affair. Again, in "The Reformation of Calliope"—a story bearing a marked resemblance to Stephen Crane's "The Bride Comes to Yellow Sky"—the loud-mouthed, free-shooting Terror of Quicksand earns absolution and reprieve from the marshall he has wounded when Calliope's aged mother providentially appears on the scene.[58] In this story, tall-tale elements provide the entertainment; and the device of mistaken identity sets up the "snapper" at the end. Mistaken identity is again the key to reformation in "A Double-Dyed Deceiver," one of the most tightly knit of O. Henry's badman plots, which develops the Llano Kid's transformation from murderous gunman to the adopted son of his last victim's wealthy South American parents through the device of a tattooed symbol. Here, the disguise motif is used skillfully, as it is also in "The Passing of Black Eagle," though this story of a scavenging hobo temporarily elevated to leadership of an outlaw gang and organizer of a train robbery that fails is too far-fetched to be anything but a tall tale. Elements of the tall tale, in fact, seldom strayed far from O. Henry's hand; he used them again in "Law and Order," another variation on the reformation theme published after his death.[59]

A third among his favorite plot situations brings together, usually in mortal combat, the opposing forces of crime and authority. Closely related to the foregoing type, this classic situation afforded O. Henry one of his earliest opportunities to reach a national audience with a story called "The Miracle of Lava Canyon," published under his real name by the McClure Syndicate shortly after he entered prison in 1898. He evidently liked the story so much that, while in jail, he revised it thoroughly and had it republished in 1902 under the title "An Afternoon Miracle." Essentially the same story is told both times—the handsome, powerful but inwardly fearful sheriff's encounter with a reckless desperado while under the watchful gaze of a threatened woman afraid of nothing—but, placed side by side, the two versions offer an illuminating study in O. Henry's maturing techniques: the "miracle" of the later version, involving a double switch between cowardice and courage, is given ironic overtones not to be found at all in the earlier one. In the earlier version the reader learns that the fearless girl after her rescue screams with genuine fright on seeing a lizard and that "the sheriff's strong arm reassured her. The miracle was complete. The soul of each had passed into the other."[60] In the later version Alvarita only pretends to be frightened by a two-inch caterpillar in order to clinch her protector Buckley's solicitude.

Again and again in his Western stories O. Henry shifted and rearranged the pieces in his "cops-and-robbers" pattern. In "A Departmental Case," the hero is an elderly government official, Luke Standifer (obviously based on O. Henry's former bene-factor, Richard Hall), who avenges the mistreated daughter of his old-time ranger pal by destroying in a gun duel her worth-less husband, Benton Sharp—"one of the most noted 'bad' men in that part of the state—a man who had been a cattle thief, an outlaw, a desperado, and was now a gambler, a swaggering bully...."[61] In "One Dollar's Worth" revenge sparks the deadly duel between Mexico Sam and Littlefield, the young district attorney who had sent him to jail four years before; but its outcome rests on Littlefield's fortuitous possession of a lead counterfeit dollar, which serves as ammunition instead of the evidence it was intended for. Thus, by a neat twist O. Henry simultaneously makes crime pay and not pay in this story; while in "The Last of the Troubadors" he reverses the twist, causing his hero, singing Sam Calloway, to destroy the bullying badman, King James, just after James has reversed his own evil intentions. Beyond a doubt, however, the most effective of all these bad-man plots is that of "The Caballero's Way," which combines the revenge and infidelity motifs in a yarn that packs a gruesome wallop comparable to Conrad's or Crane's. The story introduces the deadly Cisco Kid, O. Henry's most attractive villain, who "killed for the love of it—because he was quick-tempered—to avoid arrest—for his own amusement—any reason that came to his mind would suffice."[62] His reason in this instance is sufficient: he must avenge the insult his honor has suffered from his mis-tress, Tonia Perez, who has conspired to turn him in to her new lover, Sandridge, the Texas Ranger pursuing him; but his method of paying off her unfaithfulness is the "caballero's way" of tricking Sandridge into performing the dirty work himself. Coldly told, and almost totally free of sticky sentimentality, "The Caballero's Way" is a brilliant performance.

Despite liberal doses of "Western corn" in most of these tales, the plotting in them is often admirable, the more so in that O. Henry repeatedly reworked hackneyed situations based on primitive forms of conflict and adventure. Basically, the situations dealt with in his other Texas stories differ only slightly from those already discussed; yet each of their treatments shows the same fecundity of invention at work, warming up and flavoring an old chestnut to make it palatable. The Damon-and-Pythias motif, for instance, is developed in two versions in "A Call Loan" and "Friends in San Rosario," both stories having to do with circumvention of the banking laws through the collusion of friendly bankers. Similarly, the self-sacrifice or vindication theme is treated in two quite different ways, though with the familiar surprise ending both times, in "A Fog in Santone" and "Jimmy Hayes and Muriel": in the former a desponding young prostitute swallows the suicide pills which she has convinced a tuberculous youth he should abandon because there is so much to live for; in the latter the skeleton of the hero, who had been thought a cowardly deserter, proves that his bravery had inspired him to tackle and destroy a whole band of outlaws. The miraculous influence of a little child, another idea favored in idealistic fiction, also captured O. Henry's attention and inspired both "A Chaparral Prince" and "Georgia's Ruling"—the one a variation on the Cinderella theme in which rampaging outlaws rescue poor little Lena Hildesmuller from the misery of child-labor exploitation; the other, equally sentimental, a case of literal mortmain in which a child's dying wish saves a whole county full of settlers from eviction at the hands of greedy land sharks.

To conclude the roster of O. Henry's Texas plots, three more that deserve notice by virtue of the contrasting methods used to develop them are "The Enchanted Kiss," which employs a sequence of weird dreams vaguely reminiscent of de Maupassant to dramatize the contrast between illusion and reality; "Art and the Bronco," containing liberal infusions of tall-tale buffoonery and satire to point up the incongruity between pretentious art and the primitive society in a frontier community; and "The Hiding of Black Bill," in some ways the most sophisticated performance of the three. Based on the theme of self-preservation as the first law of nature, "The Hiding of Black Bill" is a masterpiece of plot construction. In it O. Henry employs a concealed narrator to introduce his two seedy hoboes, Ham and Snipy, one of whom then takes over to manage the story's progress in a series of reported conversations that sound as natural as something overheard. As they sit on a railroad siding waiting for a freight train, Ham reports his recent activities by telling how, while working on a lonely sheep ranch managed by a man named Ogden in a region where sheriffs' posses were hunting a bank robber called Black Bill, he managed to throw suspicion on his employer and to collect a reward when Ogden was caught with the money on his person. Snipy reacts unfavorably to this tale, saying: "I don't like your talk. You and me have been friends, off and on, for fifteen year; and I never yet knew or heard of you giving anybody up to the law—not no one. And here was a man whose saleratus you had et and at whose table you had played games of cards ... And yet you inform him to the law and take money for it. It never was like you, I say."[63] Ham simply points out that since he himself was Black Bill and had planted the stolen money on the sleeping Ogden when he saw the posse coming, Ogden had no trouble freeing himself later with an alibi.

V *Other Western Stories*

With few exceptions, the remaining seventeen stories laid in other Western states do not measure up in either color or quality to the ones O. Henry wrote about Texas; yet all but three of them are among his later work, written long after he had left Texas. Once established in New York, he apparently turned to his memories of the West from time to time to fish up a long-forgotten incident that might be quickly fashioned into a plot suitable for meeting a pressing deadline. The settings of these stories are not essentially significant. Though six of them are laid in Arizona and Colorado, four more in Oklahoma, one each in Kansas, Illinois, Indiana, New Mexico, Montana, and two others vaguely located in the West, in all of them the settings could be indiscriminately scrambled about without altering either plot structure or meaning. At least twelve of the stories can only be classified as tall tales intended to draw laughs at the absurd antics recounted by their various narrators. Only five of these stories were reprinted in the early volume *Heart of the West,* which contains Western stories which O. Henry himself regarded most highly; four others are in *The Gentle Grafter,* published only once; and the remaining eight reappeared only in the volumes containing his left-overs and published after his death.[64]

Among the dozen tall tales in this group, the most interesting from the viewpoints of content and structure are the four Jeff Peters stories in *The Gentle Grafter* and two others featuring the same narrator, though written earlier and published in other volumes. The original Jeff Peters story, published in 1902 under the title "A Guthrie Wooing" and signed as by "Olivier Henry," reappeared in *Heart of the West* under the new title "Cupid à la Carte." Though otherwise undistinguished, this is the only story in which the loquacious narrator does not speak of his swindling activities; instead, he tells a ludicrous tale of rivalry between himself and another fellow for the hand of Mame Dugan, a restaurant keeper's daughter who was so tired of dishing out hash to hungry men that she vowed to remain a spinster and raise "violets for the Eastern market."[65] The best, however, of all the Jeff Peters stories, at least in O. Henry's opinion, is the one entitled "The Atavism of John Tom Little Bear," a rollicking farce compounded of Indian medicine-show swindling, a temporary love interest, a kidnaping, and a daring rescue, complete with the scalp of the foiled villain.[66] As if Jeff's own delightful manner of telling a story were not enough to convulse the tall-tale fan, O. Henry doubles the humor of this one with his characterization of the educated Cherokee, John Tom, "a graduate of one of them Eastern football colleges that have been so successful in teaching the Indian to use the gridiron instead of burning his victims at the stake."[67] After meeting these two, one finds the remaining tall tales pretty tepid, including even the other Jeff Peters yarns.

Each of the other five stories in this Western group, however, affords an interesting insight into other areas of O. Henry's mind—specifically, his preoccupation with crime, violence, and death—as well as into his varied narrative methods. Two stories that present contrasting methods of working up his Western stories are the early piece "Hearts and Hands," published in 1902, and "The Snow Man," a story he was working on during his last illness but could not complete.[68] The first is scarcely more than an expanded anecdote; yet within its single railway-

coach scene a pathetic little drama with poignant autobiographical overtones is skillfully set forth as the young Mr. Easton,
handcuffed to the marshal conducting him to Leavenworth, saves
face while talking with a girl he knows by pretending that he
is the police officer. "The Snow Man," on the other hand, is an
elaborately designed treatment of boredom, frustration, and
rivalry shared by four men stranded in a snow-bound cabin in
Montana. The arrival of a young woman raises a problem which
O. Henry might have solved in a more daring manner had he
lived to finish his own story; but, as he left it, the conventionalized surprise ending fails to support the ominous tone introduced
in the opening pages. Even so, the feel of death lurks just
beneath the surface of this suggestive story.

Two of the other stories recall the brutality of "The Caballero's
Way." "A Technical Error," the last completed one to appear
in print before O. Henry died,[69] is another treatment of infidelity
avenged, coupled with the disguise motif; but in this one the
narrator himself claims participation in the pursuit of the fleeing
couple, who are cornered in a hotel in Guthrie. Here, the
avenger, Sam Durkee, withholds his fire because it is against
the code to shoot a man down when he is with a woman (the
victim must be "cut out of the herd" and dealt with alone);
but at the next town Sam calmly pumps six bullets into his
rival (who had exchanged clothes with the girl) when he finds
the couple sitting together. Equally brutal but quite differently
composed, "The Roads We Take" is a story of betrayal which
dramatizes, by means of a dual contrasting device involving
dream versus reality and East versus West, O. Henry's fatalistic
theory that regardless of the path followed in life the end is predetermined by what one is. The story opens with a sensational
train robbery in Arizona that reaches a climax when Dodson,
the Easterner, coldbloodedly slays his partner because Bolivar,
the one good horse they have left for a getaway, "can't carry
double."[70] Then the reader learns in a neatly turned transition
that Dodson, a well-known New York broker, has dreamed the
whole sequence of events while sitting in his office chair; but,
when his clerk comes to report that his old friend, Williams,
has been caught short in the market and will be ruined unless
Dodson agrees to settle a deal at the old price of ninety-eight,
Dodson ruthlessly asserts: " 'He will settle at one eight-five . . .
Bolivar cannot carry double.' "[71]

"The Roads We Take" presents as neat and vivid an account of a train robbery as any to be found in fiction; for within less than two pages the bandits detach the engine, blow up the express-car safe, and escape with $30,000 in loot by driving the engine two miles off to where they have tethered their horses. This portion of the narrative accordingly bears close comparison with O. Henry's longer story "Holding Up a Train," which was published a few months earlier in 1904 and which doubtless served him in part as a model for the later one. Whereas "The Roads We Take" is tight, compact, and streamlined to fit the requirements of the New York *Sunday World's* feature page, the earlier story is discursive and rambling—deliberately so, however, since it was a collaborative effort between O. Henry and his former prison mate, Al Jennings.[72] Indeed, "Holding Up a Train" is unique among O. Henry's Western stories in that it very likely contains more fact than fiction; yet there is no way of knowing exactly how much of it was written by either of its authors. The story behind the writing of it is therefore more fascinating than the account itself, for Jennings while still in prison supplied O. Henry with original data in his own manuscript. O. Henry, after analyzing it critically, suggested in detail how it might be worked up into a solid article of four to six thousand words which *Everybody's* would accept, and promised to submit another of his own composition.[73] Later, he gleefully sent his "Dear Pard" the publisher's letter of acceptance with the comment: "When you see your baby in print don't blame me if you find strange ear marks and brands on it. I slashed it and cut it and added lots of stuff that never happened, but I followed your facts and ideas, and that is what made it valuable.[74] By this time, O. Henry's Western apprenticeship had served its purpose.

He had, in fact, so thoroughly mastered the art of mingling real-life adventures and pure fantasy through the medium of the tall tale that some Eastern literary critics were unable to distinguish between the truth and the fiction in his stories. Thus, whereas they were often delighted with what they considered authentic portrayals of metropolitan life in his New York stories, they condemned his Western stories for being grossly exaggerated. The charge of exaggeration, though applicable enough to most of O. Henry's stories, has less bearing on his Western tales than on any others; for it has been demonstrated recently that his Texas "badman" types are not only based on real-life outlaws who flourished in the *brasada* or chaparral region of the Rio Grande in the 1870's and 1880's, but they are also much less flamboyant in their behavior and speech than were their real-life counterparts—men like John Wesley Hardin, King Fisher, Ben Thompson, and Ham White. These and other notorious desperadoes whom O. Henry encountered or heard of while living with the Halls were actually rendered with a greater degree of real-life authenticity than New York critics could imagine in stories like "The Last of the Troubadors," "The Passing of Black Eagle," and "The Caballero's Way." John Hardin, who had earned the distinction of being "Texas' own greatest 'singlehanded terror' of all time" for having killed forty men before reaching his majority, thus offered a solid flesh-and-blood basis for O. Henry's Cisco Kid.[75] Moreover, the exaggerated characterizations, actions, and speech condemned in these Western stories were, as we have seen, basic elements in an indigenous American literary tradition—the tall-tale humor tradition—which had flourished for many decades since its inception on the ante-bellum frontier.

VI *Lotus Land—The Latin American Stories*

One of O. Henry's biographers long ago observed that his stories generally followed in chronological order "the backgrounds against which he lived his own adventurous life."[76] There were first the Texas tales, then the New Orleans ones, then those of Central America, and finally the New York stories. In a sense this is true, but it tells less than one needs to know about the types and qualities of his stories; moreover, it is not quite accurate, since O. Henry continued writing tales about Texas, the West, and the deep South long after he had left the adventures of all those areas behind. So too, with his stories of Central America; for, while it is correct to say that "with *Cabbages and Kings* ... he invaded the Arabian Nights for the first time,"[77] it must be quickly added that O. Henry was making further trips there with the same sort of cargo as late as 1908. The question remains: aside from a place of temporary refuge, what did Central America represent in O. Henry's imagination? How did he depict it in his stories? Do they actually reflect his own life and environment—though admittedly colored by his flair for the extravagant—during the fugitive days he spent in Honduras? When all of O. Henry's Latin American stories are taken into account and analyzed, the answer to this last question is "No." They reflect rather the "far land of the lotus ... land of perpetual afternoon ... [where] life among this indolent, romantic people—a life full of music, flowers, and low laughter"[78] could be perpetually enjoyed. In largest measure, these stories represent wish fulfillment, romantic escape —and were so intended.

These stories differ from O. Henry's other Western tales in several ways, and the problem of analyzing them is complicated by a number of factors. In all, there are twenty-six Latin-American stories, eighteen of which, however, are bound up together as "chapters" in the simulated novel *Cabbages and Kings;* the remaining eight are separate stories published for the most part after that book appeared. When *Cabbages and Kings* was published in 1904, some critics noted its loose construction; one of them, for example, compared it to *The Golden Ass* of Apuleius and called it "a series of Milesian tales which have no relation to each other ... [and] no immediate relation to the principal story, which in itself is another Milesian, mechanically wedded to them."[79] Nevertheless, the book was thought to be largely an original piece of writing, the various parts of which had been artfully designed to hang together. Actually, all but two or three of its eighteen "chapters" were carved out of seven earlier stories published two or three years before in *Ainslee's, Everybody's, McClure's,* and *Smart Set;* slight changes of chapter headings and names of characters and places were made to conform to novel requirements. A thorough analysis of the book's make-up done in 1935 shows that Porter based the "plot" on his long short story "Money Maze," which he cut into segments and attached to segments of other stories, combining these and newly written portions inserted at appropriate points of the developing story. Then he wrote an entirely new chapter, which he entitled "Money Maze," and another for the conclusion, called "The Vitagraphoscope."[80] By manipulating his earlier stories in this manner, O. Henry derived a double benefit from them; he turned out—in place of the original, separate ones—what appeared to be an entirely new thing, an amusingly articulated light mystery story of embezzlers and absconders in and out of the "banana" republic of Anchuria. The book thus extended his range, giving fictional shape to his Honduran interlude, and focusing renewed attention upon him as a rival of Richard Harding Davis.

To assert, however, that the characters and action in *Cabbages and Kings* "must have been drawn from life . . . [because] sheer invention was impossible"[81] is to pay greater tribute to O. Henry's narrative skill than to the perspicacity of the critic who says so. The trap is easy to fall into because O. Henry worked over-time to conceal with seeming realism the unreality of his lotus land. When the book is read as a single entity, its illusion of reality is more persuasive than would be so if each of the original stories that went into its composition were read separately in its original context. For, if this were done, it would be seen that most of these stories, like so many others O. Henry produced, are tall tales. In fact, virtually his entire collection of Latin American stories are of this genre; of the remaining eight not included in *Cabbages and Kings*, only "The World and the Door" does not readily fall into this category.

Since none of the seven stories forming the basis of *Cabbages and Kings* has ever been reprinted, the experiment suggested above would be hard to carry out; but if one bears in mind what O. Henry told his "pard" Al Jennings about their joint production of "Holding Up a Train"—namely, that he "added lots of stuff that never happened"—one need only compare *Cabbages and Kings* as it stands with the other stories O. Henry wrote about Latin America to arrive at the same con-clusion. A good one to begin with is the story entitled "The Fourth in Salvador,"[82] a wildly ludicrous tall tale about a drink-ing spree in which four or five Americans, an Englishman, and "a buck coon from Georgia" shot up the town while celebrating the Fourth of July and incidentally contributed in doing so to the success of a revolution which made them heroes in the eyes of the new government. The whole story is utterly ridiculous but it is told in such a bland, matter-of-fact way as a remembered episode that one may readily accept its integrated details for historic fact. It should also be read, however, in the light of Al Jennings's reference to the same episode, which was allegedly the outcome of the first meeting between those two famous fugitives from American justice: "Everyone who knows O. Henry knows how three loyal prodigals celebrated the nation's birth. He has made it memorable in his story, 'The Fourth in Salvador.' What he couldn't remember he fabricated, but many

of the details ... happened just as he has narrated them."[83]
Perhaps so, but the skeptical reader may be pardoned for
suspecting that he also "added lots of stuff that never happened."

The remaining Latin American stories are cut from the same
colorful cloth, the texture of which is so cunningly woven of
a minimum of remembered actuality and a maximum of fanciful
invention that the illusion of truth is delightfully maintained.
"On Behalf of the Management" tells of an attempted revolution,
or rather a phony election campaign, cooked up and financed
in New York but abortively conducted in an imaginary postage-
stamp-sized country somewhere in the vicinity of Ecuador.[84]
"Two Renegades" likewise deals with the intervention of two
odd-ball American individuals in a Panamanian revolutionary
escapade, one of whom, a Yankee named O'Keefe, is ransomed
from a firing squad by the other, Doc Millikan, a died-in-the-wool
Rebel. When O'Keefe reluctantly swears allegiance to the Con-
federacy, the ransom of $12,000 is paid in Confederate currency,
of which Millikan has two barrels full back in Yazoo City.[85]
"Supply and Demand" is an even more fantastic yarn about the
exploitation of an innocent tribe of Central American Indians,
who, having no awareness of the exchange value of gold, supply
it freely in quantity to a swindling Irishman, Patrick Shane,
until another entrepreneur shows up with a cargo of mirrors,
cheap jewelry, and safety razors and infects them with a
knowledge of good and evil.[86] Again, "He Also Serves" is another
tale of Indian exploitation, located in the Aztec area of Mexico; it
is flavored, therefore, with pagan reincarnation rites and other
high jinks occurring in a ruined Aztec temple.[87] Still another, "A
Ruler of Men," tells of a fake revolution which an Irish giant
named O'Connor is tricked into leading in an unnamed Latin-
American republic: bilked of his funds, he is thrown in jail until
rescued by his partner, Bowers; he winds up back in New York
City, ruling men happily by cramming them into overloaded sub-
way trains.[88] Finally, "The Day We Celebrate" wearily re-echoes
the bacchanalian motif of "The Fourth in Salvador"; yet its dis-
mally farcical account of a scrap between two drunken derelicts
in Costa Rica probably comes closer to the actual conditions O.
Henry witnessed during his sojourn in Honduras than do all his
other effervescent re-creations of lotus land, including its most
elaborate presentation in *Cabbages and Kings.*[89]

In assessing O. Henry's Latin-American stories, one must

constantly bear in mind, therefore, that they are fiction; that they set forth, as do his tales of the West and the South, a newly created world of fantasy, not the environment he actually lived in, though the two are related and often made to appear convincingly identical through the narrative skill of the artist—his ability to convey realistically the surface details, the atmosphere of his setting, and the speech and action of his characters. Lotus land is exactly as Tennyson portrayed it—"a land in which it seemed always afternoon"—a world of dreams where one can "muse and brood and live again in memory."[90] In his Latin American stories O. Henry came closest to admitting the illusory nature of this realm in "The World and the Door," the story which during his last year of life he strove to refashion into a stage play. It opens, typically enough, like this: "A favourite dodge to get your story read by the public is to assert that it is true, and then add that Truth is stranger than Fiction. I do not know if the yarn I am anxious for you to read is true; but the Spanish purser of the fruit steamer *El Carrero* swore to me by the shrine of Santa Guadalupe that he had the facts from the U. S. Vice-consul at La Paz..."[91] The story tells of a romance between two well-to-do fugitives from justice: Ralph Merriam, a New York broker who has shot another man in a nightclub dispute; and Mrs. Florence Conant, who confesses to having poisoned her husband. So long as each knows of the other's guilt, both can be deliriously happy in their shared company; but when Merriam's "victim," Hedges, unaccountably shows up alive and well and bearing no grudges, and when Mrs. Conant learns from an old newspaper that her husband did not die but got a divorce, both of them quietly make plans to escape and to separate without seeing each other again.

Though this story ends in the usual O. Henry double reverse twist, there is a dash of bitters in the denouement which takes some of the curse off his sentimentalized boy-meets-girl pattern; but a more significant saving grace comes in O. Henry's own self-spoofing with his reader. He knows that he is doing a romantic bit and that the reader knows it too; hence there is no point in pretending otherwise. But while the self-ridicule directed at his "discourse in Bulwer-Lyttonese" smashes the illusion, it also reveals the deeper meaning of the theme that haunts him in the image of the world and the door—the realization that there is no lasting escape for anyone in lotus land.

CHAPTER 4

Bagdad—The New York Stories

WHEN O. HENRY first visited Irving Place, he is reported to have said while standing in front of Washington Irving's town house: "A fellow kinda feels like wearing his hat in his hand when he stands here, doesn't he?"[1] If true, the remark illuminates both O. Henry's artistic consciousness and his close relationship to the creator of Diedrich Knickerbocker, the writer who first caught the flavor of New York and who brought to the world's attention a new form of fiction developing in America. The relationship between Irving and O. Henry is thus doubly significant: both were innovators in a modern literary form; both approached and employed the materials they found appropriate to that form in much the same frame of mind. Many years before, Irving had said concerning the shifting scenes of life he had witnessed during his wanderings in search of literary materials: "I cannot say that I have studied them with the eye of a philosopher; but rather with the saunter-ing gaze with which humble lovers of the picturesque stroll from the window of one print-shop to another; caught sometimes by the delineations of beauty, sometimes by the distortions of caricature. . . . As it is the fashion for modern tourists to travel pencil in hand, and bring home their port-folios filled with sketches, I am disposed to get up a few for the entertainment of my friends."[2] But for the obvious changes of the local scene occasioned by a century of development in Manhattan, O. Henry might well have uttered precisely the same words at the outset of his career in New York; for he was to be the literary tourist of the early twentieth century who captured the beauty and picturesqueness his roving eye caught everywhere in that glamorous metropolis and who rendered these qualities in story after story "by the distortions of caricature."

During his eight years' residence in New York, O. Henry produced over 140 stories based on the life he shared in a constantly shifting backdrop suggestive of the city's colorful, endlessly varied facets. These stories, as has been noted, began appearing in popular New York magazines as soon as he arrived, and their flow, rising to a peak in the three years between 1904 and 1907, never stopped until the year after his death. More than a hundred were first published in the New York *Sunday World;* the remainder were spread through the issues of practically every other well-known periodical competing for the mass audience of those days. But long before the last of them saw magazine publication, the earlier ones were being reissued in the collected volumes that have since carried O. Henry's fame far beyond the bounds established by his magazine reputation. Beginning with *The Four Million* in 1906, the bulk of his New York stories (a total of 125) appear in this and five other volumes, two of which were published after his death;[3] but at least two or three of the New York stories, including some of his best ones, are to be found in every other volume of his *Works.*[4]

Like a mosaic patiently assembled out of thousands of minute stone particles, the New York one meets in O. Henry's stories is both real and not real. Its essence is there, firmly and indelibly embedded in scores of passages which the casual reader seeking only transitory entertainment from a story plot may feel, yet fail to grasp intellectually—the changeless, turbulent, indestructible spirit of the place, as a recent New York writer has succinctly demonstrated.[5] Speaking through one of his many masks, Raggles, the itinerant tramp who "came and laid siege to the heart of the great city of Manhattan," O. Henry struck the keynote of his love song to "the greatest of all cities." The special charms of other cities, though recognizable, "had been to him as long primer to read; as country maidens quickly to fathom; as send-price-of-subscription-with-answer rebuses to solve; as oyster cocktails to swallow; but here was one as cold, glittering, serene, impossible as a four-carat diamond in a window to a lover outside fingering damply in his pocket his ribbon-counter salary."[6] This endless allure of New York with its thousands of beckoning contrarieties, inducements and denials, he was to celebrate in story after story—sometimes in maudlin outright praise, often in the subtler awareness revealed in a carelessly turned figure of speech, always with a profound understanding of the price exacted by such a mistress from the poet who lays siege to her heart.

Fully aware of the difficulties involved, O. Henry's success in catching the essence of New York was due largely to the joyful eagerness with which he accepted the challenge, and brought into play all the blandishments his large stock of words and images could command. New York, he said, required that the outlander be either enemy or lover; and O. Henry chose to be a lover, though he never doubted that to possess the city's heart would be an unequal struggle. "Not only by blows does it seek to subdue you. It woos you to its heart with the subtlety of a siren. It is a combination of Delilah, green Chartreuse, Beethoven, chloral and John L. in his best days."[7] To record its voice would demand "a mighty and far-reaching utterance," capable of mingling in one loud note "the chords of the day's traffic, the laughter and music of the night, . . . the rag-time, the weeping, the stealthy hum of cab-wheels, the shout of the press agent, the tinkle of fountains on the roof gardens, . . . the whispers of the lovers in the parks—all these sounds must go into your voice—not combined, but mixed, and of the mixture an essence made."[8] To penetrate its mystery, one would have to turn bold adventurer, a prowler by night as well as a part of (yet apart from) "the dreary march of the hopeless Army of Mediocrity"[9] during the rush hours of the day, so as not to overlook the myriad meaningful signs visible everywhere. For "at every corner handkerchiefs drop, fingers beckon, eyes besiege, and the lost, the lonely, the rapturous, the mysterious, the perilous, changing clues of adventure are slipped into our fingers."[10] To appreciate its beauty would demand both perspective and understanding, the ability to comprehend that the city was "like a great river fed by a hundred alien streams. Each influx brings strange seeds on its flood, strange silt and weeds, and now and then a flower of rare promise. To construe this river requires a man who can build dykes against the overflow, who is a naturalist, a geologist, a humanitarian, a diver, and a strong swimmer."[11] And to know its worth would take insight and imagination enough to see beneath its "ridiculous sham palaces of trumpery and tinsel pleasures," as Blinker suddenly perceived at Coney Island, that "counterfeit and false though the garish joys of these spangled temples were, . . . deep under the gilt surface they offered saving and apposite balm and satisfaction to the restless human heart."[12]

O. Henry thus captured the essence of his beloved city because he could "distill its true meaning from a welter of deceitful immediacies."[13] But he did not overlook the immediacies; they are what registered on the sensitized film of his mental camera, the countless disparate sense impressions whose implications he could quickly synthesize and clarify. For example, "the copyrighted smells of spring" belonging to the city alone: "The smells of hot asphalt, underground caverns, gasoline, patchouli, orange peel, sewer gas, . . . Egyptian cigarettes, mortar and the undried ink on newspapers."[14] And the fire escapes, zigzagging down the front walls of pretentious flat-houses—"laden with household goods, drying clothes, and squalling children evicted by the midsummer heat."[15] And the melancholy sight of an army of "dogmen," emerging daily at twilight from these towering flats with their leashed beasts, every one of them having been "either cajoled, bribed, or commanded by his own particular Circe to take the dear household pet out for an airing."[16] Again, the devotees of curiosity, swarming like flies "in a struggling, breathless circle about the scene of [any] unusual occurrence. . . . They gaze with equal interest and absorption at a chorus girl or at a man painting a liver pill sign. They will form as deep a cordon around a man with a club foot as they will around a balked automobile. . . . They are optical gluttons, feasting and fattening on the misfortunes of their fellow beings."[17]

These are but a few of the many concrete impressions that O. Henry turned to account in his continuous round of observations. An inveterate walker, he knew the city at first hand from the Bowery to Harlem and from the Hudson River Ferry to Coney Island; and he noted down constantly the varied kinds of life inhabiting all its different neighborhoods. He noted at one extreme the jostling crowds thronging the downtown streets, the busy brokers and the trim shopgirls, the Broadway sports, the cops and con-men; and at the other, the kids playing games on quieter side streets, idlers lolling on park benches while watching the sparrows in Madison Square, and housewives exchanging gossip across front stoops or haggling with street venders over the price of strawberries. As a result of all this sharply observed detail, the settings in his stories bear the stamp of authenticity whenever he chooses to make them do so. The milieu in which his characters move, breathe, and have their being is the real New York of the four million of his day; for the accuracy of his recorded impressions makes it so. They square with the facts recorded by other media of the times such as newspaper advertisements, photographs, theatrical handbills, and the much more significant paintings of artists like Sloan and Glackens.

The authenticity of O. Henry's New York is further strengthened by the kinds of emphasis he places on his varied social scene. Though his characters are flawed by the idealization given their actions and attitudes toward whatever the problem confronting them, there is yet an air of truthfulness about the basic situations he arranges for them. Almost invariably these situations are reflections of the everyday life of the common man—at work, at home, or at play. Ikey Schoenstein behind his tall prescription desk, where his pills are "rolled out on its own pill-tile, divided with a spatula, rolled with the finger and thumb, dusted with caleined magnesia and delivered in little round pasteboard pill-boxes,"[18] is in his proper element. So are the firemen in Company 99, arguing over the merits of the Russo-Japanese War;[19] Gaines, slaving away in an office during the summer's heat and pretending to like it so that his wife and children can enjoy another month's vacation in the mountains;[20] Vesey and the other newsmen on the *Enterprise* staff, trying to interpret their foreign correspondent's coded dispatch from the Yalu River;[21] and so too, the cabby, Jerry O'Donovan, sitting "aloft like Jupiter on an unsharable seat, holding your fate between two thongs of inconstant leather."[22] In these and dozens of other analogous situations presented in O. Henry's stories, New Yorkers could see themselves reflected; and even though a half-century has wiped away many a familiar landmark, implement, vehicle, and spectacle of the period, they still can.

To find literary significance in O. Henry's treatment of this conglomerate mass of human activity, however, calls for classification of one sort or another, even though any attempt to classify his New York stories too rigidly must break down under the pressures of overlapping. One reason is that they do not conform so readily to the distinct patterns into which his Western and his Southern tales fall; moreover, no two stories are precisely alike in form and content, despite a general sameness of tone and atmosphere characterizing most of them. One basis for classifying them might be found in the kinds of activities their characters chiefly engage in; another, in the problems of adjustment these characters are obliged to face; still another, perhaps, in the several themes with which the stories deal.

But regardless of the pattern imposed, careful study of most of these stories under any legitimate criteria quickly discloses the basic unreality in the lives of O. Henry's New Yorkers. At least sixty of the stories center about the problems of men and women at work, but these problems seldom emerge from the nature or demands of their respective jobs. Another group of about thirty stories focuses on the problems of the unemployed and underprivileged, as against those of people who have more money than they know what to do with; and while a greater proportion of stories in this group do throw light on the pitiful consequences of economic disparity, they offer little if any more dramatic insight into the complex causes or possible alleviation of the social ailment. (Let the poor underpaid shopgirl meet a kind millionaire on the Coney Island steamer, or the park-bench beggar be given a generous handout by a lavish Caliph—it was the role O. Henry himself liked to play when he had the funds to spare.) Similarly, a third group, containing about twenty-five stories, deals chiefly with the living conditions and domestic affairs of representative members of the "four million"; but here again, the problems at issue tend oftener than not to arise from factitious causes rather than from normal family relationships, so that the solutions provided for them prove equally bizarre. There is, finally, a fourth group of stories in which the predominant activities of the characters are so diverse that no fully satisfactory catch-all term can be applied to them; the twenty-five stories (more or less) belonging in this miscellany, however, may be lumped under the loose heading of "Bagdad on parade," since the one trait common to most of them is the exhibition of typical, dyed-in-the-wool New Yorkers' behavior in public.

I   *O. Henry's Toilers—Men and Women at Work*

There are at least two contradictory ways of interpreting O. Henry's fictional representation of New York's toiling masses, and his Russian admirers, along with many others, seem to have adopted both at different times. On the one hand, his stories may be seen as an implied, if not an outright, criticism of the gross inequalities in the American capitalistic system, as indicated in this recent blast from the U.S.S.R.: "He gave a general idea of the absurdity of the system under which dire poverty was the source of the amassing of fantastic wealth, and under which the rich became slaves of their millions and lost all human semblance. For O. Henry they were leeches who sucked their capital out of the poor, to whom they paid a pittance so that they might keep body and soul together and help the rich make their millions."[23] On the other hand, the stories may be taken as offering a complacent, if sometimes cynical, approval of the *status quo,* and their author condemned for falseness, hypocrisy, sentimentality—for being "the great consoler," a slave of the bourgeoisie, sowing illusions, false hopes, another form of opium.[24]

By depending on a picked assortment of stories, one could perhaps make out a plausible case for either view; but neither would stand up under scrutiny. One might argue, for example, that the well-known "Gift of the Magi" and "The Furnished Room" offer a bitter indictment of the inequities which cause intense suffering in America's materialistic society; or one might point to stories like "The Shocks of Doom," "One Thousand Dollars," "A Night in New Arabia," and "The Defeat of the City"[25] as evidence of O. Henry's full support of capitalism and the concentration of wealth in the right hands. But to assess his stories in these terms is to endow him with philosophical views he never possessed; for he is neither Realist nor Naturalist in outlook. Though sincerely humanitarian in his sympathies for the underdog, his view of the human predicament is consistently that of the Romanticist. "His half-dozen Jewish characters, for example, are superficial types, revealing no serious interest in the impact which New York had on the Jewish immigrant. Nor does he show an interest in one of the crucial issues of his day, the growing fight between capital and labor. Aside from his sentimental and somewhat ambivalent concern for the under-paid shopgirl, Porter's interest in New York was that of the perennial tourist."[26]

O. Henry's portrayal of men and women at work accordingly reveals all the same Romantic postures and clichés visible in his Western and Southern stories, but his dexterity in sketching their harried existence produces the desired effect—a faint stirring of the emotions to laughter or tears, without disturbing unduly the reader's basic equanimity. Hence the widespread appeal of these stories; for, whatever the specific problem involved, the reader may remain comfortably detached, regardless of whether or not he finds that the characters and action, once his interest is aroused in them, touch his own personal concerns. Usually, the problem is pretty remote, but even if it is not, O. Henry's sleight-of-hand can quickly convert it into either a delightful farce, a touching little love story, or a shocking reversal of fortune. The problem in "The Love Philtre of Ikey Schoenstein," for example, is that Ikey, the drug clerk, is too timid to approach his adored Rosy Riddle directly; yet he is fearful that his rival, Chunk McGowan, will get her. When Chunk applies to him for an aphrodisiac to spur Rosy's desire for an elopement, Ikey gives him instead a sleeping potion intended to keep her immobilized until he can warn her father; then Ikey learns next day that the couple eloped on schedule while Rosy's dad lay soundly drugged from the potion given him by mistake.[27] In "From the Cabby's Seat" the problem is equally far-fetched: Jerry O'Donovan, half-seas over, picks up a solitary fare near McGary's Family Cafe, drives her in and around Central Park for hours, and then, finding that she has no money to pay him, angrily hauls her off to a police station—where he discovers that she is the bride he had forgotten while getting drunk at his own wedding party.[28] Again, "The Halberdier of the Little Rheinschloss" tells of the embarrassment of well-to-do young Deering when his fiancée finds him dressed in an iron suit and serving as part of the décor in a fashionable German restaurant, the only job he could get as a means of gaining her father's consent to their marriage.[29]

Synopsized in this ruthless way, the stories, of course, lose all the piquancy with which O. Henry flavors the meager substance of his little dish. His witty comparisons and turns of phrase, adroitly scattered throughout the stories, must be read in their context to see how much they add to the overall effect. So too, his clever manipulation of the angle of narration: "The Halberdier," for instance, gains considerably in comic effect by being told entirely from the point of view of sympathetic but unlettered Waiter # 18, whose fractured phraseology contrasts ludicrously with the agonizing scenes he reports: " 'He give the millionaires a lovely roast in a sarcastic way, describing their automobiles and opera-boxes and diamonds; and then he got around to the working-classes and the kind of grub they eat and the long hours they work—and all that sort of stuff—bunkum, of course. . . .' "[30] Always O. Henry's capacious bag of tricks yields up a new device or two with which he can spice up an otherwise empty or pointless plot. In "A Midsummer Knight's

Dream" it is the contrast between Gaines's dream of his courtship days in a mountain resort and the letter he receives from his wife as he sits sweating in a hot office building.[31] In "The Diamond of Kali" it is a rapidly diminishing supply of whiskey, which a newspaper reporter consumes while noting down the hair-raising details of General Marcellus B. Ludlow's pompously told story of his discovery and removal of a fabulous Indian jewel.[32] A suite of adjoining cubicles in which a divorce lawyer places all three contestants in a suit provides for the comic fiasco of mistaken identity in "The Hypothesis of Failure";[33] and miscalculations based on an eccentric editor's method of having manuscripts evaluated by elevator operators and furnace tenders lead to the downfall of a writer's hopes for publication in "A Sacrifice Hit."[34]

On the basis of these and numerous other stories like them, one is tempted to say that the more routine the occupation in real life, the more O. Henry may be counted on to embroider it in fiction. Marvey Maxwell, the broker, for instance, is so busy that when he gets to work accompanied by his stenographer, Miss Leslie, he has forgotten his previous day's instructions to his clerk to hire another stenographer and refuses to see any applicants for the job, saying that Miss Leslie can have it as long as she wants it. He has also forgotten—as he catches a glimpse of her and decides to propose to her during the one moment he can spare—that they "were married last evening at eight o'clock in the Little Church around the Corner."[35] And again, in "Witches Loaves" poor Miss Martha Meacham's misjudgment of the reason why a shabby little German buys two loaves of stale bread from her bakeshop every day brings a shocking reversal of fortune to both of them. Mistaking him for a starving artist who might respond amorously to a friendly gesture, she one day surreptitiously puts butter inside the loaves but learns very shortly from the outraged Blumberger that she has "schpoilt" him: instead of eating the bread, he had been using handfuls of stale crumbs to erase the penciled lines on his finished architectural drawings; the buttered ones ruined in a moment the results of three months' labor on a prize competition.[36]

Even in this far-fetched little tale, however, O. Henry's amused sympathy for his puppets shines through the irony of their shattered hopes, and it infects the reader. His treatment of the pathetically futile lives of striving but untalented artists, writers, and show people, in fact, covers another fairly extensive group of the working population, and he usually presents them in a nicely balanced tone of mingled irony, pathos, and humor. Sometimes the predominant tone is lightly satiric, as in the story of Miss Medora Martin, headstrong Vermonter who comes to New York with easel and paints, determined to become a professional artist. Before long she is right at the center of Bohemia's "Vortex," gabbing and drinking with other artists, whose chatter of Henry James among the tables blends oddly with the popping corks and silvery laughter—"champagne flashed in the pail, wit flashed in the pan."[37] And for a moment the reader fears that she may achieve her dream of becoming a conquering courtesan, until her old beau, Beriah Hoskins, comes to fetch her back home to Harmony. A similarly whimsical touch may be seen in "The Rathskeller and the Rose," an amusing yarn about a new Broadway star, Posie Carrington (née Boggs) who has worked her way up to stardom through the ranks of burlesque shows, musical comedy, and bit parts, though hailing originally from Cranberry Corners.[38] Now at the peak of her success, she is scheduled for the lead in a new play, "Paresis by Gaslight"; and an unknown but ambitious young actor, Hightower, hopes to secure the leading male role in it, the part of "Haytosser," a rural rube. To persuade her of his fitness for the part, he does such a convincing act of posing as her fellow townsman that, filled with nostalgia, she cancels all engagements and returns to Cranberry Corners. Still another, equally light though less beguiling, is the story "Strictly Business," which pretends to dramatize the "real" life of show people, specifically the vaudeville team of Hart and Cherry; but the punch line revealing that their strictly business relationship over a two-year road trip has also included marriage comes as no surprise to the watchful reader.[39]

Sometimes the tone in these stories of artists and showmen strikes a deeper note, the laughter shading off into sighs of sadness and even despair; and in such instances the echo of O. Henry's own personal suffering may be felt. Two stories illustrating this shift of tone are "A Service of Love" and "The Last Leaf," both of which rely on the sacrificial theme for their effect. Based on the same formula as the better known "Gift of the Magi," "A Service of Love" tells of an earnest young pair of art students, Joe and Delia Larrabee, he a painter and she a musician, who bolster each other's courage when their funds run out by pretending to have a steady income from their professional skills; it turns out that she has been ironing shirts in a laundry while he has been firing the furnace in the same building.[40] More touching yet, "The Last Leaf" has long been a universal favorite despite its glaring implausibility; for the story of kindly old Behrman, the artist *manqué* who gives up his life painting his one masterpiece—the last leaf on an outdoor vine—in order to restore a dying young girl's will to live, strikes a symbolic chord that transcends the sentimental gimcrackery of its plot.[41]

More illuminating than either of these, however, is the story of Pettit, a hopeful young writer from Alabama whose stories are rejected by New York editors because they lack "living substance." When he falls in love and writes about that experience, his story is even worse—"sentimental drivel, full of whimpering soft-heartedness and gushing egoism.... A perusal of its buttery phrases would have made a cynic of a sighing chambermaid."[42] Surviving the ending of his affair with the aid of whiskey and more writing, Pettit then finds another woman deeply in love with him, even to the point of attempted suicide over his unresponsiveness; and, when he converts this case into fiction, the editor whoops joyfully because now " 'Just as though it lay there, red and bleeding, a woman's heart was written into the lines.' " Pettit remains unimpressed, however, having discovered that " 'You can't write with ink, and you can't write with your own heart's blood, but you can write with the heart's blood of someone else. You have to be a cad before you can be an artist.' "[43] Thoroughly disillusioned, he plans to return to Alabama to sell ploughs for his father.

Perhaps the bitterest of all in this group is "The Memento," a story that embalms all the gaudy flavor of the early twentieth-century entertainment world, especially that of the cheap vaudeville circuits, as well as more than a touch of O. Henry's innate Puritanism.[44] The story is built around the notorious vaudeville act of Rosalie Ray, whose *pièce de résistance* was swinging out from the proscenium high over "bald-head row" and kicking off one of her yellow garters, which all the men below scrambled to possess. After two years of this she had quit the stage, revolted by lascivious men pawing at her; and she had gone to a village on Long Island, where she became engaged to a young minister;

but, before disclosing her own past, she learned that he owned a memento sent by a former " 'ideal love far above him in a roundabout way—yet rather direct.' "[45] Instead of feeling flattered to discover that it was one of her own yellow garters, Rosalie returned to the playhouse in high dudgeon, convinced that all men were equally bad.

In its approach to the problem of the unattached girl obliged to earn her own living in the big city, "The Memento" is similar to many other stories O. Henry wrote on the same theme, most of them equally as dated and sentimental. There are at least twenty such stories in which the underpaid shopgirl, showgirl, model, clerk, waitress, or domestic servant presents a tearful spectacle of threatened innocence or unfulfilled hopes. Seldom does one find the aggressive young woman, capable of exploiting her physical resources successfully, and never the fallen woman triumphant, such as Dreiser's Sister Carrie; but there must have been a number of both types in O. Henry's extensive circle of acquaintances. For the mid-twentieth-century reader's taste, therefore, his generally cloying treatment of the agonized working girl is perhaps the least satisfactory of all his metropolitan vignettes. In "The Trimmed Lamp," for example, two girl friends try to maintain a respectable appearance on meager wages, Lou as a laundry ironer at $18.50, Nancy as a department store clerk at only $8.00 a week. Besides her better-paying job, Lou also has Dan, a steady young electrician earning $30.00 a week and eager to marry her; she chides Nancy not only for being satisfied with a poorer job, even if it does enable her to mingle with "swell" people and to imitate in home-made clothes the "posh" styles of her rich customers, but also for turning down offers of marriage from wealthy men. But meanwhile Lou puts off marrying Dan, ditching him eventually to become a rich man's mistress; Nancy, of course, gets him. In the end Nancy adds to her trimmed lamp the unction of consolation for Lou, the foolish virgin, who on learning the outcome collapses, "crouching down against the iron fence of the park sobbing turbulently"— despite her "expensive fur coat and diamond-ringed hands."[46]

The vulnerability of the single girl, as a prey of either the wolves of starvation or those in human form, receives similar treatment in three other stories which were great favorites among O. Henry's enthusiasts forty or fifty years ago: "Elsie in New York," "The Skylight Room," and "An Unfinished Story."

The underlying implication in the first is that the very agencies
society creates specifically for the care and protection of the
innocent—including the police, the church, the welfare agencies,
and the labor unions—tend rather to thrust them into the maw
of predatory individuals. And so, poor Elsie, a little "peacherino"
who might have had a number of safely respectable jobs but
for her "protectors," winds up as a model whose fate (O. Henry
assures us by quoting Dickens) is to be numbered among the
"Lost, your Excelency."[47] For while Elsie admires herself in
Russian sables, her employer, Otter, is gleefully reserving a private dining room for two, with "the usual brand and the '85
Johannisburger with the roast." Another Elsie, the heroine of
"The Skylight Room," is granted a less harrowing fate, but not
before the poor typist, a favorite among all the occupants of
Mrs. Parker's rooming house, comes within an inch of starving
to death.[48]

The archetype of all these suffering damsels, however, is
Dulcie, heroine of what was "probably the most admired of all
O. Henry's stories" during the decade following his death.[49]
What captured the public's heart especially in "An Unfinished
Story" was the grim picture he drew of the joyless existence of
the shopgirl who, on a $6.00 a week salary, had to provide for
room rent, food, clothes, and all other needs. That Dulcie managed despite hunger and deprivation to preserve her chastity
by turning down a dinner date with Piggy Wiggins, the rat
(who "could look at a shopgirl and tell you to an hour how
long it had been since she had eaten anything more nourishing
than marsmallows and tea"[50]), gave a lift to the spirit, even
though the narrator observed ominously that on another day,
while feeling lonelier than usual, she might not be so resolute.

Not all of O. Henry's working girls suffer from malnutrition
or the menace of lost virginity. Some achieve comfort and security
in the approved manner; others have these thrust upon them,
though their inability to distinguish the real from the spurious
article may deprive them of the offered prize. Such is nearly the
fate of Miss Archer, crack model of Zizzbaum's wholesale
clothing company, whose substandard intelligence (as compared
with her hour-glass measurements, which were even better than
"the required 38-25-42 standard")[51] misinterprets a visiting execu-
tive's fumbling proposals of marriage as dishonorable advances.
And such is the fate in store for both Claribel Colby in "The

Ferry of Unfulfillment" and Maisie, the heroine of "A Lickpenny Lover": for Claribel, exhausted from a previous night's dancing and a full day's work behind the counter, misses a golden opportunity when, half-asleep, she gives the wrong answer to the rich prospector who wants to marry her;[52] while Maisie, even with her eyes open, rejects her wealthy suitor because she thinks that his promise to take her to faraway places only means that he " 'wanted me to marry him and go down to Coney Island for wedding tour.' "[53]

The strong appeal of stories like these which dramatized so glaringly the contrast between the millionaire's world of values and the shopgirl's tells us much about the taste of a period just becoming fully aware of the hardening class structure which a burgeoning industrial era had imposed on America's democratic society. To break through class barriers by applying some variation of the Cinderella formula was still held as a valid romantic hope, even though in actuality it often proved a delusion. And O. Henry, shrewdly aware of his public's wavering between hopes and fears, played the game both ways in different stories. Meanwhile, however, his sympathetic portrayal of the working girl's hard lot was a new phenomenon which drew enthusiastic response chiefly because it was so accurate in minute details. From close, firsthand observation, as reported by Anne Partlan,[54] he knew the kinds of rooms they lived in, the food they ate, the clothes they wore, the working conditions they endured, and the simple pleasures and dreams they could afford to make life bearable. Thus, however far-fetched the Cinderella motif woven about the lives of these working girls (as in "The Third Ingredient," "Springtime a la Carte," "The Purple Dress," "The Enchanted Profile," and many others),[55] there was underlying his depiction of their predicament a firm basis of truth which the public sensed and approved. Moreover, as Smith long ago pointed out, the two kinds of New York society that interested O. Henry most were "those who were under a strain of some sort and those who were under a delusion. The first stirred his sympathy; the second furnished him unending entertainment. Both are abundantly represented in his stories."[56] Since this dichotomy takes in most of us today, along with Manhattan's toiling millions of the 1900's, it is easy to see why O. Henry's stories about them still enjoy a widespread popularity.

II *The Rich and The Poor*

On the centennial anniversary of O. Henry's birth, the Soviets cannily issued a commemorative stamp in his honor, catching our own postal authorities flat-footed. And when the New York *Herald Tribune* took note of this event, observing that the Russians' tastes in American literature are curious because they have made favorites of writers like Jack London and O. Henry, "both of whom are rather out of fashion here nowadays,"[57] a dialectical riposte quickly followed in *Izvestia*. Many good American writers who criticized the "American way of life," said the writer, have gone out of fashion in the United States but will continue to be honored as classics in Russia. The implication that O. Henry—along with Steinbeck, Hemingway, Dreiser, and Mark Twain—deserves honor chiefly as a bitter critic of American capitalism can, of course be documented sufficiently to support the Communist propaganda line. But this image of O. Henry would come no closer to the truth than its exact opposite. For, although he was clearly a friend of the friendless and the poor, both in real life and in his fiction, he was certainly no publicly avowed enemy of the rich.

While portraying the horrors and pinched existence endured by his underpaid shopgirls, he does occasionally condemn in sweepingly Dickensian general terms the tight-fisted employers who keep them economically depressed. Occasionally too, he chides the idle rich, through irony and understatement, for having so much to waste while others have so little to live on. Yet, whenever he depicts the rich themselves in his stories, he generally presents them in tolerant, even affectionate terms. Blustery old Anthony Rockwall, the retired soap manufacturer in "Mammon and the Archer" is the epitome of O. Henry's type of the self-made American business tycoon: he knows that money talks, even in affairs of the heart; and he proves it to his own satisfaction by purchasing a custom-made midtown traffic jam so that his son may have ample time to propose to the girl he wants to marry before she can slip away to Europe.[58] Though he grouses over the alleged snobbishness of his aristocratic neighbors, whom we never meet, he is himself rather a lovable as well as a generous character. So too, in his own way, is old Jacob Spraggins, the multi-millionaire Caliph in "A Night in New Arabia" who alleviated his conscience by donating large sums to colleges and charitable organizations until he grew tired of trying to buy his way into heaven and decided to concentrate his attention and his wealth on his infant grandson.[59] The satirical allusions O. Henry makes in the opening passages of this story to "the powerful genie Roc-Ef-El-Er who sent the Forty Thieves to soak up the oil plant of Ali Baba; . . . [and] the good Caliph Kar-Neg-Ghe, who gave away palaces," though mildly critical of America's wealthiest "robber barons," are anything but hostile or scornful in tone. On the contrary, he implies jokingly that philanthropic millionaires in New York are stumbling over one another in their quest for the beggars whom they outnumber.

In short, O. Henry romanticizes the rich as well as the poor; he gives the impression through those he selects to represent the wealthy that money is a good thing to have if only one knows how to enjoy spending it—that is, like a Caliph. The miserly and the greedy he condemns by indirection and in broad terms, but they are seldom given a name or a character role to play in the story. At best they may be referred to by another character, as in the thinly veiled allusion to the notorious Hetty Green in "The Enchanted Profile";[60] whereas the rich men and women who do figure prominently in his stories are almost invariably open-handed, magnanimous, and sympathetic. They fulfill their role of *noblesse oblige* like knights and ladies in the *Morte d'Arthur*. Like good King Wenceslaus, Carson Chalmers, for example, the wealthy, troubled hero in "A Madison Square Arabian Night," sends his butler out on a cold January night to fetch him a dinner guest at random from among a row of homeless men he saw shivering in a bread line, requesting only that the one brought in be reasonably clean. And when the contumelious guest, Sherrard Plumer, cynically assumes that his host will want to hear his life story in exchange for the free meal (" 'Catch anybody in New York giving you something for nothing. They spell curiosity and charity with the same set of building blocks,' ")[61] Chalmers graciously reassures Plumer that he has no desire to pry into his guest's private life. Here again, although harsh criticism of the capitalistic system is implied both in the butler's explanation of the meaning of the bread line—which calls to mind Stephen Crane's "Experiment in Misery"—and in Plumer's condemnation of New York's many cheap Haroun al Raschids, Chalmers himself is depicted as a person of sensitivity and charm, not as a malefactor of great wealth. There is in his story, incidentally, more than a mere echo of Henry James's great story, "The Liar," since Plumer turns out to be a down-and-out portrait painter with skills identical to those of Oliver Lyon.

Throughout these romantic tales of affluent caliphs, there is scarcely a hint either of the ascetic Christian view of the love of money as the root of all evil, or of the liberal sociological view that the rich owe a debt to society payable through graduated income taxes. Young or old, O. Henry's opulent heroes, however blinded their riches may have made them toward the suffering of the underprivileged, miraculously see the light at the touch of a magic wand and promptly set about trying, futilely of course, to rectify the balance. Thus, bored young Alexander Blinker, heir to more downtown real estate than John Jacob Astor but too annoyed to be bothered signing the legal papers his family lawyer thrusts at him, escapes for an outing to Coney Island. There through the eyes of Florence, a lovely milliner's helper, he suddenly sees the latent beauty underlying the vulgar pleasures of the masses. He is chagrined to learn that girls like Florence must meet their dates on the street or in the park because of the cramped slums they live in; but, when he learns that he himself is the owner of Brickdust Row, he is crushed and says harshly: "Remodel it, burn it, raze it to the ground."[62]

Similarly, Dan Kinsolving, idealistic young heir to a huge flour fortune piled up by his late father, who had cornered the wheat market and raised the price of bread, seeks to restore his ill-gotten inheritance to all the little people caught in this monopolistic squeeze. His friend Kenwitz, a socialistic watchmaker, proves to him the impossibility of restitution, no matter how much wealth he might have, because during the five years he was in college and abroad, various individuals' lives were wrecked: Boyne's bakery had had to close down in bankruptcy; Boyne had died in an insane asylum after setting fire to the building; his son had turned criminal and was indicted for murder; and his pretty daughter, Mary, has had to slave away sewing shirts to pay off legal fees. When he introduces Dan to her, she angrily shows Dan the door; yet within two months Kenwitz, meeting her again in a neighborhood bakery, learns that she is no longer Miss Boyne but Mrs. Kinsolving![63]

One might argue that in Kenwitz's catalogue of horrors O. Henry does damn—as much as he dared—a system that permitted the unprincipled accumulation of wealth; but the denouement completely nullifies his criticism. But the story as a whole is a good example of how he could turn a current muckraking topic to his own uses, producing an innocuously sentimental tale that evades the harsh realities, and yet makes its mass reading public feel warm and good inside. Repeatedly this is his tactic in dealing with the rich. Old Tom Crowley, the Caliph in "What You Want" (the very titles are a giveaway), who is worth $42,000,000 but bored with all his luxuries, goes on the prowl in search of something his money cannot buy. He finds it in the person of young Jack Turner, a scholarly hat-cleaner, who scornfully rejects the older man's offer to set him up in business and subsidize his education. When Crowley calls him an impudent pup, he retaliates; and presently their scuffling lands them both in jail on a disorderly charge, neither having the necessary bail in cash. Wondering whether the old man really was rich, Turner settles down contentedly on his cot to read; and his concluding response to the officer who announces shortly afterwards that Crowley has arranged to have him bailed out is: " 'Tell him I ain't in.' "[64] The story is utterly ludicrous; yet in it O. Henry's suggestion of the New Yorker's bellicose independence, though exaggerated, is well taken.

A more fundamental implication, however, in this and most of his other stories dealing with both the rich and the poor, may be expressed by the romantic cliché: "money isn't everything." This theme receives a thorough working over in virtually every story in which money, as a symbol of desirability in life, is set forth in the scales against other less tangible values. In "The Discounters of Money," kindness and thoughtfulness toward others bring the heart's desire to young millionaire Howard Pilkins, but only after his assumption that the elegant but impoverished Alice von der Ruysling would accept his proposal for the advantages of his money has almost killed his chances.[65] In "One Thousand Dollars," the young hero Bob Gilliam gallantly foregoes his rigid uncle's $50,000 bequest by pretending to be a wastrel in order that his uncle's faithful secretary, Miss Hayden, may inherit the money.[66] The same theme is given another implausible twist in "The Shocks of Doom," which brings together on the same park bench two cousins victimized by a whimsical uncle; by reversing his decision to disinherit one in favor of the other, the uncle confers joyful relief on the disinherited cousin and pain on the other one, who gets the money unexpectedly.[67] Still other variations are played upon the same theme in "The Fool Killer," "From Each According to His Ability," and "The Marry Month of May."[68] The underlying idea in all these stories is that love, freedom, pleasure—the attainment of the heart's desire—are all preferable to wealth and that sensible people will relinquish any amount of it to obtain them.

The other side of this coin is that poverty and deprivation have their compensations, so long as one accepts his hard lot gracefully and tries to live joyously and honestly within his limitations. O. Henry dramatizes this consoling, if unrealistic doctrine from a number of contrasting points of view, most of them tending to bring out the picturesqueness rather than the grimness inherent in the lives of the poor. Nothing could be grimmer or more depressing in real life than the dope-pushing derelicts that haunt the park benches and Salvation Army soup kitchens; yet in several stories O. Henry endows these characters with qualities of nobility, grandeur, tenderness, and wisdom—tales designed to evoke mingled tears and sympathetic laughter but not an urge to confront and grapple with a disturbing social evil. In "The Caliph, Cupid, and the Clock," for instance, we meet Dopey Mike, an addict whose pipe dreams transform him into "Prince Michael of the Electorate of Valeluna," and who serves in this guise to re-unite two lovers. By urging a despondent young man to wait with him a half hour longer for the sign he expects and by promising as wedding presents a check for $100,000 and a palace on the Hudson, Mike prevails, then falls asleep; as the hour strikes, a scarf flutters from a nearby window; the young man rushes off to meet his girl; and the story ends with a bum asleep on a park bench, clutching a $50 bill.[69]

In "According to their Lights" O. Henry doubles the pathos by presenting two derelicts, Murray and Captain Maroney, a dismissed police officer, starving together on a park bench. Though neither has been able to cadge a free meal, the Captain does get an opportunity to earn a large bribe for testifying against his former superior; and, when he refuses to accept it, Murray scoffs at his naïveté. Yet, as they shuffle off toward the breadline, Murray also refuses to compromise his principles; for, when an old acquaintance recognizes and informs him that his rich uncle will take him back into favor if he agrees to marry a certain heiress, he turns the offer down flat.[70] The innate dignity of the Bowery bum is again dressed up with Christmas trimmings in "Compliments of the Season," a story refashioned from one of O. Henry's earliest Texas plots.[71] In it, Fuzzy the bum is determined to offer the season's greetings personally to the mistress of a fashionable residence after returning her child's lost doll. That the lady graciously receives him, even serves him a drink and has her chauffeur drive him off in her Mercedes, is all in keeping with O. Henry's reassuring holiday gift to his public.

Common to these and other stories—"The Higher Pragmatism," "The Cop and the Anthem," and "Two Thanksgiving Day Gentlemen"—is also the theme of appearance versus reality: things are not as they seem, nor do they turn out as expected, even under the most deceptively convincing manifestations. The hard-muscled bum lolling on a park bench has a lesson to impart of wisdom and courage if one have patience to listen to his story of conquered fear and to apply his experience to one's own problem of frustrated courtship.[72] Soapy, trying desperately to get himself arrested by breaking the law in ways not appropriate to his character, goes unobserved; he achieves his desire for a comfortable cell on Blackwell's Island only when the policeman turns him in for loitering outside a church.[73] Stuffy Pete, the Union Square bum, though already bursting from one Thanksgiving Day meal, must consume another so as not to disappoint an elderly benefactor who is himself suffering from malnutrition.[74] Irony is here the tool enabling O. Henry to switch from pathos to humor and back again to pathos within a single story and throughout a series of such stories; and each is designed to entertain his Sunday morning readers with the oddities he found or could imagine to exist among the lowly.

Only occasionally in dealing with society's cast-offs did he allow a note of genuine bitterness to stiffen the harshness of his irony, and in these few stories there are hints of what he might have done with more of his material had he chosen to present these people as the individuals he had really seen, rather than as mere puppets. In "Vanity and Some Sables," for instance, we meet "Kid" Brady, member of a tough gang of hoodlums and pickpockets from Hell's Kitchen.[75] At his girl Molly's urging, the "Kid" promises to go straight, works steadily for eight months, and then gives her an expensive set of furs, which he says were not stolen but bought with his own hard-earned money. When Molly and the "Kid" are picked up anyway on suspicion of a theft of furs from his employer, they escape arrest because her furs turn out to be cheap imitations costing only $21.50; but Brady angrily confesses that he would rather have spent six months in jail than admit he could afford so little for fake Russian sables. Though the plot is as obviously contrived as any, O. Henry did inject into the tale a shade of the realism he usually evaded. The same shade is deepened further in another story called "The Assessor of Success," which tells of Hastings Beauchamp Morley, a fellow who lives entirely by his wits. Broke one day, flush the next from gambling, picking pockets, working a confidence game, and the like, Morley is yet kindly and prepossessing in appearance, charming and witty. The only important thing in life is gulling others without being gulled; he assures a beggar to whom he gives a dollar shortly after bilking another man out of $140: " 'The world is a rock to you, no doubt; but you must be an Aaron and smite it with your rod. Then things better than water will gush out of it for you.' "[76] Nevertheless, as Morley goes jauntily on his way, he catches sight of a former schoolmate whom he can no longer face, and his last words are: " 'God! I wish I could die.' "

Stories like these, which end on a sour note, are rare in O. Henry's work, especially in his treatment of the dispossessed or the degraded. Had he chosen oftener to present life in the raw as he doubtless knew it, he would not have endeared himself to the public he was writing for. But neither would he have remained true to his own concept of life as an adventure to be confronted gaily. Whether rich or poor, one could scarcely avoid seeing life's drabness: for O. Henry the point was to transcend it.

III *New Yorkers at Home*

"I would like to live a lifetime in each street in New York. Every house has a drama in it," O. Henry is reported to have said on one occasion.[77] To understand what he meant by "drama" in this context, one would have to consider carefully two of the stories which, by common consent, still stand at the head of O. Henry favorites: "The Gift of the Magi" and "The Furnished

Room." These represent the polar opposites of joy and sadness with which his imagination clothed the domestic life of average New Yorkers; and, though both may seem somewhat dated now, they still possess a strong popular appeal based on a universal yearning for an unattainable ideal. It is not surprising that "The Gift of the Magi" still enjoys such widespread fame, for in this trite little tale of mutual self-sacrifice between husband and wife, O. Henry crystallized dramatically what the world in all its stored-up wisdom knows to be of fundamental value in ordinary family life. Unselfish love shared, regardless of the attendant difficulties or distractions—this is the idea repeatedly implied as a criterion in his fictional treatment of domestic affairs. If such love is present, life can be a great adventure transcending all drabness; if it is absent, nothing else can take its place. Conversely, because it is often absent—or when present, it exists only momentarily and in a fragile state—the world can recognize and take to heart the grim meaning of life without it. O. Henry wrote few stories of ordinary family life that approach in tenderness and universal appeal the qualities found in "The Gift of the Magi"; and fewer still of those that match the bleakness of "The Furnished Room." But among the two dozen or so in which he attempted to dramatize the family life of the four million, perhaps seven or eight deserve and can stand comparison with these.

One reason for such scarcity may be simply that O. Henry did not know very much about the home life of average New Yorkers and therefore had to rely chiefly on what he could see or hear of it from the outside. There are, for instance, almost no children involved in most of these stories, and only two of them deal specifically with the problems of childhood and child care. Except for single folk or young married couples living transiently like himself in furnished rooms, the lives he knew were largely public, they were observed externally rather than from within the family circle, and they moved predominantly on the lower economic levels. Hence the paucity of stories reflecting ordinary family problems at home, as against the many showing New Yorkers of all shades and levels in restaurants, shops, offices, and parks, on the streets, and at summer resorts. Another reason may be that O. Henry could not imagine a great variety of exciting situations taking place behind those private walls he seldom penetrated, despite his belief that every house has a drama in it. "There is a saying that no man has tasted the full flavour of life until he has known poverty, love and war.... The three conditions embrace about all there is in life worth knowing."[78] Thus he begins one of his more amusing fantasies of ordinary family life in New York, and the three conditions he lays down as essential to the full life are indicative of the kinds of drama he sought. In order to find them, and also to elicit the adventuresome qualities inherent in even the dreariest existence, the domestic situations he conceived turn out to be pretty far-fetched, as well as somehow tied up with the outside world rather than self-contained.

In O. Henry's imagination what the average New Yorker's life consisted of may be best seen in the two stories entitled "The Complete Life of John Hopkins" and "The Pendulum." The Hopkins flat, he notes, was like a thousand others, and so were its occupants, Mr. and Mrs. Hopkins and their flea-bitten terrier: the husband, a typical small wage earner holding down a non-descript job; the wife, a typical Gotham flat-dweller whose attributes included "the furor for department store marked-down sales, the feeling of superiority to the lady in the third-floor front... [and] the vigilant avoidance of the installment man."[79] After the usual "compressed dinner" they would sit staring at each other; and while she "discoursed droningly of the dinner smells from the flat across the hall," he would occasionally seek to "inject a few raisins of conversation into the tasteless dough of existence."[80] Since there was clearly neither poverty, love, nor war in such a barren routine, O. Henry would have to supply these essentials by sending Hopkins out for a cigar and by involving him in a series of wild adventures before bringing him back safely to the hornblende sofa in his flat and the resumption of conversation with his wife. Hopkins' street brawl, his escape from the police, and his accidental intrusion into a private tiff between wealthy young lovers bear some resemblance to a Walter Mitty sequence; but O. Henry does not imply that his hero dreamed this romantic excitement on his way to and from the cigar store.

In "The Pendulum" the portrayal of both the dull flat-dweller's routine and its occasional disruption is more successfully carried off. "There are no surprises awaiting a man who has been married two years and lives in a flat."[81] Thus, alighting from the elevated at 81st Street and approaching his apartment,

John Perkins can gloomily foretell to the minute exactly what will occur at each stage of the evening's progress following his inevitable pot-roast dinner: his wife will show him her quilting; at 7:30 the plaster will start falling because of overhead thumping; then the drunken vaudeville team across the hall will begin its nightly carousal; and there will be other assorted neighboring noises. At 8:15 Perkins will reach for his hat and, facing Katy's ire, announce that he's going to McCloskey's to shoot a few games of pool with his friends. This time, however, things are different. Perkins finds the place in disarray, no Katy, and a hastily scrawled note revealing her sudden departure to care for a sick mother. As he begins to set the rooms in order and to prepare his lonely meal of cold mutton and coffee, Perkins gradually realizes how important his old routine has been to him. "The night was his. He might go forth unquestioned and thrum the strings of jollity as free as any gay bachelor there. He might carouse and wander and have his fling until dawn if he liked; and there would be no wrathful Katy waiting for him, bearing the chalice that held the dregs of his joy."[82] But now there is no joy. With Katy gone, Perkins remorsefully thinks how lonely it must have been for her here during all his long evenings at McCloskey's, and he resolves, tearfully, to treat her more considerately when she returns. Then Katy opens the door and explains that the sick call was a false alarm, and the household machinery silently shifts back into its accustomed order. At exactly 8:15, in response to Katy's querulous inquiry when John reaches for his hat, he says: "Thought I'd drop up to McCloskey's . . . and play a game or two of pool with the fellows."[83]

Obviously, O. Henry could not play infinite variations on the theme of dull lives like the Hopkinses' and the Perkinses'. The only other story that approaches theirs is the one entitled "Suite Homes and Their Romance," which tells in a lightly cynical tone about a typical lower middle-class couple, the Turpins, whose income of $200 a month enables them to live high because they never pay their bills.[84] After brief but quite pointedly satirical introductory passages exposing the rootlessness and irresponsibility of such people, the story degenerates, however, into an absurdly improbable sequence of events which lead ultimately to a bookmaker's joint disguised as a Browning Society and serving as a front for an illicit ice-cream parlor.

As a commentary on middle-class domestic life, the story is too far-fetched even for effective satire, despite its wisecracks and foolery. But O. Henry could more effectively employ these tactics and achieve some variety as well by turning his attention to the more colorful lives of Irish laboring families, where his necessary ingredients of poverty, love, and war abounded. In six or seven stories, at any rate, that is what he did; and the results in several were fairly satisfactory.

Humor predominates in all but one of these Irish stories. In "Between Rounds" we have the marital scraps between John and Judy McCaskey which disturb the peace at Mrs. Murphy's boardinghouse.[85] When her little six-year old boy disappears, they become reconciled momentarily, joining in the search and thinking of him sentimentally as the child they might have had; but, as soon as he is found, the McCaskeys are at each other again hammer and tongs. In "A Harlem Tragedy" the device of marital warfare receives a different twist: Mrs. Cassidy brags to Mrs. Fink about the bruises and blackened eyes her pugnacious husband gives her because his contrition afterward brings her pretty things and dinner dates; whereas Mr. Fink, a dull, modest man who "reposed in the state of matrimony like a lump of unblended suet in a pudding," never gives his wife any trouble.[86] Mrs. Fink grows so jealous that she tries to arouse him to fury and blows by bawling him out and striking him; but, instead of thrashing her in return, he humiliates her further by knuckling under and doing her washing. Poorer than either of these, "The Harbinger" tells of three thirsty Union Square loafers, one of whom decides to tackle his two-hundred-pound wife for the dollar she earned by washing so that they can get bock beer. Impervious to his demands and excuses, the wife apparently succumbs only when he begins making ardent love to her; but instead of the dollar she brings him sarsaparilla and a tablespoon to cure his springtime malady.[87]

The best of these Irish dialect stories, accordingly, are the few that combine a more serious attitude toward family relationships with oddities of speech and mannerisms, which O. Henry always renders well. Instead of pure rackety farce, there is a certain winsomeness in the two stories entitled "The Easter of the Soul" and "The Day Resurgent," both written as special Easter feature stories for his *Sunday World* readers.[88] Young "Tiger" McQuirk, temporarily idle because the stone-cutters are on strike, cannot account for his restlessness at home; his little brother attributes it to a girl, Annie Maria; his mother, simply to spring in his bones. "Tiger" denies everything, saying there is no spring in sight; and then he goes searching for signs but finds no sure ones until he reaches Annie's house. When she assures him that spring is everywhere, he is convinced, happy, invigorated. The story, virtually plotless, is yet invested with charm and meaning through O. Henry's management of dialogue between McQuirk and the various others he meets fleetingly during his progress.

O. Henry again uses most of the same devices in "The Day Resurgent" with equal effectiveness: a gruff young hero, Danny McCree, ready to sally forth in all his finery on Easter morning, is puzzled by his blind old father's wistful reference to "the hippopotamus," which he wishes he could hear the rest of if only Danny's mother could read to him. During a series of encounters with various others, Danny tries to draw the connection between Easter and hippos: he goes to church with his girl, Katy Conlon; and finally, in the midst of the sermon, he realizes that his father was talking about a book, *The History of Greece,* from which Danny had been reading aloud to him the year before, and had remembered the account of the Pelopponesian War where the reading had stopped. Much to the old man's delight, then, his son not only picks up the reading again at that point on his return but even brushes aside gruffly the suggestion that he may want to quit to see his girl. Though oversentimentalized and far-fetched, the story firmly conveys O. Henry's purpose of bringing out the close family feeling among working-class Irish, despite their apparent harshness toward one another.

Aside from these Irish dialect stories, there are very few others in O. Henry's gallery of Gothamite family portraits that deserve more than a passing glance. He showed his versatility at combining a variety of dialects, together with other tall-tale elements and satirical overtones, in "The Gold That Glittered" and in "The City of Dreadful Night," both mildly amusing farces. The former offers another variation on one of his most overworked situations—the fomenting of Latin-American revolutions, hatched and subsidized by exiles huddling in an obscure downtown cafe called, in this story, "El Refugio."[89] But in this case he spiced the plot by injecting into it both an abortive swindle and a successful romance: General Perrico Ximenes Villablanca Falcon, about to be fleeced of his $25,000 by two Irish confidence men posing as United States cabinet ministers, falls in love with his Junoesque boardinghouse keeper, the widow O'Brien; and he buys her establishment instead of squandering his funds on a fake order of Winchester rifles for the revolution. Exaggeration, puns, ludicrous metaphors, and "fractured English" dialogue are the devices that keep the humor bubbling through this yarn as well as throughout "The City of Dreadful Night," which is a take-off on the effects of a heat wave that drove hordes of suffocating tenement dwellers to sleep in the public parks. Besides the obvious physical discomforts and multi-racial irritations that provide an "Abie's Irish Rose" flavor to this story, O. Henry undercuts the absurdity of the whole situation by having his wealthy tenement house owner resolve to raise rents fifteen per cent because of the extra benefits of grass and trees his tenants were enjoying in the park.[90]

In most of the remaining stories of the domestic group, however, even the humor fails to redeem the artificiality and pointlessness of their plots. Two of them, "Memoirs of a Yellow Dog" and "Ulysses and the Dogman," ridicule the henpecked husband who must take the family pet out for an airing each evening.[91] Another pair, "Girl" and "The Struggle of the Outliers," develop the identical problem of the suburbanite's efforts to secure a household maid by making it appear that the hero is contending with a rival for the girl's affection.[92] Frustrated love overcoming either self-imposed obstacles or the machinations of assorted rivals stretches the reader's credulity in at least five or six others.[93] In one story, "Tommy's Burglar," O. Henry spoofs the typical juvenile fiction of his day by having the burglar and the little boy who apprehends him discuss critically the appropriate methods and clichés employed in writing a story involving a burglar and a little boy. In another called "A Newspaper Story" he shows how a single copy of a cast-off newspaper can link together through fortuitous events the disparate lives of various families unknown to one another.[94]

The preponderance of light foolery and romance in nearly all these stories, most of them written under contract to fill the *Sunday World* page each week, offers fairly convincing proof that O. Henry not only gauged the taste of his mass reading public quite accurately but also knew how to satisfy it. That he was likewise more concerned with this problem of producing a weekly diet of light entertainment than with the more demanding problem of rendering artistically the manifold dramas inherent in Manhattan's domestic life also seems evident. If he could achieve now and then incidental criticism of greedy landlords, miserly employers, or crooked public officials along with his entertainment, well and good; but the entertainment took precedence over everything else. For the only other exception to his common practice (aside from "The Gift of the Magi" and "The Furnished Room") is in "The Guilty Party—An East Side Tragedy," a grim tale of parental neglect which "was made a full-page feature by the Sunday [World] Magazine editor, with a prize contest announced for the best letter regarding it."[95] Somewhat reminiscent of Crane's Maggie, "The Guilty Party" tells of a twelve-year-old girl, Liz, who grows up to become a drunkard, murderess, and suicide because of her father's unwillingness to play with her as a child. Employing his typical "envelope" technique consisting of a brief opening scene and of a swift transition to the main scene couched in the form of a dream, O. Henry achieved in this story a meaningful domestic drama that suggests more truthfully than most of his others some of the festering social problems underlying the picturesque surface of metropolitan life. Like most of the others, it too suffers from an overdose of maudlin sentimentality in its conclusion; but it deserves nevertheless to be taken as seriously as "The Furnished Room."

IV   Bagdad on Parade—New Yorkers in Public

"O. Henry's favorite coign of vantage was the restaurant. From his seat here . . . he gazed at his peep-show with a zest and interpretative insight that never flagged."[96] No characteristic of O. Henry's writing more clearly stamps his individuality than his unceasing fascination with the passing show, which he could observe at greater leisure and possibly with deeper insight while seated at a restaurant table, alone or with friends, than he could while ambling about the city's highroads and byways. The stories told of his fondness for dining out in all manner of eating places are, of course, numerous and colorful; but one would not need to know any of them to sense the excitement he must have felt in the presence of New York's constantly changing scene. Far more clearly than any recollections at second hand, his own stories convey both the impressions and their effect upon him—a sea of faces arriving and departing, the hum of lively talk, the flashing colors of women's clothes, the tinkle of silver and glassware, the popping of corks, and the savor of varied dishes served forth by hurrying waiters—as he presents the public image of New York in its scores of food and drink emporiums, from the most fashionable of dining halls to the obscurest of the Bohemian rathskellers. These stories show, even more convincingly than do his tales of family life, that the public spotlight was his special arena. The restaurant, not the furnished room, was where he found the real drama of New York life.

There is scarcely a story dealing with New York public life in which the restaurant does not somehow play a part, either as the central scene of action or as a point of reference against which life elsewhere in the city can be measured. The dispensing and consumption of food and drink in public are therefore major symbols—sometimes consciously, sometimes unwittingly employed—in O. Henry's portrayal of what he took to be the significant actions in the lives of his fellow New Yorkers. Indeed, the kinds of places they patronized, as well as their conduct in those places, were apparently the chief means he relied on for classifying and evaluating the patrons and would-be patrons who served as models for his fictional characterizations. For as C. A. Smith correctly pointed out many years ago, O. Henry divided these people into two broad classes: "those who knew and those who thought they knew, the real thing and those who would be considered the real thing."[97] Viewed from the vantage point of the restaurant table, the passing throng of O. Henry's New York society accordingly receives its most picturesque treatment in this group of thirty or more stories, nearly all of which present a highly idealized version of romantic adventure framed in an illusorily realistic setting.

The basic themes dramatized in these stories, however, are fundamentally the same as those underlying his others; they are neither simpler nor more complex in their analysis of human motives, though perhaps oftener dressed in a more attractive package. As a commentary on the follies and ambitions of human nature, they can hardly be called trenchant; yet their appearance in such a variety of forms exposes another illuminating facet of O. Henry's artistic skill. Four themes recur often enough to be singled out and examined separately: (a) pretense and reversal of fortune—"turning the tables on Haroun";[98] (b) discovery and initiation through adventure; (c) the city as spiritual playground for the imagination; and (d) the basic yearning of all human nature. One or more of these themes may be detected in virtually all his stories of New Yorkers on parade, but in some of them the theme may be coyly concealed beneath several layers of seemingly irrelevant chaff.

Without doubt the theme of pretense—the desire to pose for what one is not, if only for a few brief moments and regardless of the price exacted—is the most persistent one in O. Henry's writing; for it crops up again and again in nearly all his stories from the earliest to the last few he left unfinished at his death. It is the foundation of "While the Auto Waits," one of the first tales that aroused the curiosity of editors and critics in the writing of an unknown author who called himself James L. Bliss.[99] Still one of his best, the story dramatizes the pathos of false pretenses in the transparent claims to family grandeur with which a comely young woman seeks to impress a young man who stops to chat with her in a park. Taking his cue from her pretentiousness, he too masks his real identity by pretending to be a humble restaurant cashier, which is actually the position she fills; he is also the wealthy owner of the chauffeured car waiting for occupancy, which she has pointed to as hers. The loss to both individuals as a result of a natural human urge toward one-upmanship is pointedly driven home with an irony unmarred by either sentimentality or gratuitous moralizing.

O. Henry simply reversed the same situation in "Lost on Dress Parade," this time portraying the man as victim of his own folly, but heightening the poignance of lost hopes with several additional touches of characterization. Towers Chandler, the hero in this instance, is a likable, generous young chap who scrimps along on a meager salary; he saves one dollar a week so that every tenth week he can blow himself to an expensive dinner at a fashionable Broadway restaurant. But on this icy evening he encounters a pretty girl, rather shabbily dressed, who has slipped on the sidewalk and sprained her ankle. Helping her up, he introduces himself and invites her to dine with him; she accepts reluctantly; and he brags throughout the meal about being an idle man about town, an habitué of clubs and fine restaurants, impressing the poor working girl. But, after thanking and bidding him good-bye, she returns to her wealthy home, saddened by the thought that although she could cheerfully marry a poor man so long as he had "some work to do in the world," she could never love a social butterfly, "even if his eyes were blue and he were so kind to poor girls whom he met in the street."[100] Again, the double loss is what gives the story its special tang.

Sometimes, however, O. Henry could present situations similar to these in which profit rather than loss accrues to one or more of the persons involved without necessarily injuring others. The therapeutic effect of playing the poseur temporarily is quite amusingly set forth, for example, in "Transients in Arcadia," which opens with a mouth-watering description of the elegant but unobtrusive Hotel Lotus on Broadway: "an oasis in the July desert of Manhattan" where one can get "brook trout better than the White Mountains ever served, sea food that would turn Old Point Comfort—'by Gad, sah!'—green with envy, and Maine venison that would melt the official heart of a game warden."[101] Enter next the lovely, well-groomed Madame Heloise D'Arcy Beaumont, whose graciousness promptly charms bellboys and management alike; she stays a few days, seldom going out; and she soon meets handsome young Harold Farrington, also well groomed and obviously a leisured man of the world. They congratulate each other for having found this quiet retreat away from all the blatant foreign resorts, already overrun and cheapened by tourists. But after three days of such pleasant chit-chat, the lady confesses that she is actually Mamie Siviter, a hosiery clerk at Casey's Mammoth Store, who has but a dollar left from the fund she saved up for a year in order to enjoy this one week's glorious holiday; and that dollar must go to pay the installment due on her dress. Unperturbed, Farrington scribbles a receipt and takes her dollar, confessing on his part that he is actually Jimmy McManus, bill collector for O'Dowd and Levinsky; he too has saved up out of a paltry salary because, like her, he "'always wanted to put up at a swell hotel.'"[102] Both have got more than their money's worth with the *lagniappe* of blossoming romance to boot (for in parting at the elevator Jimmy and Mamie have made a date to go to Coney Island the following Saturday) in a brilliantly contrived idyll that combines all four of O. Henry's major themes within fewer than nine pages.

With slightly more daring than he usually allowed himself, he wove them together again in a later story which flirts with the fringes of neurosis and the divided personality, though it too is a study in wish-fulfillment, of the urge to kick off the shackles of convention and to live a free, uncommitted life, if only for a short while.[103] The narrator, Elwyn Bellford, is a prominent Denver lawyer who seemingly cracks under the strain of hard work, forgets his past, and boards a train for New York with $3,000 in his pocket but no baggage. Surrounded by Western pharmacists en route to a convention, he pretends to be one, invents the name Edward Pinkhammer, and registers at the same hotel with the others. O. Henry casually drops the hint that the amnesia bit is merely a hoax pulled by a smart fellow who wants to run off. Though soon recognized by a traveling salesman acquaintance who greets him in the hotel lobby, Bellford brushes him off and changes hotels. Meanwhile, reveling in his anonymity, he enjoys all the varied glamor of Broadway; and once again O. Henry waxes lyrical about the gold and silver delights of New York, available to those who possess imagination and intelligence enough to partake of them within the framework of the order of things—"the key to liberty is not in the hands of License, but Convention holds it. Comity has a toll-gate at which you must pay, or you may not enter the land of Freedom."[104] Then he runs into another old friend in a quiet off-Broadway restaurant, a lovely lady in her mid-thirties, who recognizes him at once as the lover she had had fifteen years before. But Bellford still insists that he is Pinkhammer and has forgotten everything, despite her recalling specific intimacies they shared plus details she knows of his subsequent career. To his persistent denial of all memory of these things, she says quietly with a soft laugh of mingled bliss and misery, " 'You lie, Elwyn Bellford, ... Oh, I know you lie!' "[105] and then climbs into her carriage, and disappears unidentified. On returning to his hotel, Bellford is confronted by his family physician and by his distraught wife; and, though still brazening out the Pinkhammer disguise, he gradually cracks under the doctor's grilling, and admits that he may have been a victim of aphasia during the two weeks spent in New York. " 'But, oh, Doc,' " he concludes after confessing that he's rather tired of the whole experience now, " 'good old Doc—it was glorious!' "

Few others among O. Henry's remaining stories that develop

the pretense theme can match these in either technical virtuosity or general appeal; yet the mere fact that he found numerous other ways of varying his treatment of the theme effectively is in itself remarkable. In "The Social Triangle," for example, he used it to cast an ironic beam of light on the pretentiousness of three different levels of New York society by showing how the poverty-stricken Ikey Snigglefritz spends his hard-earned week's pay to set up drinks for his ward boss, Billy McMahon; he in turn later sits with his wife in a fashionable restaurant and suffers despair until he can figure out a scheme for being publicly accepted by Cortlandt Van Duyckink, a multimillionaire philanthropist sitting nearby. Then, to complete the triangle, Van Duyckink, while looking over a slum-clearance project he is sponsoring, impulsively leaves his limousine to grasp "the hand of what seemed to him a living rebuke" and, quite sincerely expressing a desire to be friendly and helpful, drives off with a glow in his heart, not knowing that "he had shaken the hand of Ikey Snigglefritz."[106] Still other devices are used in "The Caliph and the Cad," "The Poet and the Peasant," "The Country of Elusion," and "From Each According to his Ability,"[107] to juxtapose ironically the pretenses of different social levels and the effects of pretense among members of the same social class. Sometimes painful, at others pleasant, these are brought out with varying skill in four or five more tales.[108] In each case, the surprise ending, O. Henry's trademark, is carefully contrived to cut off all further exploration into the problem raised; but, by the time it is reached, the theme and its implications have, nevertheless, usually been nailed down.

Though the two main themes of pretense and discovery through adventure often unfold concurrently in O. Henry's stories, they are not invariably yoked together or mutually dependent. The idea of eagerly confronting the unknown, with or without the protective coloration of a disguise, seems to have excited O. Henry throughout life, the more so during his last years when so little of it remained. And since he constantly saw life itself as an uncertain adventure at best, his eagerness to crowd in all possible chances spilled over into his stories like water flowing over a dam. Thus, the character he most admires is clearly a person like his hero Rudolph Steiner in "The Green Door," to whom "the most interesting thing in life seemed . . . to be what might lie just around the next corner."[109] Steiner, a true adventurer, is willing to pay the toll that will be charged for following up a lead, even though aware from past experience that the fee may come high. And there are many others like him in O. Henry's stories, most of them clearly projections of their author's own personality.

Nor are they necessarily always men. In an absurd yet charming tale called "A Philistine in Bohemia," the adventurer is a winsome Irish lass, Katy Dempsey, who with her mother keeps one of the cheap rooming houses below Union Square. Ardently courted by one of their lodgers, the meticulous Mr. Brunelli, Katy is wary of him, first, because he is Italian and, second, because, in her mother's view, he seems a bit "too coolchured in his spache for a rale gintleman."[110] Still, Katy accepts his invitation to dine at a real Bohemian restaurant in the Village, patronized by poor artists and sporty characters and managed by a fellow named Tonio. After escorting her to a table, Mr. Brunelli excuses himself; but presently one of the waiters brings her a truly Lucullian meal before he returns. Fascinated by the gay atmosphere and overcome by the excellence of her food, Katy nevertheless begins to suspect Brunelli of being a titled patrician, "glorious of name but shy of rent money," and she wonders why he left her to dine alone. Meanwhile, all the other patrons are clamoring for Tonio, who treats them like a prince; and when the crowd thins out a little, Brunelli reappears at Katy's table, disclosing himself as "the great Tonio" and once more professing his "loaf" for her. Stuffed to the gills with fine food, she accepts him gratefully: " 'Sure I'll marry wid ye. But why didn't ye tell me ye was the cook? I was near turnin' ye down for bein' one of thim foreign counts!' "[111]

Nor does the adventure and its consequent discovery have to be among the more sensational experiences that the big city provides. It can be the simplest departure from routine behavior and yet yield rich rewards—as Big Jim Dougherty, a typical Broadway "sport," discovered when he took his wife out to dinner. Though married over three years, he had scarcely noticed his Delia except to swap a few meaningless phrases with her at breakfast; but, while escorting her up the street on the evening of their dinner date, he soon noted the admiring glances and murmurs cast upon his stunning spouse, altered his original plan to take her to an ordinary joint, and steered her instead to swank Hoogley's—"the swellest slow-lunch warehouse on the line"—where she shone like a solitary star. Chatting gaily and joyously over their meal, she soon attracted the attention of "the Honorable Patrick Corrigan, leader in Dougherty's district" who, after the introductions, accused Big Jim of hiding a treasure.[112] His eyes opened at last, Dougherty can only mutter to himself over the time he has lost with this dazzling creature, his own wife, as she goes on charming a tableful of his politician friends. Although the story is somewhat overdone for comic effect, the fact that the situation is not too far-fetched to appeal to tastes more elevated than those of Dougherty's level suggests another insight into O. Henry's grip on his public; quite often the underlying moral of his story, though woven neatly into its dramatic texture as it is here, is nevertheless so obvious and so broadly logical that sage and dunce alike cannot help applauding it.

The burden of his best stories that dwell on this theme is that both awareness and simplicity are as essential as courage in the pursuit of the adventurous life. Even his less impressive performances, such as "Psyche and the Pskyscraper," in which his flagging imagination can be seen straining to produce an effect, still manage to convey this idea with a modicum of force. To Daisy, the ignorant little shopgirl heroine of this story, the love of down-to-earth Joe, who runs a tiny newsstand, makes more sense than the attentions of his rival Dabster, a self-assured philosophical snob, who takes her to the top of a skyscraper and, with the broad view before them, belabors her with statistics about the smallness of human affairs. Frightened by all these figures signifying the cold, heartless immensity of things in the universe, Daisy in rebellion flees back to Joe's little newsstand where it is "cozy and warm and homelike," and one cannot help admiring her wisdom in offering herself to him whenever he is ready to take her.[113]

O. Henry's most ambitious effort on the theme of adventure and discovery, however, as well as one of his most interesting stories is the late one entitled "The Venturers," published only a few months before his death.[114] The story grew out of a brief seminal idea recorded as follows in his notebook: "Followers of chance—two 'Knights errant' one leaves girl and other marries her for what may be 'around-the-corner.' "[115] On one level the story quite plainly expresses what Smith referred to as O.

Henry's "revolt against the calculable," a problem that remained central with him from the beginning to the end of his career. But a deeper level, based on the immediate specific problem of his own second marriage can likewise be readily picked out; for in the two knights errant of the tale, Forster and Ives, are visible the unresolved halves of their creator himself: O. Henry, the adventurous literary artist, and Porter, the man who had taken a second wife in what was turning out to be a sadly mistaken venture for him. This element of the divided self accounts for both the story's depth of meaning and for what Smith notes as its seemingly misplaced center.[116]

The story proper opens with John Reginald Forster's wondering where he can seek an exciting dinner as he leaves his exclusive Powhattan Club. He stops on the corner, fumbles through his pockets, and, though personally wealthy, discovers that they are all empty. Another well-groomed chap, Ives, noting his predicament, strikes up an acquaintance and, confessing that he too possesses only two pennies, proposes that they dine together in style at the swank restaurant across the way and then match coins to see which of them will have to deal with the proprietor's outraged wrath. Forster takes him up and the two men order a typical O. Henry meal, complete with fancy wines and exotic dishes, meanwhile entertaining each other with tales of their fondness for encountering unexpected but eagerly sought adventures in odd corners of the world. Ives has had more varied experiences than Forster, who has been largely confined to New York, though he too has always dreamed of doing things that would not lead to clearly predictable ends, such as their shared dinner.

At the dinner's end, however, both men have to confess that even this adventure was predictable, since it turns out that Forster, on losing the toss, has only to sign a credit chit and that Ives himself owns the place. But Forster, reluctant to break off their friendship, now discloses that he is engaged to be married to a lovely woman within a month and cannot decide whether to go through with the marriage or cut out for Alaska; for, although he loves the girl, it is the dead certainty of all their future that makes him doubtful. The two men agree to meet for another dinner on the following Thursday. Ives then goes to call on a beautiful girl, Mary Marsden, and the dialogue between them reveals that they've known each other since childhood and that he could have married her three years before if he had not decided to take off on another of his periodic jaunts around the world; but now it is too late—she is about to be married to another man. Seeing her in her unchanged, predictable surroundings, Ives thinks that she will always be the same there; the certainty of it was what had driven him away before. On Thursday Forster tells Ives that the dinner will have to be postponed, for he had decided to sail round the world and has explained this need to his fiancée in a letter. Ives, of course, tells him not to bother, for he has married the girl himself; he has discovered that this is the Venture, the one hazardous course that a man may follow all his life without ever knowing, even to his dying day, whether it is to end in the highest heaven or the blackest pit.

Whether or not "The Venturers" is actually a veiled commentary on the misgivings O. Henry felt toward his own marriage, the story does reveal his deep-seated conviction, the result of painful personal experience, that one cannot escape one's destiny regardless of the road taken, and that accordingly it is better to accept willingly the chances that come than to try to manipulate one's fate. Neither withdrawal nor escape will serve, for both lead to unsatisfactory ends, as he shows in another odd tale, "To Him Who Waits," the story of a man who made a hermit of himself because the woman he had wanted chose a richer husband.[117] Then, when the same woman, divorced and contrite and still desirable, offered him a second chance, he compounded his folly by rejecting her to pursue a younger one whom he could not obtain. The essence of the adventurous life lies in confrontation and in eager acceptance of the chances offered; for, even though these too may lead to sad ends, the ends themselves are unforeseen in any case; hence, satisfaction can only be derived from the kind of race one runs. Such is O. Henry's treatment of this theme repeatedly.

That the great city is the inevitable spot for pursuing the adventurous life, simply because its store of chances is inexhaustible, marks another prominent thematic thread in O. Henry's work. Unlike the foregoing themes, however, the city as a spiritual reservoir for the imagination is a more pervasive one, appearing in many scattered passages, hints, and overtones, as in "The Voice of the City" and other tales already cited, rather than as the predominant motif of entire stories.[118] Still, its prominence among the other themes can often be seen in the presentation of contrasting viewpoints or attitudes which O. Henry employs as a standard device in many stories. In "A Little Local Color," for example, his main purpose is to satirize, spoofingly, himself and other feature-writing journalists in New York, all of whom are questing for the picturesque word, phrase, image, and metaphor with which to describe the city because their livelihood depends on giving the public what it wants. The writer-narrator accordingly badgers his friend, a "young-man-about-town and a New Yorker by birth, preference and incommutability,"[119] to show him around where he can note down the real local color in the people's polyglot speech, their mannerisms and idiosyncrasies. Wherever they go, however, the unexpected rather than the typical turns up—college professors talk Bowery slang, while a dyed-in-the-wool native Boweryite, using impeccable English, mercilessly ridicules the literary commercialization of alleged Bowery argot. In the end both are forced to admit that New York is too colorful and variegated to be easily stereotyped and classified. That the city does produce the unexpected where one is least prepared to find it is the real source of its charm, even though pulp feature writers thrive on their standardized but faked local-color portrayals.

This is a theme that O. Henry expresses continuously, even when poking fun at the city's manifest discomforts in midsummer heat. In the story "Rus in Urbe" he uses it as flavoring for an otherwise stale plot involving rich man versus poor man in pursuit of the same girl and manages to make both men's patently deceitful praise of the city's summer delights nevertheless sound quite authentic.[120] Again, in "The Call of the Tame" he puts over the same theme by relating it to another of his favorite situations: the contrast between the confirmed Gothamite's viewpoint and that of the bluff, hearty man of the West, who becomes a convert as soon as he sees the light.[121] Baffled and bored by all the metropolitan hubbub of Sixth Avenue, Greenbrier Nye can hardly wait to return to his native heath in Arizona, despite the luxury surrounding him in the exclusive café where his former partner, Longhorn Merritt, has taken him for luncheon. He scorns the effete drinks and dishes Merritt orders—dry Martinis, green Chartreuse, squab en casserole, etc.—and sticks to straight whiskey, saddened by the realization that city life has softened and feminized his old cowpunching pal of bygone days. Then his eye lights on the elegantly dressed woman in speckled silk at a table nearby, and before long the comforts of city life thus viewed in a new framework have cast their spell upon him.

Whether O. Henry found his symbol in a woman's stylish dress, an absinthe frappé, or a restaurant table's glittering array of silverware, his loyalty to the city's endless lure could be so fervently expressed that one need not wonder why New Yorkers loved him fifty years ago—and still do. But to appreciate his method of singing the city's praises one must often look beneath the insouciance and bravura of his approach. His most concentrated paean to the enchantment of New York occurs in the last few pages of "The Duel," a story that resembles "The Venturers" in that again it offers two contrasting views, both of them his own, which are brilliantly synthesized in a concluding passage of poetic prose. The two young Westerners, William and Jack, who meet at luncheon after four years' residence in the city, are both projections of O. Henry's personality. William, the successful businessman, defends the city in rather crude, slangy terms, and for the wrong reasons—he is making his pile, meeting important people, seeing the plays he does not understand. Jack, the successful artist, condemns the city in more literate terms as "a monster to which the innocence, the genius, and the beauty of the land must pay tribute." He hates it because it is crude, base, materialistic—a city controlled by its lowest ingredients— and would return to the purer air of the West at once if he could, rather than sell his soul to it as his friend has done. Then at midnight Jack throws up his window and looks out over the city far below, catching his breath at the massive beauty of a sight he has seen and felt hundreds of times. As a Westerner, he sees its irregular background shapes in terms of canyons, cliffs, and gulches; but as an artist he responds to the implications of its myriads of glowing lights like a rapt devotee before an altar: ". . . out of the violet and purple depths ascended like the city's soul sounds and odors and thrills that make up the civic body. There arose the breath of gaiety unrestrained, of love, of hate, of all the passions that man can know. There below him lay all things, good or bad, that can be brought from the four corners of the earth to instruct, please, thrill, enrich, despoil, elevate, cast down, nurture, or kill. Thus the flavor of it came to him and went into his blood."[122]

O. Henry leaves it up to the reader to decide which of the two men won the battle against the city; but, after such a purple passage as this, there is little doubt in the reader's mind concerning the effect of the city's "cup of mandragora" on O. Henry himself. It was the draught of vintage enabling him in imagination to escape all leaden-eyed despairs.

Though New York provided the stimulus for O. Henry's fertile imagination, the city as a microcosm in each of his 140 stories is, after all, simply the objective correlative that serves to pin down the broadest of his themes: namely, the idea of oneness at the heart of things in human society. A typically romantic approach to life, this notion that a strong common bond unites all people sweeps away or ignores as irrelevant superficialities the infinite gradations and distinctions existing between rich and poor, strong and weak, intelligent and stupid, good and evil, in order to focus attention on the centralizing principle or ideal for which all humanity strives. It is an approach abhorred by Realists who insist on the importance of those distinctions in the world as we know it and who urge the literary artist not to ignore them in his fictional portrayal of the world round about him. Whatever the tie between them may be, says the Realist, saints and sinners are not the same; and the differences between them are more significant than the Romanticist will admit.

Still, there is something indestructibly appealing in the Romanticist's creed which the world cherishes and clings to. And that is what explains O. Henry's hold on the world's reading public, despite the critic's scorn. The reader knows very well that things do not work out in the world as they do in O. Henry's stories; but in his heart he would like to believe they might. He would like to believe that all brides are not only beautiful, but, beneath their beauty, sisters of the golden circle; that all bums and millionaires alike are redeemable; that all lads and lasses, regardless of their hue, seek the blue flower of contentment together in the far fields of the human heart. O. Henry's stories about New Yorkers, Westerners, Southerners, and Latin Americans are but part of a vast literature of Romanticism that has always fed this basic human hunger—"the search for those common traits and common impulses which together form a sort of common denominator of our common humanity."[123] Their ultimate theme, as his first biographer aptly concludes, "is your nature and mine."

CHAPTER 5

O. Henry's Technical Achievements

THE ELEMENTS of his art were not many.... He knew
precisely how much of the sugar of sentimentality the
great average reading public must have, and how much of
the pepper of sensation, and the salt of facts, and the salad
dressing of romance.... But brilliant as were the possibility of
his powers, and distinctive as was his technique, his final place
can never be high even among the writers of short stories. He
did not take literature seriously: he was a victim of Momus
and the swift ephemeral press. His undoubted powers were
completely debauched by it. He became exclusively an entertain-
er, with no thought but of the moment, and no art save that
which brought instant effect upon his reader. To accomplish
that he would sacrifice everything, even the truth."[1]

Thus arbitrarily does F. L. Pattee, historian of the American
short story in the 1920's, dispose of O. Henry. The severity of
the tone is indicative of the strong reaction against O. Henry's
popularity and influence which had set in during the debunking
period of World War I after the first wave of critical enthusiasm
for O. Henry's writings was spent. Critics like Pattee and N.
Bryllion Fagin roundly denounced these stories on the grounds
of superficiality and falseness; they could not forgive O. Henry's
failure, as they saw it, to take himself and his art seriously
because they felt that the very brilliance of his technical skill,
so misapplied, wrought great mischief upon the corpus of the
American short story as a whole. At its best, said Fagin, O.
Henry's work "discloses an occasional brave peep at life, hasty,
superficial and dazzlingly flippant.... At its worst, his work
is not more than a series of cheap jokes renovated and expanded.
But over all there is the unmistakable charm of a master trickster,
of a facile player with incidents and words."[2]

The problem presented by O. Henry, however, was more
readily dismissed than analyzed. Primarily, it was the problem
of technique—one analogous to that with which Poe in the
preceding century had baffled his contemporary critics. How

should one approach, explain, and judge the elements which, in combination, resulted in that "unmistakable charm of a master trickster"? What criteria should be applied? Poe's critics likewise had accused him of playing fast and loose with his materials, of sacrificing truth and reality for the sake of achieving sensational effects; but they recognized that he too was a master craftsman whose technical dexterity enabled him to achieve the precise literary effects which he deliberately intended to produce. The American critics' tendency to deplore technique, or at least to relegate it to a subordinate role while focusing their attention on the artist's alleged "content," can thus be seen at work in Pattee's attack on O. Henry just as strongly as it originally operated against Poe. And it is instructive to find Pattee, while condemning O. Henry as "a harlequin Poe with modern laughter in place of gloom," arguing nevertheless that "he was utterly without Poe's reverence for the literature of power, he was without his simplicity, without his universality, without his ability to stand with the great serious literary creators of the world."[3]

In reaching this unfavorable judgment, Pattee did not overlook O. Henry's technical skills: he listed a number of the more prominent ones, pointing out that *manner* rather than *matter* is the significant element in O. Henry's art; that he is primarily a humorist with a journalist's ability to fashion a "good one," like a commercial traveler's yarn, but with a "punch" in every sentence; that, even better than Mark Twain, he can manipulate the narrator's function so that "to read him is at times almost to feel his physical presence"; and that, paradoxically, despite his outrageous use of modern slang, he is a master of felicitous expressions and amazingly strange verbal flavors such that "not even Henry James could choose words more fastidiously or use them more accurately."[4] But, while noting these by no means negligible feats, Pattee nevertheless condemned O. Henry for not using his gifts as he, the critic, would have preferred. Pattee's was the typical critic's disapproval of the artist for being himself rather than some other writer. Instead of accepting O. Henry as he stood, as determinedly the master of the revels for a popular audience, and going on from there to analyze the skills that gave him such pre-eminence, the critic must chastize him as one who could not be trusted, as a writer who prostituted his great gifts for the sake of a laugh.

To condemn O. Henry's stories *in toto* for not being realistic and serious, for depending too heavily on coincidence, and for playing to the gallery is an evasion of the critic's responsibility—unless it can be shown that these characteristics invariably result in badly written stories. This, O. Henry's severest critics have seldom been willing to do. His intention rather than his achievement has been the object of their censure, and the result is that O. Henry criticism over the past five decades has swung from the one extreme of thoughtless adulation to the opposite one of hasty and ill-considered dismissal, based too cavalierly upon the examination of individual stories, as in the well-known analysis of "The Furnished Room" by Brooks and Warren.[5]

What needs to be done, on the contrary, is to recognize first, as Langford suggests, that, like him or not, O. Henry is a minor classic who occupies a permanent, unique spot in American literature; and, second, to seek to understand his uniqueness in the light of his total accomplishment.[6] When this effort is made, O. Henry's techniques as seen in isolated instances become of less moment than his technique as a whole; his individual imperfections and peculiarities are of less significance than his pervasive, overall literary personality. This pervasive wholeness may then be seen as a subtle amalgam of disparate, recognizable qualities which add up to an entity that is more impressive—and baffling—than the mere sum of its parts.

I   *Delight in the Unexpected: Surprise Endings*

One way to account for this mysterious afflatus is to recognize that at the core of O. Henry's being lies an element of surprise or wonder, as though everything his eye lighted on were sufficient cause for startled pleasure. Van Wyck Brooks has noted that New York City seemed to belong to O. Henry because of "the fresh curiosity with which he approached it, his feeling of wonder about it . . . which made for a literary virtue transcending his occasional cheapness and coarseness, his sometimes unbearable jocularity and meretricious effects."[7] No shrewder observation of O. Henry's art has been made, but it might also be extended to cover not only his New York stories but his entire approach to the problem of fiction. For the element of surprise is the keynote of his technique as well.

The most obvious technical manifestation of O. Henry's delight in the unexpected is, of course, in his famous surprise endings; for scarcely a single story among his nearly three hundred fails to meet his specifications for a conclusion other than the one the reader is apparently being prepared for. In sheer quantity O. Henry's surprise endings are therefore impressive, though qualitatively too many of them are so patently contrived that the sophisticated reader soon tires of the guessing contest which their anticipated discovery interposes between himself and the author. Invariably the result of some trick of reversal based on essential information withheld or only partially disclosed, the surprise ending was a well-worn device long before O. Henry's day; it entered the short story with the emergence of the form itself and was developed at the hands of many writers from Washington Irving on. Nor did O. Henry add any significant features to it which had not already been employed by writers like Poe, Bret Harte, Stockton, Bierce, Aldrich, and others.[8] In its various forms, the surprise ending included the hoax and the practical joke, the anti-conventional or distorted revelation of events, the paradoxical or antithetical disclosure, the manipulation of psychological concepts, the double reversal, the problem close—all of which had been worked with varying success by O. Henry's predecessors and contemporaries. He, however, paid them the sincere flattery of imitating all their methods, using at least seven different variants of the surprise ending, the most nearly original of which were those disclosing sudden proof of the tyranny of habit or of environment, as in "The Girl and the Habit" and in "The Lickpenny Lover."[9]

Any list of plot summaries would immediately show that most if not all of these surprise endings that O. Henry contrived were based on sheer coincidence, the plausibility of which is unacceptable to those who seek in fiction a reasonable reflection of events in actual life. This is the source of much of the adverse criticism leveled at O. Henry by critics nurtured in the Realistic tradition, and insofar as his stories violate a cardinal principle of fiction expressed by Melville—that "it should present another world, and yet one to which we feel the tie"[10]—their criticism is valid. But there is another side even to this coin. Many of his stories, as H. E. Rollins noted, are as brilliantly contrived for achieving the single effect as those of Poe and de Maupassant, and O. Henry's so-called surprise endings are logically prepared for within the framework of the narrative; so that his technique does decidedly conform to the rules "that he affected to despise."[11] A good example of such contrivance may be seen in "The Ransom of Mack," one of his lighter Western yarns in which the plot, turning on a partly concealed misunderstanding, works out to a ludicrous conclusion that throws the laugh back on the narrator, yet is both logical and morally justifiable.[12]

With no preliminaries, the story opens: "Me and old Mack Lonsbury, we got out of that Little Hide-and-Seek gold mine affair with about $40,000 apiece. I say 'old' Mack; but he wasn't old. Forty-one, I should say; but he always seemed old." The narrator, Andy, goes on from there to tell how, with their wealth, the two men set up housekeeping in a little town near Denver, hired a Chinese cook, and planned just to enjoy life by reading, chatting, learning to play the banjo. Inevitably they discussed women, Mack regretfully admitting that he had never understood them and thus had forfeited the joys of marriage; Andy boasting that he did understand them and knew therefore that both he and Mack had avoided considerable discontent. At this point Andy tells of having had to go off to New Mexico on business and of having found on his return two months later that Mack had been elected justice of the peace and now wore fancy clothes and ogled the girls. After one of them bowed to him on the street, he made the astounding announcement that he would be marrying her that same evening. Upset, Andy rushed off to intercept the girl, tried vainly to dissuade her from marrying, and then asked her what time the wedding was to take place. When she replied that it would be at six o'clock, Andy offered her a thousand dollars to marry at five o'clock a young man she admitted she was fond of. Puzzled but delighted, both the girl and her young man agreed to take the money on those terms. But when Andy returned to his house at 5:30, he found Mack again in old clothes, explaining in answer to his query about the wedding that it had been performed at five—that he, in fact, had "operated" it because with the preacher away, he was the only one in town qualified to do the job.

The entire plot is neatly managed on the basis of misinterpreted dialogue firmly contained within a narrator's disingenuous recital of events that seemingly followed one another in a perfectly natural order. Tricky and clever, yet deceptively simple, the technique results in an ending that is unexpected yet satisfactory, logically prepared for and quite amusing. And though it might be objected that no two human beings, even uneducated miners, could be so witless as Andy and Mack, such argument would be irrelevant to the point that within the framework of the narrative O. Henry has carefully—and economically—set up the means of reaching its inevitable outcome. Granted that the characters are mere types, altogether lacking individuality even though their portrayal seems convincingly realistic; granted also that their behavior is naïve and their problem of no significance, the fact still remains that their creator succeeds in making them appear to be momentarily important through the dexterity with which he manages their humorous predicament. For in the same simple passages of dialogue he not only reveals their concern and masks from the reader their ignorance of the truth (thus achieving a measure of characterization), but also keeps the plot moving dramatically forward. The following colloquy between Andy and the young girl, Rebosa, illustrates how his method functions.

Having ascertained that she is to be married and that his friend Mack is involved in the wedding because "'he was the only chance there was,'" Andy protests that a pretty girl like her might pick any man rather than such an old codger as his friend. He then repeats his question:

"Rebosa, are you bent on having this marriage occur?"

"Why, sure I am," says she, oscillating the pansies on her hat, "and so is somebody else, I reckon."

"What time is it to take place?" I asks.

"At six o'clock," says she.

I made up my mind right away what to do. I'd save old Mack if I could. . . .

"Rebosa," says I, earnest, drawing upon my display of knowledge concerning the feminine intuitions of reason—"ain't there a young man in Pina—a nice young man that you think a heap of?"

"Yep," says Rebosa, nodding her pansies—"Sure there is! What do you think! Gracious!"

"Does he like you?" I asks. "How does he stand in the matter?"

"Crazy," says Rebosa. "Ma has to wet down the front steps to keep him from sitting there all the time. But I guess that'll be all over tonight," she winds up with a sigh.

"Rebosa," says I, "you don't really experience any of this adoration called love for old Mack, do you?"

"Lord! no," says the girl, shaking her head. "I think he's as dry as a lava bed. The idea!"

"Who is this young man that you like, Rebosa?" I inquires.

"It's Eddie Bayles," says she. "He clerks in Crosby's grocery. But he don't make but thirty-five a month. Ella Noakes was wild about him once."

"Old Mack tells me," I says, "that he's going to marry you at six o'clock this evening."

"That's the time," says she. "It's to be at our house."

"Rebosa," says I, "listen to me. If Eddie Bayles had a thousand dollars cash—a thousand dollars, mind you, would buy him a store of his own—if you and Eddie had that much to excuse matrimony on, would you consent to marry him this evening at five o'clock?"

The girl looks at me a minute: and I can see these inaudible cogitations going on inside of her, as women will.

"A thousand dollars?" says she. "Of course I would."

"Come on," says I. "We'll go and see Eddie."[13]

The charm of the master trickster is certainly visible in these lines: first in his manner of having the narrator present himself as a Mr. Fix-it type, so selfishly bent on managing things to suit his own ends that he fails to ask the one question which would explain everything (as well as destroy the story); second, in the deceptively innocent remarks he puts in the girl's mouth to signify her attitude and relationship to both Mack and her fiancé; third, in his juxtaposition of successive comments between the two speakers which can be taken two ways, as in the girl's reference to Eddie's impecunious salary and former sweetheart and Andy's immediate rejoinder. Here too can be seen another aspect of O. Henry's technical legerdemain: his skill in making seemingly irrelevant, offhand remarks do double duty. For the girl's comment that Ella Noakes was once wild about Eddie not only throws a fresh and unexpected light on her own attitude, but at the same time enhances the young man's desirability and also helps confirm the reader's suspicion that she too, for prudential reasons, would nevertheless consider passing him up to marry an older man whom she cares nothing for.

II *Verbal Trickery: Dialect and Word Coinages*

Compression thus applied to seemingly realistic dialogue and to descriptive phraseology containing the unlooked-for term constantly operates in O. Henry's stories to produce fresh surprises and incidental delights. In many of his Western and Central American stories, for example, his liberal use of the Spanish-American vernacular, gracefully inserted into specific names for things and people and into many common colloquial expressions, again serves this dual purpose by conveying both a subtle flavor of the place itself and a humorous (or violent) turn of the story.[14] The whole tone of humorous exoticism in *Cabbages and Kings* is set in the brief glimpse of a native messenger boy dashing down Coralio's "grass-grown" street, shrieking: "*'Busca el Señor* Goodwin. *Ha venido un telégrafo por él!'*" (11). Similar examples of this sort may be seen in Ylario's way of explaining to his boss how the ranch doctor mistakenly examined him instead of the right patient: "He put his ear here and here and here, and listen—I not know for what. He put little glass stick in my mouth. He feel my arm here. He make me count like whisper—so—twenty, *treinta, cuarenta.* Who knows . . . for what that doctor do those verree droll and such-like things?"[15] Again, in the Mexican desperado's retort when the heroine calls him a *coon:* "*'Hidalgo, Yo!* . . . I am not neg-r-ro! *Diabla bonita,* for that you shall pay me.'"[16] Or in the *vaquero,* Gregorio Falcon's polite yet reproachful complaint over the lack of tobacco in his camp: "*'Ah,* Don Samuel, . . . escuse me. Dthey say dthe jack-rabbeet and dthe sheep have dthe most leetle *sesos*—how you call dthem—brain-es? Ah don' believe dthat, Don Samuel—escuse me. Ah dthink people w'at don' keep esmokin' tobacco, dthey—bot you weel escuse me, Don Samuel.'"[17] Or again, finally, in this bit of dialogue between a ranch boy and the hero, Ranse, as he walks out toward the *jacals* (cabins) of the Mexican ranch hands:

"Manuel, can you catch Vaminos, in the little pasture, for me?"
"Why not, señor? I saw him near the *puerta* but two hours past. He bears a drag-rope."
"Get him and saddle him as quick as you can."
"*Prontito,* señor."[18]

Scores of similar examples may be picked out of other stories in *Heart of the West, Cabbages and Kings,* in *Roads of Destiny,* and in *The Gentle Grafter.* In "The Caballero's Way" alone, for example, there are nearly twenty terms such as *cañoncito, tienda, lavandera, chica, alma, muy caballero, canciones de amor, que mal muchacho, pues señor.*[19]

While the precise effect of these dialectal contributions cannot be scientifically assayed in any given story, it is nevertheless plain that over the whole stretch of O. Henry's writings his facility in rendering the speech patterns and rhythms of incidental common folk adds much to the vivacity, variety, and interest of his stories. This fact is demonstrable not only in his Western tales but also in those of other settings; for comparative analysis has shown that he employed with astonishing accuracy at least five different native American dialects along with as many foreign ones.[20] Besides Texas cowpoke language, these include the colloquial speech of Cumberland Mountain whites, as well as the mixtures of Spanish-English, German-English, French-English, and Italian-English. Moreover, it is of major significance that despite O. Henry's "lack of any scientific study of dialects, his genius for keen observation by sight and sound enabled him to use these dialects with a trueness that compares favorably with authentic dialects which have been set up through scientific study; [secondly, that] he was impartial in his use of dialects resulting from locale, race, class, and foreign language influence."[21] As a single example of O. Henry's subtle management of Cumberland Mountain speech in the story "The Whirligig of Life," the following commentary is illuminating:

> O. Henry describes the timbre of this speech, which tends toward the nasal, when he says the woman speaks "in a voice like the wind blowing through pine boughs." He sets the tempo, which is often very slow and drawled, by phrases describing the characters. "The imperturbability of the mountains" hung upon Ransie, and the woman was "weary with unknown desires." The Justice of the Peace "stirred deliberately to his duties," . . . The rhythm, which is revelatory of the thought processes, O. Henry changes as the thought processes change. A deliberate four-four rhythm is found in the final statement, "We-all wants a divo'ce." A more rapid two-four rhythm is found in expressing the mental process of justification in the statement, "But when she's a-spittin' like a wildcat or a-sullin' like a hoot-owl in the cabin, a man ain't got no call to live with her.[22]

This writer's findings support Rollins' judgment concerning the broadly democratic appeal found in O. Henry's stories: the fact that he succeeded in making all his romanticized types seem important—even the dregs of humanity—by portraying them sympathetically and humorously through their own language. As a stylist, in fact, his most striking trait is humor; and once again, it is worth noting that O. Henry's humor is his own, a unique quality, not a mere shadow of Twain's or Stockton's or that of any of their predecessors. Rather, as Langford has mentioned, it is closer in both flavor and technique to the humor of later writers like Dorothy Parker, Robert Benchley, James Thurber, and E. B. White (or, he might have added, S. J. Perelman); that is, an intellectualized humor based on a fondness for and a firm grasp of odd, esoteric, yet precise terminology.[23]

Humor resulting from clever turns of phrase, from unusual and unexpected word combinations and distortions—the humor of surprise—is thus central to O. Henry's technique. Puns, coinages, sophistries, slang, malapropisms of various kinds are all among the standard logomachic devices he used over and over again to keep his readers on the *qui vive*. He usually concentrated them in his opening passages but he also sprinked them liberally throughout his stories. A few typical examples of his breezy method of story-opening are:

> George Washington, with his right arm upraised, sits his iron horse at the lower corner of Union Square, forever signalling the Broadway cars to stop as they round the curve into Fourteenth Street. But the cars buzz on, heedless, as they do at the beck of a private citizen, and the great General must feel, unless his nerves are iron, that rapid transit gloria mundi.[24]

.   .   .   .

> The spectacle of the money-caliphs of the present day going about Bagdad-on-the-Subway trying to relieve the wants of the people is enough to make the great Al Raschid turn Haroun in his grave. If not so, then the assertion should do so, the real caliph having been a wit and a scholar and therefore a hater of puns.[25]

.   .   .   .

> A story with a moral appended is like the bill of a mosquito. It bores you, and then injects a stinging drop to irritate your conscience. Therefore let us have the moral first and be done with it. All is not gold that glitters, but it is a wise child that keeps the stopper in his bottle of testing acid.
>
> Where Broadway skirts the corner of the square presided over by George the Veracious is the Little Rialto. Here stand the actors of that quarter, and this is their shibboleth: " 'Nit,' says I to Frohman, 'you can't touch me for a kopeck less than two-fifty per,' and out I walks."[26]

.   .   .   .

> *Habit*—a tendency or aptitude acquired by custom or frequent repetition.

The critics have assailed every source of inspiration save one. To that one we are driven for our moral theme. When we levied upon the masters of old they gleefully dug up the parallels to our columns. When we strove to set forth real life they reproached us for trying to imitate Henry George, George Washington, Washington Irving, and Irving Bacheller. We wrote of the West and the East, and they accused us of both Jesse and Henry James. We wrote from our heart—and they said something about a disordered liver. We took a text from Matthew or—er—yes, Deuteronomy, but the preachers were hammering away at the inspiration idea before we could get into type. So, driven to the wall, we go for our subject-matter to the reliable, old, moral, unassailable vade mecum—the unabridged dictionary.[27]

Such sprightly passages as these, however, though capable of being matched many times over by similarly unorthodox treatment, still give but a hint of the elaborate word-play that O. Henry's ingenuity contrived in order to spice his tales and keep his readers chuckling. Like Shakespeare and Sheridan, he enjoyed tampering with standard idioms, both English and foreign, so as to produce both pure and antithetical malapropisms, blundering misquotations, and word-mutilations and distortions, often brilliantly original in conception. One student has noted hundreds of these, of which the following are a brief sampling:[28]

"I reckon in New York you get to be a conniseer; and when you go around with the '*demi-tasse*,' you are naturally bound to buy 'em stylish grub."[29]

. . . .

"I never saw a man eat with so much earnestness—not hastily like a grammarian or one of the canal, slow and appreciating like a anaconda, or a real 'vive bonjour.' "[30]

. . . .

What's this? Horse with the heaves [*hors d'oeuvres*]?"[31]

. . . .

"Our friend, Lee Andrews, will again swim the Hell's point to-night."[32]

. . . .

"Now, there was a woman that would have tempted an anchovy to forget his vows. A kind of welcome seemed to mitigate her vicinity."[33]

. . . .

"It's right plausible of you . . . to take up the curmudgeons in your friend's behalf; but it don't alter the fact that he has made proposals to me sufficiently obnoxious to ruffle the ignominy of any lady."[34]

. . . .

"Ain't you ashamed of yourself, you whited sculpture?"[35]

. . . .

"He was traveling impromptu like kings, I guess."[36]

. . . .

". . . to see if he was real or only a kind of stuffed figure like they burn in elegy."[37]

. . . .

"He got three or four bullets planted in various parts of his autonomy."[38]

III *Literary Allusions: Shakespeare and the Classics*

Still further examples of O. Henry's artistry with words may be seen in his numerous literary allusions, chiefly to well-known Shakespearean plays and the ancient Classics as well as to his favorite *Arabian Nights;* but occasionally he alludes also to the writings of standard modern authors. His purpose again here is generally humorous; for as one writer has noted, in most of the hundred or so extended allusions to Shakespeare found in his stories, "he shows a tendency to word-play or to an unexpected turn similar to that manifest in the plots of his stories."[39] Among the numerous parallels cited by this scholar, the few following perhaps best illustrate O. Henry's deftness in turning to account his breezy familiarity with the Bard, whose phrases he usually wove "into his own sentences with a deliberate, occasionally somewhat artificial 'twist.' "[40]

1. Far better to linger there . . . than sit upon the horsehair sofa . . . and . . . drivel in the ears of gaping neighbors sad stories of the death of colonial governors.
    (*The Head-Hunter*)

For God's sake, let us sit upon the ground.
And tell sad stories of the death of kings.
    (*Richard II*, II:ii)

2. Twill serve—'tis not so deep as a lobster à la Newburgh, nor so wide as a church festival doughnut; but 'twill serve.
    (*The Third Ingredient*)

'Tis not so deep as a well, nor so wide as a church-door, but 'tis enough—'twill serve.
    (*Romeo and Juliet,* III:i)

3. "I've noticed you, Sam," says I, "seeking the bubble notoriety in the cannon's larynx a number of times."
    (*The Moment of Victory*)

Seeking the bubble reputation. Even in the cannon's mouth.
    (*As You Like It,* II:vii)

4. On the Rio Grande border if you take a man's life you sometimes take trash; but if you take his horse, you take a thing the loss of which renders him poor indeed, and which enriches you not—if you are caught.
    (*A Double-Dyed Deceiver*)

Who steals my purse steals trash, 'tis something, nothing . . .
But he that filches from me my good name
Robs me of that which not enriches him
And makes me poor indeed.
    (*Othello,* III:iii)

5. As for Tonia, though she sends description to the poorhouse, let her make a millionaire of your fancy.
    (*The Caballero's Way*)

For her own person,
It beggar'd all description.
    (*Antony and Cleopatra,* II:i)

Thanks to another scholar's labor, there is even more abundant evidence of O. Henry's use of the ancient Classics; for a total of some 450 "clearly recognizable allusions" to them have been spotted in his various writings.[41] Curiously enough, most of these allusions reflect a serious intent on O. Henry's part; and they indicate that, even though frankly appealing to a mass audience, he could still take for granted that many of his readers would recognize and appreciate his references to Homer, Cicero, Caesar, and to other Greek and Latin poets. Still, in at least seventy-five separate instances his purpose in making them was clearly humorous; and his methods were primarily those of punning and word mutilation. A Pittsburgh millionaire, for instance, becomes "Midas Americanus" and a Texan one, "an oil-Grease-us"; their common ailment, presumably, is "optikos needleorum camelibus—or rich man's disease."[42] An angry but shapely young dress model retorts: "Fudge for your Prax Italys. Bring one of your Venus Anno Dominos down to Cohen's."[43] Another character is described as one whose "hair waved a little bit like the statue of the dinkus thrower in the Vacation at Rome";[44] and Jeff Peters, posing as Dr. Waugh-hoo, modestly disclaims being "a regular preordained disciple of S. Q. Lapius."[45] Dozens of similar classical high jinks pop up unexpectedly again and again, as O. Henry goes on merrily distorting "lotus" into "lettuce," Mount Olympus into "Mount Catawampus" and "Mount Amphibious," Jupiter Pluvius into "Juniper Aquarius" ("Juniper Aquarius was sure turning on the water plugs on Mount Amphibious"[46]), Croesus into "greasers," and Scylla and Charybdis into "Squills and Chalybeates."[47]

Unfortunately, when such word-play loses much of whatever freshness it once possessed, it becomes sadly dated, if not downright cheap and tawdry; for O. Henry with the punning bit firmly between his teeth was not noted for restraint. Some of his misused or garbled Latin phrases—such as "adjourn sine qua non," "requiescat in hoc signo," "requiescat in pieces," "sine qua grata," "non compis vocis," etc.—no longer sound as funny as they once did, possibly because the original phrases themselves have become virtually standard English or because too many other jokesters have similarly garbled them. And yet, many of his linguistic capers still sound both apt and witty to the tolerant ear of a Classics specialist:

> A newspaper office is a "sanctum asinorum," and by the same token the office of a public stenographer is a "sanctum Remingtorium." Two fugitives alight from a train in Arizona, happy to return once more to "terra cotta," perhaps true in that climate. Commended for examination in context is "I'll fry some fat out of this ignis fatuus." The uproar in a railroad station evokes "Ad noisyam." Broadway, as the gathering place for the rural element, is, for O. Henry, the "Yappian Way.". . .
> Enough to make Vergil shudder is "fussily decency Averni—which means it's an easy slide from the street faker's dry goods box to a desk in Wall street." It is left to O. Henry to provide the translation to end all translations of Caesar's opening lines: "Omnes Gallia in tres partes divisa est: we will need all of our gall in devising means to tree them parties."[48]

Besides these deliberately ludicrous examples of O. Henry's tampering with the Classics, however, the same writer has shown that much oftener he employed classical allusions for a serious and significant purpose: "The 375 serious allusions in his short stories vary from the obvious and usual to references which assume a rather advanced classical knowledge for full comprehension. The average reader may have no difficulty with Cupid, Psyche, Jupiter, Juno, Mars, Minerva, *et al.*, but an appreciation of . . . an 'Autolycan adventurer' demands more than average classical background."⁴⁹ Some of the ways in which the Classics are thus widely used in O. Henry's stories are in the names of places, institutions, and persons—often with symbolic overtones, as in the Hotel Lotus, the *Minerva Magazine*, Caligula Polk, Aglaia, Artemisia, etc. Other uses are made of them as symbols of the cultured individual, or as figurative comparisons to heighten personal descriptions, as in the quite effective portrait of Ida Bates, the young typist at the Hotel Acropolis who "was a hold-over from the Greek classics. There wasn't a flaw in her looks. . . . I saw her turn pink, perfect statue that she was—a miracle that I share with Pygmalion only."⁵⁰ Many other classical comparisons appear in references to the weather, the social and economic competition prevalent in New York, the political solidarity of the South, the carnival gaiety of New York night life, the Western landscape at different seasons and times of day, the composition of literature and song, and, inevitably, the swift passage of time. From a classicist's point of view, many of O. Henry's serious classical allusions are both apt and pointed; often they are subtle as well in conveying complex moods and attitudes through the medium of a single sharp image, as in the glimpse of young Mary Ann Adrian cowering in her parents' rigid Calvinistic church beneath the disapproving glare of the congregation—"a hundred-eyed Cerberus that watched the gates through which her sins were fast thrusting her."⁵¹

IV *The Light Touch: Style and Rhetorical Mastery*

It may be doubted whether a great many of O. Henry's vast audience ever possessed a sufficiently broad classical background to appreciate as fully as he did the aptness of his allusions. But what they could appreciate and readily respond to was his lightness of touch in making them, to his easy assumption that he and his reader together stood on the same ground, sharing the same point of view, and that only a matter of chance therefore caused him rather than his reader to think of the appropriate comparison first. This, too, was part of the charm of the master trickster, capable of selecting repeatedly the unexpected word or phrase, which yet seemed in its context the inevitable choice to fit the occasion and thus contribute to that "absolute harmony of tone so essential to the short-story writer."[52] How many New Yorkers would have conceived the fanciful idea of an aerial conversation on the state of things in Manhattan between the statue of Diana atop Madison Square Garden and the Statue of Liberty down the bay? Or conceiving it, would have found the perspective and the details for setting it in motion? In a single vaulting passage, O. Henry sets the scene for his reader:

> Three hundred and sixty-five feet above the heated asphalt the tip-toeing symbolic deity on Manhattan pointed her vacillating arrow straight, for the time, in the direction of her exalted sister on Liberty Island. The lights of the great Garden were out; the benches in the Square were filled with sleepers in postures so strange that beside them the writhing figures in Dore's illustrations of the Inferno would have straightened into tailor's dummies. The statue of Diana on the tower of the Garden—its constancy shown by its weathercock ways, its innocence by the coating of gold that it has acquired, its devotion to style by its single, graceful flying scarf, its candour and artlessness by its habit of ever drawing the long bow, its metropolitanism by its posture of swift flight to catch a Harlem train—remained poised with its arrow pointed across the upper bay. Had that arrow sped truly and horizontally it would have passed fifty feet above the head of the heroic matron whose duty it is to offer a cast-ironical welcome to the oppressed of other lands.[53]

As a rhetorician, O. Henry is often at his best in descriptive passages of this sort, lightly sketching in the vivid yet characteristic details—such as the park-bench sleepers and Diana's scarf and long bow—and relating them to their temporal and spatial environment, often with a pun or *double-entendre* half concealed in the texture of his prose. In an even briefer paragraph consisting of only four sentences, he brings to life vividly both the appearance and the flavor of Jackson Square in New Orleans' Vieux Carré by drawing the reader's eye up to it, swiftly sketching its major peripheral features, focusing then upon its central compelling monument, and finally using that as a means of pointing off toward the opposite horizon. Moreover, in the actual details chosen are suggested simultaneously the mingled history enveloping the scene:

O. Henry's Technical Achievements

The Rue Chartres perishes in the old Place d'Armes. The ancient Cabildo, where Spanish justice fell like hail, faces it, and the Cathedral, another provincial ghost, overlooks it. Its centre is a little, iron-railed park of flowers and immaculate gravelled walks, where citizens take the air of evenings. Pedestalled high above it, the general sits his cavorting steed, with his face turned stonily down the river toward English Turn, whence come no more Britons to bombard his cotton bales.[54]

Whether serious or in a jesting mood—but often both by rapid turns—O. Henry's sheer love of words may break loose unexpectedly at any moment into colorful passages which, even though not wholly germane to his plot, nevertheless seize the reader's attention and achieve Conrad's stated purpose of making him *see, hear,* and *feel* the life relived on the printed page. Rhythm, movement, the right collocation of vowels and consonants, sound and sight images—all coalesce in these passages to produce a significant bit of experience. And even though they are rarely sustained beyond a page or so, as Pattee correctly noted, there are a great many of them. There is a passage, for instance, in which he depicts the "glorious and sonorous" motion of things going on daily in "one of those palaces of marble and glass," evidently a precursor of Horn and Hardart's, though comparable only to Valhalla:

The classic marble on which we ate, the great, light-flooded, vitreous front, adorned with snow-white scrolls; the grand Wagnerian din of clanking cups and bowls, the flashing staccato of brandishing cutlery, the piercing recitative of the white-aproned grub-maidens at the morgue-like banquet tables; the recurrent leit-motif of the cash-register—it was gigantic, triumphant welding of art and sound, a deafening, soul-uplifting pageant of heroic and emblematic life.[55]

Another passage, too long to quote in its entirety, matches the sound and significance of the early morning newsboys' cries in a superb crescendo of nouns suggesting the sensational headlines "heralding the chances that the slipping of one cogwheel in the machinery of time had made; apportioning to the sleepers while they lay at the mercy of fate, the vengeance, profit, grief, reward, and doom that the new figure in the calendar had brought them. Shrill and yet plaintive were the cries, as if the young voices grieved that so much evil and so little good was in their irresponsible hands. Thus echoed in the streets of the helpless city the transmission of the latest decrees of the gods, the cries of the newsboy—the Clarion call of the Press."[56] Among still other passages of like quality and import there is the one describing the actors' aptly named refuge, Hotel Thalia, which "looks on Broadway as Marathon looks on the sea," where "the player-bands gather at the end of their wanderings to loosen the buskin and dust the sock";[57] and another that fulfills the dual purpose of painting "with hard, broad strokes a marvelous lingual panorama of the West" and of revealing its electrifying effect upon a group of bored New York clubmen.[58]

Repeatedly in O. Henry's stories, passages like these are cunningly fitted into the structure of his narrative so that they are made to appear not simply gratuitous lingual ornaments but integral parts of the tale. This is where his art of compression and subtle joinery comes into play to justify and support the daring self-assurance with which he tosses together ingredients of a seemingly indissoluble nature, only to surprise the reader with a blend that is both light and satisfying and that possesses its own independent, distinctive characteristics. Much of his successful craftsmanship, as well as his popularity, rests on his sureness of touch, his confidence that the very process by which he makes a tale unfold will keep his reader on the alert for new surprises—will keep him, in fact, diverted and puzzled fully as much by the sleight-of-hand movements of the performing artist as he is by the substance of the story itself. Thus, scarcely has the story got under way than the reader has become an unwitting participant in its development: he supplies its unwritten portions, fills in its gaps and swift transitions, looks ahead in an effort to anticipate its forthcoming twists, turns, and outcome. Though possibly unexpressed, the question in the reader's mind "How will he pull this one off?" becomes no less important than "What happens next?"

V *Art that Conceals Art: O. Henry's Irony*

To test the assertion just made, one need only examine closely the structural pattern of a typical O. Henry story—not necessarily one of his better-known ones—and note one's own reaction to it on a first reading. "The Poet and the Peasant," for example, combines a number of his favorite ingredients, devices, and situations.[59] The story opens as a first-person narrative, the speaker telling of "a poet friend of mine" who wrote a nature poem recently and submitted it to an editor. Having spent his entire life in close contact with nature, he had produced "a living pastoral"; yet the editor rejected it as being too artificial. And so while lunching together, "several of us," the narrator continues, indignantly condemned the editor. Among the group was Conant, a successful, city-bred fiction writer, who despised "bucolic scenes"; he, however, wrote another poem called "The Doe and the Brook," described by the narrator as "a fine specimen of the kind of work you would expect from a poet who had strayed with Amaryllis only as far as the florist's windows, and whose sole ornithological discussion had been carried on with a waiter" (73-74). He signed it, "and we sent it to the same editor."

At this point the reader's curiosity has been thoroughly whetted; his only concern is to learn the fate of the second poem. But O. Henry coyly turns the whole matter aside with his offhand remark: "But this has very little to do with the story." Yet the next sentence raises the possibility that Conant's poem does have something to do with the story, for it reveals that "just as the editor was reading the first line of the poem, on the next morning, a being stumbled off the West Shore ferryboat, and loped slowly up Forty-second Street." Now follows a fairly detailed, ludicrous description of a typical young rustic carrying a battered valise; he is so obviously the hayseed, however, that—although passersby smile knowingly at first sight of him—they quickly decide upon closer scrutiny that his antics and manner, like his appearance, are too patently overdone to be real. A confidence man, Bunco Harry, even sidles up to advise him quietly, as he stands gawking into a jeweler's window, that his make-up is "too thick." Nothing the innocent young rube can say to justify his identity can convince the swindler that he is not also a crook in disguise; and, while Bunco Harry tolerantly invites him to have a drink, he cannily declines the young man's offer "to play a game or two of seven-up."

By now the reader is puzzled as to whether any relationship exists between the poet and this peasant, but the problem of Haylocks has already begun to complicate his puzzlement. It is now a question of finding out what lies in store for him, besides that of linking him up somehow with Conant. In rapid order everyone he meets suspects him of chicanery: Bunco Harry is convinced that the $950 he flashes in a roll as big as a teacup is counterfeit; the bartender and other assorted hoodlums take him for a poorly disguised detective; a second bartender to whom he entrusts the valise knows without opening it that the only nine-fifty in it is "a ninety-eight cent Waterbury that's stopped at ten minutes to ten." Everyone on Broadway sardonically regards him as "the oldest of 'gags' that the city must endure." Even the newsboy spurns his proffered twenty-dollar "yellow back" as stage money; and a gambling-house steerer whom he appeals to for guidance toward a sporting house angrily accuses him of being a police decoy. At each turn of events the irony of Haylocks' predicament receives a further complicating, humorous twist; and the reader wonders how many more variations of it the author will be able to crowd into his swift-moving narrative before it grows tedious.

Thoroughly rebuffed by "the great city that is so swift to detect artificialities," Haylocks now decides that his difficulties have been due to his clothes, which make him look like a hayseed; he therefore spends part of his fortune for a complete outfit (brilliantly described by O. Henry in four compact sentences); then, resplendantly, he sets forth once again down Broadway "with the easy and graceful tread of a millionaire." And within a few minutes he is spotted by a trio of hold-up men, who size him up immediately as "the juiciest jay" they have encountered in months. O. Henry wastes no further words explaining what happens next: his narrator simply indicates that at half-past eleven "a man galloped into West Forty-seventh Street Police Station" to report breathlessly that he has been robbed of $950, his entire share of his grandmother's farm. At this point the story of Haylocks (or Jabez Bulltongue, the name he gives the desk sergeant) ends, and with no further transition, the narrator proceeds, in four more short paragraphs, to wrap up also the unfinished account of Conant and the story as a whole.

Conant's poem, "The Doe and the Brook," of course, receives high praise from the editor as " 'the work of one whose life has been heart to heart with Nature,' " its finished artistry forcibly reminding him of a homely comparison—" 'it was as if a wild, free child of the woods and fields were to don the garb of fashion and walk down Broadway. Beneath the apparel the man would show'" (p. 82). Conant himself laconically accepts both the praise and his check, and O. Henry ironically offers the reader his choice of mixed morals suggested by the story: either "'Stay on the Farm'" or "'Don't Write Poetry.'" Only the naïve reader, however, will fail to recognize that neither of these touches the underlying meaning of the story, which has to do with the age-old theme of appearance versus reality, as well as with the basic human tendency to rely on snap judgments derived from an inadequate interpretation of the former. Granted that O. Henry's flimsy little tale offers no very profound commentary on these matters, is it after all just an idle piece of jugglery, devoid of art and perhaps even of truth, as Pattee insisted? Is it mere pointless prestidigitation, designed to flatter and cajole the unthinking masses? If so, one might still bear in mind the import of Anatole France's "Jongleur de Notre Dame," the hero of which found favor in the Virgin Mother's eyes by performing humbly the one skill he possessed. For if O. Henry's story is jugglery of the same sort, it is at least unpretentious in its appeal to a mass audience; moreover, its essential cleverness is artfully concealed beneath a surface level of pseudo-cleverness sufficient to delight the many who read on the run.

On the one level "The Poet and the Peasant," like so many other O. Henry stories, is simply an entertaining bit of fluff. Its power to divert and amuse springs from a series of obvious related ironies; from O. Henry's absurdly comic portrayal of the young Ulsterman, and from his narrator's slangy insouciance in juxtaposing the two seemingly unrelated accounts, welding them together as though there were nothing out of the ordinary in doing so, and applying two different idioms to his two groups of characters. All this superficial trickery provides ample entertainment for the typical O. Henry fan. But beneath this surface level there is suggested also a cluster of related truths about art and life, about knowledge and ignorance, and about human fallibility in distinguishing the genuine from the spurious. That O. Henry's technique enabled him to compress so much within the compass of a Sunday supplement page—and with such seeming artlessness—is the true measure of his artistry.

CHAPTER 6

Reputation and Revaluation

I *The O. Henry Vogue: 1910-1930*

DURING THE YEARS immediately following his death, O.
Henry's popularity rose to unprecedented heights. No other
American writer of stories had ever been so widely read, enjoyed,
discussed, approved of, and imitated. By 1920 nearly five million
copies of his books had been sold in the United States,[1] and
proportionately large sales were being made in other English-
speaking countries, where Kipling was his only rival. Moreover,
though O. Henry while still alive had been merely the darling of
the Sunday-supplement reader—Mr. Everybody—he had now
become the mute oracle of the critics and literary intelligentsia;
his writings were the norm against which all other short stories
were judged and, in the main, found wanting.

This favorable tide began about 1908 with the appearance of
H. J. Forman's frankly laudatory essay in the *North American
Review*.[2] No one, Forman asserted, had yet "brought so much
fun and humour to the Western story . . . material of the 'dime
novel,' but all treated with the skill of a Maupassant, and a
humour Maupassant never dreamed of."[3] Thereafter the comparison stuck: O. Henry became the "Yankee Maupassant,"[4] a
soubriquet skillfully ballyhooed by his publishers; and a succession of critical essays, stimulated in part by blatant sales-promo-
tion devices, soon kept his name prominently before the public
that looked to periodicals like the *Bookman, Cosmopolitan,* and
Current Opinion for its literary guidance. Between 1910 and
1915 numerous essays about him and his work were published
in these magazines, some of them encouraged by a prize contest
engineered by his good friend and literary executor, Henry
Peyton Steger, a brilliant young employee of Doubleday, who
was scheduled to write the first biography of O. Henry.[5]

As literary adviser to Doubleday, Steger, in furthering O.

Henry's reputation, displayed both his close personal friendship for the dead author and his commercial acumen. He had helped assemble the stories for the volumes published just before, and after O. Henry's death, assisted in the funeral arrangements, and been named Margaret's guardian. And since O. Henry died owing Doubleday thousands of dollars paid him in advances, Steger planned to recover these funds as well as to aid the family by publicizing the author extensively and thus augmenting the sales of his books. While gathering materials for his biography, Steger discovered in a barn in Austin the only nearly complete file of *The Rolling Stone*. He discussed it and other facts about O. Henry in a series of articles in the *Bookman* during 1910 and 1911; but, although his book was announced for publication in 1912, Steger himself died suddenly that year at the age of thirty, and his unfinished work was taken over by Professor C. Alphonso Smith. Steger's last job as literary adviser to Doubleday, however, was to plan and sell the famous limited first edition of O. Henry's complete works, consisting of 250 de luxe printings of twelve volumes at $125 a set, each separate volume of which bore the unique distinction of containing a single yellow sheet of O. Henry's manuscript folded and tucked into an inside pocket. This edition sold out at once, and it has rarely been offered on the market since—at any price.[6]

With Steger removed from the scene, O. Henry's publicity suffered little if any diminution, for numerous other essayists continued appraising his work in tones of growing respect.[7] The leading figure in this group was O. Henry's boyhood chum, Professor Smith, whose *O. Henry Biography*, published in 1916, firmly established its subject's claim to rank among America's major authors. Based on years of patient research, the book had been eagerly awaited and was well received, but Smith's high praise for O. Henry's work naturally aroused some negative reaction among the more fastidious academic critics. Their adverse criticism was focused in charges by Katherine Fullerton Gerrould, who deplored the "pernicious influence" of O. Henry's stories and condemned them as merely "expanded anecdotes" shorn of serious intellectual content.[8] Later, F. L. Pattee likewise dismissed them as specious journalization.[9] These attacks, however, brought forth swift counterattacks, notably by Stephen Leacock, the Canadian humorist, who brushed aside all such animadversions as sheer nonsense, unworthy a serious reply; for, if O. Henry's stories were only anecdotes, said Leacock, "let's have another barrelful,"[10] and he concluded another highly adulatory essay with a fervent prediction that soon "the whole English-speaking world will recognize in O. Henry one of the great masters of modern literature."[11] Leacock's extravagant praise was at least matched, if not surpassed, by that of another enthusiast, Frank Newbolt, whose ten-page essay, a sustained love song written in imitation of O. Henry's slangiest style, re-echoed the delight he had found in every volume and climaxed his tribute in the words of one of the master's own characters: " 'You're the goods, duty free, and half-way to the warehouse in a red waggon.' *Au revoir.*"[12]

Thanks to steadily mounting praise like this, O. Henry's image quickly overshadowed all others in the field of the short story. By 1919, when the annual volume of selections called the *O. Henry Memorial Award Prize Stories* was inaugurated, his name was the inevitable choice with which to symbolize pre-eminence in this art form because his work stood—for the time being—as the highest standard of what the short story was meant to be. Most authorities agreed that the four masters of the American short story were Poe, Hawthorne, Bret Harte, and O. Henry; and many were positive that O. Henry surpassed the others in the genre. Handbooks and college courses professing to teach the technique of short story writing had proliferated during the preceding two decades ("Why not be an O. Henry yourself and make money? Here were the rules");[13] and, although O. Henry himself was not alone responsible for this trend toward mechanization, "his artistry was so striking and his methods so evident that even the novice was inspired to codify his laws and imitate his devices."[14] It is hardly surprising therefore that within a few more years he had become a "contemporary classic," confidently placed by Archibald Henderson as on a par with Hardy, Meredith, Henry James, Tolstoy, and Kipling, and as decidedly above Conrad, Bourget, Galsworthy, Edith Wharton, and H. G. Wells.[15] In fact, said Henderson, Kipling was really his only equal among contemporary short story writers, since for over a dozen years there had been a clamorous demand for a selected edition of O. Henry's "best" stories, although no two individuals could ever agree as to which were his best.

II *Spread and Variety of O. Henry's Influence*

Meanwhile, O. Henry's stories had rapidly gained an enthusiastic following abroad, first in England but shortly afterward in France and other European countries, where the problem
of translating his slangy American vernacular must have posed
formidable difficulties. Within six months after Leacock's pane-
gyric appeared, an English essayist, St. John Adcock, agreed
that the reading public in England had only recently begun to
take to O. Henry, but he blamed this neglect on his fellow
critics and publishers rather than on the indifference of British
readers. For it was obvious now that, with the assured sale of
half a million copies of a newly published shilling edition, "at
long last O. Henry is triumphantly entering into his kingdom."[16]
And well did he deserve to in the opinion of this writer, who
wholeheartedly endorsed Leacock's evaluation of O. Henry's
artistry, particularly his easy, colloquial style and his deftness
in leading toward an apparently ingenious ending which, with
a sudden quick turn, became "a still more ingenious climax."[17]

O. Henry's dexterity in ordering and controlling his materials
likewise delighted the French, one of whom, Raoul Narcy,
upheld the short story as an art form worthy of respect because
"its compactness cannot tolerate either disorder in the construction or weakness in the style...[it] has its own law; which
requires the exactness of measures and proportions."[18] Since O.
Henry's writings admirably fulfilled these requirements, they
were fit to stand beside those of Irving, Hawthorne, and Poe;
for they revealed not only skill in selecting detail, but also a
sharp, amused observation, "abounding *verve*, [and]...intel-
ligence armed with irony; he dominates his characters rather
than suffering them."[19] Moreover, from a Frenchman's point of
view, it was a pleasure to encounter an American writer who
avoided moral preachments, presented life as he saw it, and
let the reader form his own judgments; yet O. Henry managed
also to reveal sordid slum conditions and Western violence and
bloodshed without creating an "impression of misanthropy or
pessimism."[20]

Of all the European countries, however, O. Henry seems to
have made his strongest impression in Russia, where for forty
years he has been a top favorite from among a small number

of American writers.[21] Shortly after appearing there in 1923 his stories quickly won enthusiastic acclaim, nearly a million volumes of them being published within the next four or five years; and despite changing fashions and new names—such as Dreiser, Steinbeck, Erskine Caldwell, and Hemingway—they continue through frequent reprintings to be widely read and enjoyed in the 1960's.[22] Like the French, the earliest Soviet critics esteemed O. Henry for the style and structure of his stories, especially for the vigor and freshness of his language and for his adroitness in plot construction. But they also found a strong appeal in his treatment of urban life, notably that of humble workers, and in his ability to divert and amuse, even though some deplored his lack of moral fervor in condemning the evils of bourgeois society revealed in his tales of New York. To some he became "the American Rousseau"; to others "the American Chekhov"; but in either case, a classic. Later critics even professed to find in his stories a bitter denunciation of the capitalist system, but the prevailing view since the 1930's has been that they offer only frothy, sentimental entertainment—" 'magnificent railroad reading.' "[23] Whatever the critic's strictures, however, the point is that for the masses of Russian readers, O. Henry remains even today, almost the sole representative of American "mass" or "escape" literature, possibly because his stories, if not ideologically useful to the Party, are at least harmless, but more likely because their light, swiftly moving, suspenseful excitement and their uncomplicated moral and intellectual texture make them ideally suited to the average reader's tastes. Their values and standards "must seem 'sound' to the Soviet reader, despite their political backwardness from the Marxist point of view. This accounts for the pronounced inclination of many critics to value O. Henry as a poet of the 'little man,' despite the simultaneous insistence of other critics that the author ran away from real social problems."[24]

Very likely the same reasons would account for O. Henry's continuing popularity throughout other foreign countries, from Scandinavia to Latin America and from the Balkans to the Far East. For, as Langford indicates, not only have his stories "been industriously pirated all over the world, but even the list of authorized foreign reprintings in the last two decades is impressive."[25] There is thus no way of estimating accurately how many separate editions, let alone copies, of O. Henry's tales have been printed and distributed to date throughout the world. But one can safely assume that they have brought an appealing image of America, however outdated, to tens of millions of foreigners.

In other than their original versions, moreover, the stories have also continued to delight millions of Americans down to the present day. First on the stage, later in motion pictures, and finally through the medium of radio and television dramatizations many of the favorite O. Henry tales—"A Retrieved Reformation," "A Double-Dyed Deceiver," and "The Caballero's Way"— have appeared and reappeared, sometimes in versions so far-fetched that O. Henry himself might have ridiculed them. Here again, precise figures are hard to establish: a carefully prepared but admittedly incomplete record of statistics furnished by Doubleday and Company shows that up to 1960 there had been produced in the United States alone at least forty separate radio and stage dramatizations, 130 motion picture versions, and forty more television adaptations of the various stories, most of the last group having appeared as recently as the mid-1950's on the "O. Henry Television Playhouse."[26] How many further adaptations in these different media have appeared outside the United States is anybody's guess; but it is known, for example, that the first two titles above each had a play and three different motion pictures based on their plots, while "The Caballero's Way" provided the source not only for several motion pictures but also for some nineteen or twenty other "Cisco Kid" productions, which bear no relation whatever to the original story except that of the hero's name.[27] This tenuous connection alone, however, was sufficient to supply O. Henry's widow with substantial royalties as late as 1952.[28]

Among the first to publicize as well as to exploit the dramatic resources of O. Henry's stories was the young Broadway actor, Norman Hackett, who played the lead in *Alias Jimmy Valentine* for two full seasons at Wallack's Theatre. Later, Hackett took both that play and the *Double-Dyed Deceiver* on the road for long runs.[29] To support the continuing box-office appeal of his performances he not only relied on lavish newspaper advertisements, but also delivered public lectures heaping high praise on O. Henry's genius.[30] Meanwhile, motion picture rights to more than a dozen of the stories had been sold as early as May, 1914, chiefly from among O. Henry's most colorful Texas tales.

"The Caballero's Way," filmed in Tucson that year and subsequently released under the title *In Old Arizona,* was characterized by *Motion Picture Magazine* as the finest "western" produced up to that time.[31] The most elaborate dramatic adaptation of O. Henry's work, however, appeared ten years later, when the indefatigable Upton Sinclair published at his own expense *Bill Porter: A Drama of O. Henry in Prison,* a play he had written based about equally on some of Porter's most popular stories and on his real-life experiences as an inmate of the Ohio Penitentiary.[32]

Surely the ultimate in sentimentality, Sinclair's play nevertheless offers an impressive, if somewhat bewildering, view of the degree of reverence O. Henry could still inspire among other writers as late as the mid-1920's. According to Sinclair, his play "follows as literally as possible the facts concerning Bill Porter's life and behavior in prison, as revealed in his letters and other published records ... [It] deals with the soul of a creative artist, working despite ill fortune ... [and] tries to show a writer at work; how he takes the experiences of his life, and revises and reshapes them according to his temperament."[33] Actually, the play appears to have been drawn largely from extensive talks with Al Jennings, who also read and approved the text besides figuring prominently in it.

Whatever its genesis, the play attempts through a manipulation of the stage lighting to fuse reality and fantasy in alternating scenes. As a result, characters representing real individuals, such as Athol, Margaret, Jennings, the bank examiners, and some of Porter's fellow prisoners become transformed into creatures of his own brain, characters who would later appear in eight of his best-known stories, including "A Municipal Report," "A Retrieved Reformation," and "An Unfinished Story."[34] As the play develops, familiar scenes from these stories are linked to alleged or imagined activities Porter engaged in while still a prisoner—for example, his tendency to drink and his services as a pharmacist—but the underlying purpose of each scene is to justify and applaud Porter's conduct both as man and as writer. Thus, the shade of Jimmy Valentine urges the propriety of his romanticized tales of miraculously reformed criminals because "people will get some good out of them"; and the dead Athol's ghost excuses his reticence about prison brutality on the grounds that her husband will help millions of people instead by representing their poor, pinched lives imaginatively with a little kindness and humor:

> "Write about them, Will! Write *for* them! I see them, eager, hungry, craving just the sort of pity mixed with laughter that is your gift. Yes, I see them! Will! Will—look at them! (she points; a searchlight behind the scenes is suddenly turned upon the audience through an aperture in the back drop; it plays here and there, and Athol's voice rises with excitement) Faces! Faces! Millions of faces—and all of them your lovers! Eager faces, shining, with gratitude, with hope, with fun—all of them ready to cheer you, to shout to you—to tell the affection they bear you! Go forth, Will Porter! Do your work, and take your place as their story teller—the voice of the Four Million!"[35]

Though crudely overdone, Sinclair's rhapsodic speech at the climax of his play is probably a less exaggerated characterization of Porter's young wife, the real Athol of the 1890's, than today's reader can imagine. Furthermore, it expresses not only Sinclair's own sincere evaluation of O. Henry's achievement, but also that of the many times four million readers who have continued to see themselves affectionately reflected in O. Henry's stories.

Declining Reputation and Restored Perspectives: 1930-1960

Among the literary critics the falling off of O. Henry's reputation in the United States after the 1920's was nearly as swift and precipitous as its original ascent. Though attacked even earlier by critics like Pattee and H. L. Mencken, who sneered at his "smoke-room and variety-show smartness,"[36] as well as by Sherwood Anderson, who deplored his mechanized plots, O. Henry was at least noticed by these writers if only to be condemned occasionally for faults that belonged more properly to a host of cheaper imitators. This was the era of the "new" fiction which, in its youthful revolt against all the accepted moral standards, taboos, and conventions of an older generation, as well as against the older fiction's exclusive reliance upon plot structure, was seeking its effects through experimentation in indirection, symbolism, and understatement; and these writers accordingly made O. Henry's clever contrivances seem all the more dated and passé. As embodied in Anderson's own *Wines-*

burg, Ohio tales and the still more daringly fashioned pieces in Hemingway's *In Our Time* and in *Men Without Women,* these new techniques were causing even Fitzgerald's best short stories to lose favor at the very time that they were being published.[37]

By the 1930's the "new" fiction had gained so much respect among critics and younger aspirants to literary prominence that O. Henry's style of writing no longer seemed important enough to notice, even unfavorably; and his stories seemed destined, whatever their merits or defects, to almost total critical oblivion. Though an occasional tribute such as Davis and Maurice's *The Caliph of Bagdad* might appear on the scene, the critical consensus during this decade increasingly indicated that O. Henry's works—despite their massive popular appeal—were rapidly becoming a mere footnote to American literary history. John Chamberlain, for example, questioned whether many of his stories would in time "even provide a good laugh"; Ludwig Lewisohn found in them a certain degree of "creative honesty . . . that was new and has not wholly faded yet" but felt that O. Henry had penetrated to the permanently significant only in scattered glimpses of New York "somehow captured and held fast." And A. H. Quinn, amazed upon re-reading the stories "to think how seriously he was taken at the time of his death," found scarcely a dozen out of the entire canon that might be called "first-rate" and possibly a dozen more that seemed "creditable."[38]

During the same decade scholarly interest in O. Henry, though slightly more abundant, sharply reflected this decline in critical esteem. Throughout the entire nation about ten or a dozen masters' theses on O. Henry were written, only two or three of which at the University of Texas disclosed significant new data concerning his early career as a journalist in Austin and Houston; and, except for the single volume entitled *O. Henry Encore* (1939), all of this material remained unpublished. In addition to this work, the only other important scholarly material on O. Henry published during the 1930's included several articles of a biographical nature which appeared in the *South Atlantic Quarterly* and in the *Southwest Review;* another article in *American Literature,* by P. S. Clarkson, which clarified the composition of O. Henry's first book; and, of greatest value to the student of O. Henry, the same author's *A Bibliography of William Sidney Porter.*[39] For the rest, there were at most three or four books of personal reminiscences such as W. W. Williams' *The Quiet Lodger of Irving Place* which, while adding valuable data to the record of O. Henry's life, did little to enhance his literary stature.[40]

Slight as this overall critical and scholarly concern may appear to be for a writer who had dominated the literary scene only twenty years before, it was still ample when compared with the almost total neglect O. Henry's reputation suffered in the United States during the 1940's and most of the 1950's. Except for a few more masters' theses, a single published dissertation, and one scholarly article that re-examined the facts in his embezzlement trial, O. Henry was virtually dismissed as unworthy of any further serious consideration. "The world of O. Henry is an intellectual Sahara," concluded George F. Whicher in one of the two major literary histories published during these decades;[41] while the other scarcely bothered to mention his name at all in its revised edition.[42] That O. Henry with his trickery and cheap wisecracks had all but debased the art of the short story beyond redemption had become the standard attitude of these and several other authorities, such as Brooks and Warren, who took the trouble to re-examine an occasional sample of his work.[43] It is thus hardly surprising to find the author of an elaborate recent treatise on the development of the American short story in the 1920's bluntly asserting that O. Henry's reputation has died and accordingly ignoring his work altogether.[44]

Whether such judgments as these will hold, however, remains to be seen. Just as the original adulation lavished upon O. Henry proved to be laughably excessive, so may the more recent deprecation of his work turn out to be both imperceptive and unjustified. For his individuality and popular appeal—however dead and dated his mannerisms, contrivances, and influence— vigorously continue to resist interment. Possibly his most perceptive biographer, Gerald Langford, is overoptimistic in conjecturing that "at long last the time has come when O. Henry can be given his rightful place in American literature."[45] He is nevertheless correct in asserting that O. Henry, as a *minor* classic who is here to stay, deserves his permanent niche by virtue of a uniqueness of flavor in his work compounded of humor, enchantment, and pity for all who suffer from a sense of isolation and frustration. Nearly forty years ago Upton Sinclair, perceiving these same durable values in O. Henry's stories, expressed them in the bit of doggerel that rang down the curtain of his play:

He comes with vaudeville, with stare and leer.
He comes with megaphone and specious cheer.
His troupe, too fat or short or long or lean,
Step from the pages of the magazine
With slapstick or sombrero or with cane:
The rube, the cowboy or the masher vain.
They overact each part. But at the height
Of banter and of canter and delight
The masks fall off for one queer instant there
And show real faces: faces full of care
And desperate longing: love that's hot or cold;
And subtle thoughts, and countenances bold. . . .[46]

Notes and References

Many of the references below are to manuscript materials included in the large O. Henry Collection belonging to the Public Library of Greensboro, North Carolina. Now available on microfilm, this collection consists of two large groups of papers, referred to here as *Greensboro Papers* and as *Smith Papers*. The Smith papers include notes on interviews, letters from Porter's friends and acquaintances, and other materials gathered by C. Alphonso Smith during the preparation of his authorized biography published in 1916. Besides these, the Greensboro Public Library has accumulated a vast number of clippings, reviews, typescripts, and other manuscript materials pertaining to O. Henry.

To secure brevity in notes referring to several frequently used sources, the following abbreviations have been used:

Alias O. Henry, by Gerald Langford (New York, 1957), is referred to simply as "Langford."

The *O. Henry Biography*, by C. Alphonso Smith (New York, 1916), is referred to as "Smith."

The Caliph of Bagdad, by Robert H. Davis and Arthur B. Maurice (New York, 1931), is referred to as *Caliph*.

O. Henry From Polecat Creek, by Ethel Stephens Arnett (Greensboro, North Carolina, 1962), is referred to as "Arnett."

A Bibliography of William Sydney Porter, by Paul S. Clarkson (Caldwell, Idaho, 1938), is referred to as "Clarkson."

Wherever possible, references to O. Henry's stories and sketches are to individual volumes, indicated by the volume title, in the thirteen-volume edition published by Doubleday, Page and Company (1920). A few other references are made to *The Complete Works of O. Henry* (2 vols.) (New York, 1953), which are here referred to as "*Works.*"

Chapter One

1. Ethel Stephens Arnett, *O. Henry From Polecat Creek* (Greensboro, North Carolina, 1962), p. 1.
2. Gerald Langford, *Alias O. Henry* (New York, 1957), Chapter 1.
3. Arnett, pp. 2; 207-11.
4. C. Alphonso Smith, *O. Henry Biography* (Garden City, N.Y., 1916), pp. 25-33, 41.
5. Quoted in Arnett, p. 46.
6. Langford, p. 6.
7. John H. Dillard: Letter to C. A. Smith, *Smith Papers,* quoted in Langford, pp. 5, 7.
8. Smith, pp. 76, 89. See also Arnett, pp. 92-95.
9. Smith, p. 41.
10. Langford, p. 9.
11. Arnett, pp. 129-33.
12. Smith, p. 73.

13. S. W. Porter, "O. Henry as His Brother Knew Him," Greensboro *Daily News*, May 12, 1929: in *Greensboro Papers;* also quoted in Arnett, p. 131.

14. William P. Beall, "Young Porter Looked upon as Second Nas[t]," Greensboro *Daily News*, July 2, 1919; and "Will Porter's Home Town Pays His Memory a Belated Tribute," Greensboro *Daily News*, March 28, 1924: in *Greensboro Papers;* quoted in Arnett, pp. 144-45.

15. Arnett, pp. 149-52.

16. *Ibid.*, pp. 147-48.

17. A. W. McAllister: Letter to C. A. Smith, November 25, 1914; A. W. Page, "Little Pictures of O. Henry: I," *Bookman* (June, 1913), p. 386; Cecile Lindau, "Will Porter and Uncle Charlie," *Homespun*, October, 1925: all in *Greensboro Papers* and cited in Arnett, pp. 153-66, *passim*.

18. Arnett, inserts, pp. 168-69. For a good brief discussion of Tourgée's activities and reputation in Greensboro, see Smith, pp. 60-68. See also T. L. Gross, *Albion Tourgée*, TUSAS, Vol. XXXIX (New York, 1963).

19. Arnett, pp. 114, 145-46.

20. Langford, pp. 14-15; Arnett, pp. 193-97.

21. Arnett, pp. 184-92.

22. Anne Partlan: interview quoted by Smith: "The grind in the drug store was agony to me." In *Smith Papers;* also quoted in Arnett, p. 193.

23. Langford, pp. 14-17.

24. Arnett, pp. 201-3.

25. Dora Neill Raymond, *Captain Lee Hall of Texas* (Norman, Oklahoma; 1940), Chapter 1. See also Edmund King, *The Great South*, (Hartford, Conn., 1875), pp. 178-79.

26. See, e.g., "An Afternoon Miracle," a rewritten version of one of O. Henry's earliest stories, "The Miracle of Lava Canyon"; also "The Caballero's Way" and others in the volume *Heart of the West*, Vol. IV.

27. Langford, pp. 21-25.

28. "The Last of the Troubadors," in *Sixes and Sevens, Works*, VIII, 5.

29. Langford, pp. 29-30.

30. *Ibid.*, pp. 22, 27.

31. *Ibid.*, pp. 27-29.

32. See letters to Dr. W. P. Beall, *Works*, II, 1072-75.

33. Arthur W. Page, "Little Pictures of O. Henry," *Bookman* XXXVIII (July, 1913), 498-99. Quoted in Langford, p. 32.

34. *Smith Papers;* cited in Langford, p. 33.

35. Dan Hollis, "The Persecution of O. Henry," Austin *American-Statesman Magazine* (August 30, 1925), p. 10. Quoted in Langford, pp. 37-38.

36. Letters to Beall, cited in Langford, p. 30.

37. For a more detailed treatment, see Langford, pp. 38-44.

38. Smith, p. 118.

39. See, e.g., Frances G. Maltby, *The Dimity Sweetheart* (Richmond, Virginia, 1930); Lollie Cave Wilson, *Hard to Forget* (Los Angeles, California, 1939); Mary S. Harrell, "O. Henry's Texas Contacts," University of Texas Master's Thesis, 1935.

40. Langford, pp. 55-60.

41. *Ibid.*, p. 62.

42. In *Roads of Destiny, Works,* VI, 155-70.

43. For an excellent descriptive analysis of *The Rolling Stone,* see Langford, pp. 75-81 and Appendix, pp. 251-58.

44. *Ibid.,* pp. 71-74.

45. *Ibid.,* p. 86.

46. *Ibid.,* pp. 82-84, 89-90.

47. For a brief but careful analytic summary of these, see Langford, pp. 92-96; also Mary S. Harrell, *O. Henry Encore* (New York, 1939), for the entire collection.

48. Langford, p. 101.

49. In *Whirligigs,* XIII, 259-87.

50. Langford, pp. 102-3.

51. *Ibid.,* p. 110.

52. *Ibid.,* Chapter 7, pp. 112-30.

53. Dan McAllister, "Negligently, Perhaps; Criminally, Never," *South Atlantic Quarterly* (October, 1952), pp. 562-73.

54. See L. W. Courtney, "O. Henry's Case Reconsidered," *American Literature,* XIV (January, 1943), 361-71. See also interviews in Rollins papers, cited in Langford, pp. 124-25.

55. Letter quoted in Smith, p. 148.

56. See *ibid.,* pp. 158-66.

57. The titles of these 14 are: "Whistling Dick's Christmas Stocking," "Georgia's Ruling," "An Afternoon Miracle" (rewritten version of "The Miracle of Lava Canyon"), "A Medley of Moods" (first published as "Blind Man's Holiday"), "Money Maze," "No Story," "A Fog in Santone," "A Blackjack Bargainer," "The Enchanted Kiss," "Hygeia at the Solito," "Rouge et Noir," "The Duplicity of Hargraves," "The Marionettes," and "A Chaparral Christmas Gift."

58. Letter quoted in Smith, p. 157.

59. Al Jennings, *Through The Shadows With O. Henry* (London, Duckworth & Co., 1923), p. 222; quoted in Langford, pp. 145-46.

60. For various alleged sources of the pseudonym, some as early as Porter's Texas ranch days, see Langford, pp. 149-50.

61. In *Roads of Destiny,* pp. 134-43; but first published in the *Cosmopolitan,* April, 1903. Cf. Langford, p. 147.

62. Jennings, *Through the Shadows,* p. 252.

63. Langford, p. 148.

64. *Ibid.,* pp. 152-55.

65. The titles of these are listed in Langford, p. 276; but Langford overlooks one story, "Bulger's Friend," which is listed in Paul S. Clarkson, *A Bibliography of William Sydney Porter* (pp. 68, 111) as published in the *Youth's Companion,* December, 1901.

66. The complete letter is reprinted in *Complete Works* (1953) II: 1092-93.

67. Jennings, p. 257.

68. Jennings, pp. 297-98.

69. Smith, p. 173.

70. Clarkson lists publication in ten different periodicals for the year 1902: pp. 103-11.

71. Langford, pp. 160-62.

72. Davis & Maurice, *The Caliph of Bagdad* (New York, 1931), p. 260.
73. "The Gold That Glittered," *Strictly Business,* pp. 21-23.
74. Langford, p. 169.
75. *Caliph,* p. 260.
76. Mabel Wagnalls, *Letters to Lithopolis* (New York, 1922); Ethel Patterson, ."O. Henry and Me," *Everybody's Magazine* (February, 1914), pp. 206-10; both cited in Langford, pp. 162-64, 197-200.
77. John D. Barry, "O. Henry," Greensboro *News,* April 12, 1915; in *Greensboro Papers* and quoted in Langford, p. 171.
78. Langford, p. 182.
79. *Ibid.,* pp. 187-91.
80. "The Memento," *Voice of the City,* p. 236, 243.
81. Quoted in *Caliph,* p. 309.
82. Langford, p. 184.
83. "O. Henry," *The Texas Review,* II (April, 1917), 254.
84. Langford, pp. 187-90.
85. *Caliph,* pp. 331-32.
86. Langford, p. 207.
87. *Ibid.,* p. 190.
88. See Smith, pp. 194-99.
89. Langford, pp. 204-5.
90. For complete information on these volumes, see Clarkson, pp. 17-76.
91. H. J. Forman "O. Henry's Short Stories", *North American Review* (May, 1908), p. 781; quoted in Langford, pp. 217-18.
92. *Nation,* November 28, 1907, p. 496; quoted in Langford, p. 212.
93. Langford, p. 208.
94. *Ibid.,* pp. 210-11, 214-17, 219-22.
95. *Ibid.,* pp. 224-26, 231-32.
96. Most of O. Henry's biographers have mistakenly asserted that the play *Lo!* was based on his story "To Him Who Waits," published in *Collier's* January 23, 1909; whereas the actual source, "He Also Serves," was an earlier story on an entirely different theme, but also published in the same magazine on October 31, 1908 (See Note #87 to Chapter 3 and Note #117 to Chapter 4 below.). The chain of errors responsible for this confusion of titles is fully explained in a recent master's thesis by Eleen Mitchell, *The Dramatizations of O. Henry's Short Stories,* Auburn University, 1964, pp. 20-26.
97. Published July, 1910 in *Cosmopolitan* and included in *Sixes and Sevens,* pp. 154-73. Cf. Clarkson, p. 56.
98. Langford, pp. 234-35, 237-38.
99. *Ibid.,* pp. 239-40; see also *Caliph,* pp. 387-92.
100. Published in *Hampton's* (August, 1910), and included in *Waifs and Strays,* pp. 102-26. Cf. also Clarkson, p. 65, for correction of information in headnote concerning Porter's share of work done.
101. Langford, pp. 243-47.

Chapter Two

1. See, e.g., Walter Blair, *Native American Humor* (New York, 1937), pp. 62-101; Franklin J. Meine, *Tall Tales of the Southwest* (New York, 1930); Arthur Palmer Hudson, *Humor of the Old Deep South* (New York,

Notes and References

1936); Constance Rourke, *American Humor, A Study of the National Character* (New York, 1931).

2. Lucy L. Hazard, "The American Picaresque," *The Trans-Mississippi West*, quoted in Blair, *op. cit.*, p. 87.

3. E. Current-Garcia, " 'York's Tall Son' and his Southern Correspondents," *American Quarterly*, VII (1955), 380-82; and "Mr. 'Spirit' and *The Big Bear of Arkansas*," *American Literature* XXXVII (November, 1955), 332-46.

4. Blair, *op. cit.*, pp. 92-99.

5. Critical purists and reviewers in the 1880's and 1890's often attacked local colorists because of alleged vulgarity in the dialect used in their stories. See Claude M. Simpson, *The Local Colorists* (New York, 1960), p. 13, note 7.

6. Langford, p. 232.

7. Simpson, *op. cit.*, pp. 12-13.

8. The titles of these five are "Jeff Peters as a Personal Magnet," "A Midsummer Masquerade," "Shearing the Wolf," "The Man Higher Up," and "The Ethics of Pig." The three remaining titles of the eight southern tall tales referred to are "Hostages to Momus" (also in *The Gentle Grafter*), "Phoebe" (in *Roads of Destiny*), and "The Ransom of Red Chief," one of the most popular of all O. Henry favorites (in *Whirligigs*).

9. See *Caliph*, pp. 355-58.

10. *Ibid.*, p. 379. The story was first published in the *Saturday Evening Post* (July 6, 1907) and collected in *Whirligigs*, pp. 100-15. See Clarkson, p. 50.

11. In *Roads of Destiny*, pp. 88-106; first published in *Everybody's* (November, 1907).

12. These six were first published and later collected as follows: "A Blackjack Bargainer," in *Munsey's* (August, 1901) as by "Sydney Porter" and in *Whirligigs*, pp. 166-87; "The Duplicity of Hargraves," in *Junior Munsey* (February, 1902) and in *Sixes and Sevens*, pp. 133-53; "The Guardian of the Accolade," in *Brandur Magazine* (October 11, 1902), and again in *Cosmopolitan* (May, 1903), on both occasions under the title of "The Guardian of the Scutcheon," and as by "Olivier Henry," and in *Roads of Destiny*, pp. 29-39; "The Emancipation of Billy," in *Everybody's* (May, 1904) and in *Roads of Destiny*, pp. 184-96; "Blind Man's Holiday," in *Ainslee's* (December, 1905) and in *Whirligigs*, pp. 259-87; "A Municipal Report," in *Hampton's* (November, 1909) and in *Strictly Business*, pp. 148-72. For further bibliographical data on all these, see Clarkson, pp. 47-56.

13. Almost certainly O. Henry had in mind William Garret's book: *Reminiscences of Public Men in Alabama for Thirty Years* (Atlanta, 1872).

14. *Sixes and Sevens*, p. 137.

15. In *McClure's* (December, 1899). For further bibliographical information on these, see Clarkson, pp. 39, 40, 43, 56, 57, 68.

16. See Clarkson, Appendix, pp. 143-44, for O. Henry's letter awarding prizes for the best solutions of the problems set forth in this story.

17. *Ibid.*, p. 99.

18. *Ibid.*, pp. 39, 43, 44, 50, 52, 64, 73, 99, 103, 107, 108, 111.

19. In *Roads of Destiny*, p. 144.

20. *Ibid.* p. 153.
21. In *Options,* p. 7.
22. Clarkson, p. 44.
23. In *Sixes and Sevens,* pp. 154-73; see Clarkson, pp. 52, 56.
24. John Milton, "Lycidas," *Complete Poetical Works* (Cambridge, 1941), pp. 117-18.

Chapter Three

1. Letter to Mrs. Hall, November 31, 1883. *Works,* II, 1071.
2. Letter to Dr. W. P. Beall, February 27, 1884. *Works,* II, 1075.
3. Letter to Dave (David Scott?) April 28, 1885. *Works,* II, 1077.
4. *Ibid.,* pp. 1079-80.
5. *Rolling Stones,* pp. ix-xv, 199-233.
6. *Ibid.,* pp. 64, 80, 96, 128, 160, 176, 232-33, 242-43.
7. H. E. Rollins, "O. Henry," *Sewanee Review,* XXII (April, 1914), 213-32; "O. Henry's Texas Days," *Bookman,* XL (October, 1914), 154-65. See also by same author, "O. Henry's Texas," *Texas Review,* IV (July, 1919), 295-307.
8. "O. Henry," *Sewanee Review,* XXII (April, 1914), 217.
9. "O. Henry's Texas Days," *Bookman,* XL (October, 1914), 164.
10. *Caliph,* pp. 77-78.
11. *Rolling Stones,* pp. 146-66, 199-211.
12. *Ibid.,* p. 230. See also Langford, pp. 78-80.
13. Langford, pp. 58-60.
14. Credit for the discovery of this treasure trove of O. Henryana belongs to two young graduate students at the University of Texas who, in the mid-1930's, established beyond question the authenticity of their findings. One of them subsequently published a book containing some, though not all, of O. Henry's *Post* stories; but since the companion volume promised in her introduction has never appeared, the only extant collection of all these stories, aside from the original newspaper files, is in the unpublished thesis of her fellow student, Grace M. Watson, *O. Henry On The Houston 'Post,'* Master's Thesis, University of Texas, 1934; Mary S. Harrell, *O. Henry's Texas Contacts,* Master's Thesis, University of Texas, 1935. For Miss Harrell's findings, see *O. Henry Encore* (New York, Doubleday, 1939), Preface and Introduction, pp. vii-xvii. Miss Harrell's claim to have "discovered" this material is debatable, however, as Miss Watson's thesis antedates hers by a full year.
15. A misleading statement concerning these *Post* stories appears in the foreword of the latest so-called *Complete Works* published in 1953: "A number of unsigned stories taken from the files of the Houston *Post* and thought to have been written by O. Henry were published in 1936, but they are of indifferent quality and not positively identified as his" (Vol. I, p. vii). Watson's thesis shows that many of the stories were not only signed "W.S.P." and "The Postman," but also identical in theme, characterization, and style to later ones published by O. Henry.
16. In *O. Henry Encore,* pp. 119-29.
17. *Ibid.,* pp. 101-15, 221-26.
18. In Watson thesis, pp. 319-20.
19. *O. Henry Encore,* p. xv.

20. "A Tragedy," *ibid.*, pp. 35-36.
21. "In Mezzotint," *ibid.*, pp. 11-14.
22. "The Bruised Reed," "Simmons' Saturday Night," "Nothing New Under the Sun," "How She Got in the Swim," "Barber Shop Adventure," *ibid.*, pp. 38-43, 60-78, 132-34, 149-51, 158-66.
23. *Ibid.*, p. 73.
24. *Ibid.*, pp. 98-100.
25. In *Strictly Business*, pp. 83-89.
26. *O. Henry Encore*, pp. 79-82.
27. Langford, p. 93.
28. In *Strictly Business*, pp. 209-30.
29. In *The Four Million*, pp. 221-31.
30. In *Voice of the City*, pp. 170-78.
31. In *Sixes and Sevens*, pp. 258-64.
32. In *Voice of the City*, pp. 58-66.
33. "Night Errant," *O. Henry Encore*, pp. 1-10.
34. "An Odd Character," *ibid.*, pp. 93-97.
35. "An Aquatint," Watson Thesis, pp. 340-44.
36. "A Story for Men," *O. Henry Encore*, pp. 145-48.
37. "A Departmental Case," in *Roads of Destiny*, p. 213.
38. *Ibid.*
39. Dana M. Howell, *Settings and Characters of O. Henry's Texas Stories*, Master's Thesis, George Peabody College, 1937.
40. "Madame Bo-Peep of the Ranches," *Whirligigs*, pp. 288-314.
41. "Hearts and Crosses,"*Heart of the West*, pp. 3-20.
42. "Hygeia at the Solito," *ibid*, pp. 93-113.
43. "The Higher Abdication," *ibid.*, pp. 132-61.
44. "The Missing Chord," *ibid.*, pp. 228-39.
45. "Madame Bo-Peep," *Whirligigs*, p. 293.
46. "A Poor Rule," *Options*, p. 240.
47. "An Afternoon Miracle," *Heart of the West*, p. 120.
48. "Hygeia at the Solito," *ibid.*, p. 106.
49. "The Higher Abdication," *ibid.*, p. 157.
50. "The Marquis and Miss Sally," *Rolling Stones*, pp. 93-97.
51. "The Passing of Black Eagle," *Roads of Destiny*, p. 128.
52. "The Reformation of Calliope," *Heart of the West*, pp. 303-4.
53. "The Lonesome Road," *Roads of Destiny*, pp. 308-9.
54. "Georgia's Ruling," *Whirligigs*, p. 246.
55. "The Red Roses of Tonia," *Waifs and Strays*, p. 4.
56. "The Indian Summer of Dry Valley Johnson," *Heart of the West*, p. 260.
57. Howell thesis, pp. 112-37.
58. See Clarkson, p. 30, for data on this story's reprint history.
59. In *Everybody's* (September, 1910); see Clarkson, p. 57.
60. See Clarkson, pp. 134-40, for helpful editorial comment and a complete reprint of the earlier story.
61. In *Roads of Destiny*, p. 219.
62. *Heart of the West*, p. 187.
63. *Options*, pp. 54-55.
64. The five titles in *Heart of the West* are "Christmas by Injunction,"

"The Ransom of Mack," "Telemachus, Friend," "The Handbook of Hymen," and "Cupid a la Carte." The five in *The Gentle Grafter* are "The Octopus Marooned," "Modern Rural Sports," "The Chair of Philanthromathematics," "The Exact Science of Matrimony," and "Conscience in Art"; the two other tall tales are "New York by Campfire Light" (in *Sixes and Sevens*, pp. 197-203), and "The Friendly Call" (in *Rolling Stones*, pp. 112-26).

65. *Heart of the West*, p. 168. See Clarkson, p. 29.

66. In *Rolling Stones*, pp. 34-52; see also Clarkson, p. 60.

67. *Ibid.*, p. 35.

68. Both in *Waifs and Strays*, pp. 72-75, 102-26; see Clarkson, pp. 64-65.

69. In *Whirligigs*, pp. 125-34; see Clarkson, p. 50.

70. *Ibid.*, p. 163.

71. *Ibid.*, p. 165.

72. In *Sixes and Sevens*, pp. 46-63; see Clarkson, p. 55.

73. "The Story of 'Holding up a Train,'" *Rolling Stones*, pp. 288-92.

74. *Ibid.*, p. 292.

75. See J. S. Gallegly, "Backgrounds and Patterns of O. Henry's Texas Badman Stories," *Rice Institute Pamphlet*, XIII (October, 1955), 1-32; cited in Langford, pp. 212-14.

76. *Caliph*, p. 103.

77. *Ibid.*

78. *Cabbages and Kings*, p. 32. Citing this passage, Langford notes that in conversations with Anne Partlan, Porter " 'spoke of Honduras as Mecca' where he had found 'freedom . . . infinite peace,' " and that he would even urge that they go there together. Surely, he was idealizing his memories even then.

79. Quoted in *Caliph*, pp. 105-6.

80. P. S. Clarkson, "A Decomposition of Cabbages and Kings," *American Literature*, VII (May, 1935), 195-202. See Langford, pp. 280-81 for a detailed summary of Clarkson's findings.

81. *Caliph*, p. 104.

82. In *Roads of Destiny*, pp. 171-83.

83. *Through the Shadows*, p. 75.

84. In *Roads of Destiny*, pp. 243-57.

85. *Ibid.*, pp. 289-301.

86. In *Options*, pp. 89-103.

87. *Ibid.*, pp. 134-49. This was obviously the story which served as a basis for the musical comedy *Lo!*, jointly composed by O. Henry and Franklin P. Adams in 1909. See Note #96 to Chapter 1 above and Note #117 to Chapter 4 below.

88. In *Rolling Stones*, pp. 8-33.

89. In *Sixes and Sevens*, pp. 275-83.

90. Alfred Tennyson, "The Lotus Eaters," *Works* (1908).

91. In *Whirligigs*, pp. 3-21.

Chapter Four

1. William Wash Williams, *The Quiet Lodger of Irving Place* (New York, 1936), p. 121: quoted in Langford, p. 169.

2. "The Author's Account of Himself," *The Sketchbook* (New York, 1848), p. 4.

3. As indicated in Chapter 1, the titles of these volumes in chronological order are *The Trimmed Lamp, The Voice of the City, Strictly Business, Whirligigs,* and *Sixes and Sevens.*

4. The numbers of New York stories in other volumes are as follows: *The Gentle Grafter,* 2; *Roads of Destiny,* 3; *Options,* 7; *Rolling Stones,* 4; *Waifs and Strays,* 6; and *O. Henryana,* 3.

5. Gilbert Millstein, "O. Henry's New Yorkers and Today's," New York *Times Magazine* (September 9, 1962), pp. 36-38, 132-38.

6. "The Making of a New Yorker," *The Trimmed Lamp,* pp. 104-6.

7. "The Duel," *Strictly Business,* p. 295.

8. "The Voice of the City," *The Voice of the City,* p. 8.

9. "Extradited from Bohemia," *ibid.,* p. 200.

10. "The Green Door," *The Four Million,* p. 153.

11. "A Little Local Color," *Whirligigs,* p. 238.

12. "Brickdust Row," *The Trimmed Lamp,* p. 95.

13. Millstein, *op. cit.,* p. 36.

14. "The Marry Month of May," *Whirligigs,* pp. 117-18.

15. "Girl," *ibid.,* p. 83.

16. "Ulysses and the Dogman," *Sixes and Sevens,* p. 64.

17. "A Comedy in Rubber," *Voice of the City,* pp. 67-68.

18. "The Love-Philtre of Ikey Schoenstein," *Four Million,* p. 119.

19. "The Foreign Policy of Company 99," *Trimmed Lamp,* pp. 139-49.

20. "A Midsummer Knight's Dream," *ibid.,* pp. 189-97.

21. "Calloway's Code," *Whirligigs,* pp. 55-65.

22. "From the Cabby's Seat," *Four Million,* p. 165.

23. Roman Samarin, "O. Henry–'A Really Remarkable Writer,'" *The Soviet Review* (December, 1962), p. 57.

24. Deming Brown, "O. Henry in Russia," *The Russian Review,* XII (1953), 253-58.

25. In *Voice of the City,* pp. 75-104; and in *Strictly Business,* pp. 209-30.

26. Langford, pp. 218-19.

27. In *Four Million,* pp. 119-27.

28. *Ibid.,* pp. 165-73.

29. In *Roads of Destiny,* pp. 278-88.

30. *Ibid.,* pp. 286-87.

31. *Trimmed Lamp,* pp. 189-97.

32. *Sixes and Sevens,* pp. 265-74.

33. *Whirligigs,* pp. 37-54.

34. *Ibid.,* pp. 152-58.

35. "The Romance of a Busy Broker," *Four Million,* p. 214.

36. In *Sixes and Sevens,* pp. 32-37.

37. "Extradited from Bohemia," *Voice of the City,* p. 204.

38. *Ibid.,* pp. 179-87.

39. In *Strictly Business,* pp. 3-20.

40. In *Four Million,* pp. 58-68.

41. In *Trimmed Lamp,* pp. 198-208. Cf. *Caliph,* pp. 323ff. for location of the house on Grove Street said to be exact site.

42. "The Plutonian Fire," *Voice of the City,* p. 111.

43. *Ibid.,* p. 113-14.

44. In *Voice of the City*, pp. 230-44. See Clarkson, *Bibliography*, p. 34 for reference to particular vaudeville act forming background of this story.

45. *Ibid.*, p. 241.

46. In *Trimmed Lamp*, p. 21.

47. *Ibid.*, p. 260.

48. In *Four Million*, pp. 47-57.

49. Smith, p. 221.

50. In *Four Million*, p. 180.

51. "The Buyer from Cactus City," *Trimmed Lamp*, p. 73.

52. *Ibid.*, pp. 233-39.

53. In *Voice of the City*, p. 30.

54. Quoted in Smith, pp. 185-87.

55. In *Options*, pp. 20-37; *Four Million*, pp. 140-50; *Trimmed Lamp*, pp. 130-38; *Roads of Destiny*, pp. 48-56.

56. *Op. cit.*, p. 184.

57. Quoted in Greensboro *Daily News*, September 30, 1962, p. A19.

58. In *Four Million*, pp. 128-39.

59. In *Strictly Business*, pp. 209-30.

60. In *Roads of Destiny*, pp. 48-56.

61. In *Trimmed Lamp*, p. 26.

62. "Brickdust Row," *ibid.*, pp. 89-101.

63. "The Unknown Quantity," *Strictly Business*, pp. 109-17.

64. *Ibid.*, p. 310.

65. In *Roads of Destiny*, pp. 40-47.

66. In *Voice of the City*, pp. 75-84.

67. *Ibid.*, pp. 95-104.

68. *Ibid.*, pp. 157-69, 219-29; and in *Whirligigs*, pp. 116-24.

69. In *Four Million*, pp. 186-96.

70. In *Trimmed Lamp*, pp. 179-88.

71. In *Strictly Business*, pp. 194-208. The earlier title was "An Aquatint."

72. "The Higher Pragmatism," *Options*, pp. 199-209.

73. "The Cop and the Anthem," *Four Million*, pp. 90-100.

74. "Two Thanksgiving Day Gentlemen," *Trimmed Lamp*, pp. 50-58.

75. *Ibid.*, pp. 111-20.

76. *Ibid.*, p. 68.

77. Quoted in Smith, p. 233.

78. "The Complete Life of John Hopkins," *Voice of the City*, p. 11.

79. *Ibid.*, p. 12.

80. *Ibid.*, p. 13.

81. In *Trimmed Lamp*, p. 42.

82. *Ibid.*, p. 46.

83. *Ibid.*, p. 49.

84. In *Whirligigs*, pp. 135-42.

85. In *Four Million*, pp. 36-46.

86. In *Trimmed Lamp*, pp. 165-66.

87. In *Voice of the City*, pp. 141-48.

88. *Ibid.*, pp. 149-56; and *Strictly Business*, pp. 43-53.

89. In *Strictly Business*, pp. 21-23.

90. In *Voice of the City*, pp. 141-48.

91. In *Four Million*, pp. 110-18; and *Sixes and Sevens*, pp. 64-73.

92. In *Whirligigs*, pp. 81-88; and *O. Henryana*, pp. 75-89.

93. "The Count and the Wedding Guest," *Trimmed Lamp*, pp. 209-18; "Schools and Schools," *Options*, pp. 56-71; "The Marry Month of May," *Whirligigs*, pp. 116-24; "Nemesis and the Candy Man," *Voice of the City*, pp. 115-24; "Mammon and the Archer," *Four Million*, pp. 128-39; "The Defeat of the City," *Voice of the City*, pp. 85-94; and "The Rubber Plant's Story," *Waifs and Strays*, pp. 25-31.

94. In *Whirligigs*, pp. 215-22; 209-14.

95. Clarkson, p. 26; the story appears in *Trimmed Lamp*, pp. 169-78.

96. Smith, p. 187.

97. *Ibid.*, p. 188.

98. *Ibid.*

99. In *Voice of the City*, pp. 58-66.

100. *Four Million*, p. 23.

101. *Voice of the City*, p. 170.

102. *Ibid.*, p. 177.

103. In *Strictly Business*, pp. 130-47. The term "aphasia," derived from the Greek, is now defined as "total loss of power to use or understand words, usually caused by brain disease or injury"; it is not defined as loss of memory. The question is whether O. Henry deliberately misused the term for "Amnesia."

104. *Ibid.*, p. 138.

105. *Ibid.*, p. 142.

106. *Trimmed Lamp*, p. 129.

107. In *Sixes and Sevens*, pp. 258-64; *Strictly Business*, pp. 73-82; *Trimmed Lamp*, pp. 219-32; *Voice of the City*, pp. 219-29.

108. "A Bird of Bagdad," *Strictly Business*, pp. 182-93; "The Coming Out of Maggie," *Four Million*, pp. 69-81; "Past One at Rooney's," *Strictly Business*, pp. 255-75; "The Rubaiyat of a Scotch High Ball," *Trimmed Lamp*, pp. 32-41.

109. *Four Million*, p. 153.

110. *Voice of the City*, p. 213.

111. *Ibid.*, p. 218.

112. "Dougherty's Eye-Opener," *Voice of the City*, pp. 35, 38.

113. *Strictly Business*, pp. 173-82.

114. *Ibid.*, pp. 276-93.

115. Quoted in Langford, p. 191; and in Smith, pp. 214-15.

116. *O. Henry Biography*, pp. 214-16.

117. *Options*, pp. 119-33. For an account of how this story was allegedly transformed into the musical comedy *Lo!* by Porter and Franklin P. Adams, see Langford, pp. 226-28. Adams' fuller discussion including songs from the play appears in the essay "The Misadventures in Musical Comedy of O. Henry and Franklin P. Adams," *Waifs and Strays*, pp. 205-21. See Note #96 to Chapter 1 and Note #87 to Chapter 3 above.

118. Other variations on the same theme, less skillfully managed, may be found in "Roses, Ruses, and Romance," *Voice of the City*, pp. 132-40; "The Badge of Policeman O'Roon," *Trimmed Lamp*, pp. 81-88; and "The Enchanted Kiss," *Roads of Destiny*, pp. 197-212.

119. *Whirligigs*, p. 231.

120. *Options*, pp. 227-39.

121. *Strictly Business,* pp. 100-8.
122. *Ibid.,* pp. 300-1.
123. *O. Henry Biography,* p. 243.

Chapter Five

1. F. L. Pattee, *The Development of the American Short Story* (New York, 1923), pp. 360-63.
2. N. Bryllion Fagin, *Short Story Writing: An Art or a Trade?* (New York, 1923), p. 41.
3. *Op. cit.,* p. 364.
4. *Ibid.,* pp. 361-62.
5. *Understanding Fiction* (New York, 1943), pp. 114-18.
6. Langford, *op. cit.,* Foreword, pp. xvi-xvii.
7. *The Confident Years* (New York, 1952), p. 276.
8. Graves Glenwood Clark, *The Development of the Surprise Ending in the American Short Story from Washington Irving to O. Henry,* M. A. Thesis, Columbia University, 1930, pp. 1-3.
9. *Ibid.,* pp. 123-33.
10. Herman Melville, *The Confidence Man* (New York, 1955), p. 216.
11. "O. Henry," *Sewanee Review,* XXII (April, 1914), 226.
12. *Heart of the West,* pp. 21-29.
13. *Ibid.,* pp. 26-27.
14. F. M. Kercheville, "O. Henry and Don Alfonso," *New Mexico Quarterly Review,* I (November, 1931), 367-88.
15. "Hygeia at the Solito," *Heart of the West,* p. 110.
16. "An Afternoon Miracle," *ibid.,* p. 127.
17. "The Higher Abdication," *ibid.,* pp. 139-40.
18. *Ibid.,* p. 148.
19. *Ibid.,* pp. 187-204.
20. Arminda T. Yates, *Dialects in O. Henry's Stories,* M. A. Thesis, Hardin-Simmons University, 1948.
21. *Ibid.,* Introduction, pp. ix-x.
22. *Ibid.,* pp. 5-6.
23. Langford, p. xvii.
24. "A Philistine in Bohemia," *Voice of the City,* p. 210.
25. "The Discounters of Money," *Roads of Destiny,* p. 40.
26. "The Gold that Glittered," *Strictly Business,* p. 21.
27. "The Girl and the Habit," *ibid.,* p. 231.
28. V. S. Woodward, *"O. Henry's Use of the Malapropos and Related Devices,* M. A. Thesis, Stetson University, 1935.
29. "Hostages to Momus," *The Gentle Grafter,* p. 203.
30. *Ibid.,* p. 213.
31. "The Call of the Tame," *Strictly Business,* p. 107.
32. "Hearts and Crosses," *Heart of the West,* p. 8.
33. "Telemachus, Friend," *ibid.,* p. 32.
34. "The Handbook of Hymen," *ibid.,* p. 52.
35. "The Man Higher Up," *The Gentle Grafter,* p. 145.
36. "The Halberdier of the Little Rheinschloss," *Roads of Destiny,* p. 280.

37. *Ibid.*, p. 281.

38. "The Moment of Victory," *Options*, p. 162.

39. W. B. Gates, "O. Henry and Shakespeare," *Shakespeare Association Bulletin*, XIX (January, 1944), 20.

40. *Ibid.*, p. 25.

41. Edward C. Echols, "O. Henry's 'Shaker of Attic Salt,'" *Classical Journal*, XLIII (October, 1947–May, 1948), 488-89.

42. "A Night in New Arabia," *Strictly Business*, p. 217.

43. "Extradited from Bohemia," *Voice of the City*, p. 206.

44. "The Ethics of Pig," *The Gentle Grafter*, p. 225.

45. "Jeff Peters as a Personal Magnet," *ibid.*, p. 24.

46. "The Octopus Marooned," *ibid.*, p. 5.

47. All Classical allusions noted here are listed in Mr. Echols' article.

48. *Ibid.*, p. 489.

49. Echols, "O. Henry and the Classics–II," *op. cit.*, XLIV (October, 1948–May, 1949), 109.

50. "The Enchanted Profile," *Roads of Destiny*, pp. 49, 56.

51. "The Country of Elusion," *Trimmed Lamp*, p. 229.

52. H. E. Rollins, "O. Henry," *Sewanee Review*, XXII (April, 1914) 231.

53. "The Lady Higher Up," *Sixes and Sevens*, pp. 214-15.

54. "Blind Man's Holiday," *Whirligigs*, p. 263.

55. "The Plutonian Fire," *Voice of the City*, pp. 107-8.

56. "The Clarion Call," *ibid.*, p. 198.

57. "The Memento," *ibid.*, p. 230.

58. "From Each According to his Ability," *ibid.*, pp. 225-26.

59. In *Strictly Business*, pp. 73-82.

Chapter Six

1. Langford, p. xiii.

2. In *Waifs and Strays*, pp. 277-80; see Clarkson, p. 118.

3. *Ibid.*, p. 280.

4. *Ibid.*, pp. 271-76.

5. See Clarkson, pp. 119-23; also Langford, pp. 228-29.

6. J. A. Lomax, "Henry Steger and O. Henry," *Southwest Review*, XXIV (April, 1939), 299-316. Steger offered the Greensboro Public Library a set of the de luxe "Manuscript Edition" for the pre-publication price of $70.00 ("absolutely confidential"); but the Library evidently did not accept his offer. Letter dated April 19, 1912: *Greensboro Papers*.

7. See, e.g., A. W. Page, "Little Pictures of O. Henry," *Bookman*, XXXVII (June, July, August, 1913), 381-87, 498-508, 607-16; XXXVIII (October, 1913), 169-77; A. B. Maurice, "About New York with O. Henry," *Bookman*, XXXVIII (September, 1913), 49-57; H. E. Rollins, "O. Henry," *Sewanee Review*, XXII (April, 1914), 213-32; Caroline R. Richardson, "O. Henry and New Orleans," *Bookman*, XXXIX (May, 1914), 281-87; H. E. Rollins, "O. Henry's Texas Days," *Bookman*, XL (October, 1914), 154-65; Archibald Henderson, "O. Henry and North Carolina," *Nation*, C (January 14, 1915), 49-50.

8. Lecture delivered in Princeton and reported by Joyce Kilmer in the Philadelphia *Public Ledger*, July 23, 1916; also reprinted in New York

Times Book Review of same date. Mrs. Gerrould held up Hawthorne, Henry James, Bret Harte, and G. W. Cable as masters of the American short story but saw nothing of value in the work of either O. Henry or Poe. In *Greensboro Papers.*

9. "Journalization of American Literature: the Work of O. Henry," *Unpopular Review,* VII (April, 1916), 374-94.

10. "O. Henry and his Critics," *New Republic,* IX (December 2, 1916), 121; see also W. T. Larned, "Professor Leacock and the Other Professors," *ibid.,* IX (January 13, 1917), 299. Larned gently chided Leacock for his counterattack on the professors, reminding him that Americans had a tendency to "canonize too quickly, without the tempering aid of *advocatus diaboli*"; that they enthroned overnight idols with flashy tricks of style and then kicked them to pieces shortly afterwards.

11. "The Amazing Genius of O. Henry"; originally published in his *Essays and Literary Studies* (1916), the essay is reprinted in *Waifs and Strays,* pp. 171-95.

12. Frank Newbolt, "Letter to a Dead Author," *Nineteenth Century,* LXXXII (October, 1917), 825-34.

13. Pattee, *op. cit.,* p. 365.

14. *Ibid.,* p. 368.

15. Archibald Henderson, "O. Henry—A Contemporary Classic," *South Atlantic Quarterly,* XXII (July, 1923), 270-78. This essay was based on the fact that C. A. Smith had recently edited the first selected edition of O. Henry's stories, Doubleday having finally given in to the pressure for such a collection.

16. A. St. John Adcock, "O. Henry: An English View," in *Waifs and Strays,* pp. 197-98.

17. *Ibid.,* p. 203.

18. Raoul Narcy, "O. Henry Through French Eyes," *Living Age,* CCCIII (October 11, 1919), 87.

19. *Ibid.*

20. *Ibid.,* p. 88.

21. Deming Brown, *Soviet Attitudes Toward American Writing,* Princeton, 1962, pp. 21, 22, 53, 138, 170, 177.

22. *Ibid.,* pp. 230ff.

23. *Ibid.,* p. 236.

24. *Ibid.,* p. 238.

25. *Op. cit.,* p. xiv. The list includes reprinting rights granted to nearly twenty separate countries between 1940 and 1955.

26. Letter dated August 14, 1963, from Dorothy M. McKittrick to this writer, listing titles of individual stories, dates and names of producing companies that secured rights to the stories.

27. *Ibid.*

28. Walter Carroll, "An Afternoon with O. Henry's Widow," *Prairie Schooner,* XXVI (Summer, 1952), 138-44.

29. He opened with the latter play at the Greensboro Grand Opera House on November 18, 1913. *Greensboro Papers.*

30. A copy of Hackett's lecture included among the *Greensboro Papers.*

31. Letter from A. W. Page to C. A. Smith dated May 22, 1914. In *Greensboro Papers.* The other titles listed by Page included "The Badge

of Policeman O'Roon," "A Blackjack Bargainer," "A Chaparral Christmas Gift," "A Chaparral Prince," "The Halberdier of the Little Rheinschloss," "The Higher Abdication," "Jimmy Hayes and Muriel," "Hearts and Crosses," "The Ransom of Red Chief," "The Reformation of Calliope," "The Shamrock and the Palm," and "The Whirligig of Life." See *Motion Picture Magazine* (January, 1915), in *Greensboro Papers*.

32. Published by the Author, Pasadena, California, 1925.

33. "Foreword," *ibid.*, p. 5.

34. The other five stories treated in Sinclair's play were "Holding Up a Train," "Makes the Whole World Kin," "The Day We Celebrate," "A Fourth in Salvador," and "The Guardian of the Accolade."

35. *Ibid.*, pp. 54, 57-58.

36. *Prejudices, Second Series* (1920), p. 43. It should be noted that Mencken superciliously dismissed virtually all other contemporary American writers, except the younger post World War I rebels, as hopelessly derivative.

37. K. E. Eble, *F. Scott Fitzgerald* (New York, 1963), p. 62.

38. Langford, pp. xiv-xv.

39. See "A Decomposition of *Cabbages and Kings*," *American Literature*, VII (May, 1935), 195-202; Clarence Gohdes, "Some Letters by O. Henry," *South Atlantic Quarterly*, XXXVIII (January, 1939), 31-39; Margetta Jung, "O. Henry in Manhattan," *Southwest Review*, XXIV (July, 1939), 410-15; J. A. Lomax, "Henry Steger and O. Henry," *ibid.*, pp. 299-316; and Trueman O'Quinn, "O. Henry in Austin," *Southwest Historical Quarterly*, XLIII (October, 1939) 143-57. See also H. E. Rollins' generally favorable review of Clarkson's *Bibliography* in *American Literature*, XI (May, 1940), 107-9.

40. Other books in this group include Frances G. Maltby, *The Dimity Sweetheart* (Richmond, Virginia, 1930); Florence Stratton and Vincent Burke, *The White Plume* (Beaumont, Texas, 1931); and Lollie Cave Wilson, *Hard to Forget* (Los Angeles, California, 1939).

41. A. H. Quinn *et al.*, *The Literature of the American People* (New York, 1951), p. 838.

42. R. E. Spiller *et al.*, *Literary History of the United States* (New York, 1953), pp. 755, 1385.

43. Cleanth Brooks and R. P. Warren, *Understanding Fiction* (New York, 1943), p. 118.

44. Austin M. Wright, *The American Short Story in the Twenties* (Chicago, 1961), p. 6.

45. Langford, p. xvii.

46. *Op. cit.*, p. 58-59.

Selected Bibliography

PRIMARY SOURCES

The following list of O. Henry first editions is taken from the exhaustive bibliography compiled in 1938 by Paul S. Clarkson. Titles, dates, and original sources of publication for all known stories by O. Henry may also be found in Clarkson's work.

A. *Books (First Editions)*

Cabbages And Kings. New York: McClure, Phillips and Company, 1904.
The Four Million. New York: McClure, Phillips and Company, 1906.
The Trimmed Lamp. New York: McClure, Phillips and Company, 1907.
Heart of The West. New York: The McClure Company, 1907.
The Voice Of The City. New York: The McClure Company, 1908.
The Gentle Grafter. New York: The McClure Company, 1908.
Roads Of Destiny. New York: Doubleday, Page and Company, 1909.
Options. New York and London: Harper and Brothers, 1909.
Strictly Business. New York: Doubleday, Page and Company, 1910.
Whirligigs. New York: Doubleday, Page and Company, 1910.
Sixes And Sevens. New York: Doubleday, Page and Company, 1911.
Rolling Stones. New York: Doubleday, Page and Company, 1912.
Waifs And Strays. New York: Doubleday, Page and Company, 1917.
O. Henryana. New York: Doubleday, Page and Company, 1920.
Letters To Lithopolis. New York: Doubleday, Page and Company, 1922.
Postscripts. Edited with an Introduction by Florence Stratton. New York: Harper and Brothers, 1923.
O. Henry Encore. Edited with an Introduction by Mary S. Harrell. New York: Doubleday and Company, 1939.

B. *Collective Editions*

The Manuscript Edition of the Complete Works. (14 vols.) New York: Doubleday, Page and Company, 1912.
The Authorized Edition (12 vols.) New York: Doubleday, Page and Company, 1913.
The Memorial Edition (14 vols.) New York: Doubleday, Page and Company, 1917.
The Biographical Edition (18 vols.) New York: Doubleday, Doran and Company, 1929.
The Complete Works of O. Henry (2 vols.) New York: Doubleday, 1953.

SECONDARY SOURCES

Only the most important commentary on O. Henry's life and writings is here listed. Further bibliographical data of this type may be found in Clarkson's work and in more recently published studies by Ethel Stephens Arnett, Gerald Langford, and E. Hudson Long.

A. *Books*

ARNETT, ETHEL STEPHENS. *O. Henry From Polecat Creek.* Greensboro, North Carolina, Piedmont Press, 1962. Contains hitherto undisclosed facts concerning Porter's birthplace and childhood environment.

BROWN, DEMING. *Soviet Attitudes Toward American Writing.* Princeton University Press, 1962. Excellent summary and interpretation of O. Henry's popularity in Russia during past forty years.

CLARKSON, PAUL S. *A Bibliography of William Sydney Porter.* Caldwell, Idaho; The Caxton Printers, Ltd., 1938. Though incomplete, the most exhaustive listing of works by and about O. Henry; hence an invaluable aid to the student.

COLEMAN, SARA LINDSAY. *Wind of Destiny.* New York: Doubleday, Page and Company, 1916. Fictionalized treatment of O. Henry's second courtship (by his wife) and marriage.

DAVIS, ROBERT H. AND ARTHUR B. MAURICE. *The Caliph of Bagdad.* New York: D. Appleton and Company, 1931. Engaging but unscholarly memoir based on personal recollections.

FAGIN, N. BRYLLION. *Short Story Writing: An Art Or a Trade?* New York: Thomas Seltzer, Inc., 1923. Valuable as example of early adverse critical reaction to O. Henry's work in the United States.

JENNINGS, AL. *Through The Shadows With O. Henry.* London: Duckworth and Company, 1923. Colorful but not wholly trustworthy account of Porter's Latin-American and prison experiences.

LANGFORD, GERALD. *Alias O. Henry: A Biography of William Sidney Porter.* New York: The Macmillan Company, 1957. The most carefully documented and, on controversial matters, the most evenly balanced treatment of Porter's life as a whole now available.

LONG, E. HUDSON. *O. Henry, The Man And His Work.* Philadelphia: University of Pennsylvania Press, 1949. Competent, scholarly dissertation, but largely superseded by Langford's biography.

MALTBY, FRANCES G. *The Dimity Sweetheart.* Richmond, Virginia: Dietz Printing Company, 1930. Contains intimate biographical data about both Athol Estes and William S. Porter.

PATTEE, F. L. *The Development of the American Short Story.* New York: Harper and Brothers, 1923. Contains chapter on O. Henry's methods, techniques, and influences; biased but vigorously expressed.

SINCLAIR, UPTON. *Bill Porter: A Drama Of O. Henry In Prison.* Pasadena, California; Published by the Author, 1925. Highly sentimentalized but fascinating dramatization of Porter's prison experiences as contributing influences in the growth of his creative imagination.

SMITH, C. ALPHONSO. *O. Henry Biography.* New York: Doubleday, Page and Company, 1916. First full-length, authorized biographical treatment of Porter and, though outdated by subsequent findings, still an authoritative source.

WILLIAMS, WILLIAM WASH. *The Quiet Lodger of Irving Place.* New York: E. P. Dutton and Company, 1936. Delightfully informal portrait of Porter in New York, based on personal recollections of an intimate friendship.

B. *Unpublished Studies*

CLARK, GRAVES GLENWOOD. *The Development of the Surprise Ending in the American Short Story from Washington Irving Through O. Henry.* Master's Thesis, Columbia University, 1930. Attempts to show that O. Henry added nothing of significance to technique to the surprise ending, but illustrates numerous varying examples of it employed by him.

CONNALLY, LUCY BELLE. *A Study of the Social Background of the Characters in O. Henry's New York Short Stories.* Master's thesis, Texas State Teachers College, 1940. Analysis of O. Henry's social attitudes as reflected in varied social types, chiefly lower class, treated in his stories.

FELKNER, VIOLET E. *A Study of O. Henry's Southeastern Types.* Master's thesis, J. B. Stetson University, 1935. Analysis similar to Connally's above based on O. Henry's Southern stories.

HOWELL, DANA MONTEVILLE. *Settings and Characters of O. Henry's Texas Stories.* Master's thesis, George Peabody College, 1937. Elaborate summary and analysis showing relationships between settings and characters in fifty-six Texas stories, classified by geographical sections.

MITCHELL, ELEEN. *The Dramatizations of O. Henry's Short Stories.* Master's thesis, Auburn University, 1964. A careful study of all available data relating to the various dramatic media—including the stage, motion pictures, radio, and television—in which more than a hundred of O. Henry's stories have been presented from 1909 to the present.

WATSON, GRACE MILLER. *O. Henry on the Houston Post.* Master's thesis, University of Texas, 1934. Important discussion and facsimile reproduction of all sketches and stories by Porter originally published in Houston *Post* and not previously noted in work by Stratton entitled *Postscripts.*

WOODWARD, VINOLA SALA. *O. Henry's Use of the Malapropos and*

Related Devices. Master's thesis, Stetson University, 1935. Careful analysis of O. Henry's varied use of word mutilations, coinages, misquotations, and distortions for securing humorous effects.

YATES, ARMINDA TIMMONS. *Dialects in O. Henry's Stories.* Master's thesis, Hardin-Simmons University, 1948. Classified demonstration of O. Henry's accuracy in his use of six different dialects, both foreign and domestic.

C. *Essays*

ADCOCK, J. ST. JOHN. "O. Henry." *Bookman* (London), L (September, 1916), 153-57; *Littell's Living Age,* CCXCI (November 25, 1916), 482-88. Good examples of early British enthusiasm for O. Henry.

BARBAN, ARNOLD M. "The Discovery of an O. Henry Rolling Stone." *American Literature,* XXXI (1959), 340-41. Recent example of scholarly interest in Porter's earliest writings.

BOYD, DAVID. "O. Henry's Road of Destiny," *Americana,* XXXI (October, 1937), 579-608. Superficial but interesting critical study of O. Henry as a "despairing artist."

BROWN, DEMING. "O. Henry in Russia," *Russian Review,* XII (1953), 253-58. Brief but careful scholarly analysis of O. Henry's continuing popularity among Soviet critics and readers.

CESARE, MARGARET PORTER. "My O. Henry," *Mentor,* XI (February, 1923), 17-20. Part of series of memorials to O. Henry printed in this issue: contains intimate biographical details recorded by his daughter.

CLARKSON, PAUL S. "A Decomposition of Cabbages and Kings," *American Literature,* VII (May, 1935), 195-202. Important scholarly analysis showing how original stories were cut and spliced together to produce O. Henry's first book.

COURTNEY, L. W. "O. Henry's Case Reconsidered," *American Literature,* XIV (January, 1943), 361-71. First scholarly proof that Porter received a fair trial and was unquestionably guilty of embezzlement.

ECHOLS, EDWARD C. "O. Henry's 'Shaker of Attic Salt,'" *Classical Journal,* XLIII (October, 1948–May, 1948), 488-89.

————. "O. Henry and the Classics–II," *Classical Journal,* XLIV (October, 1948–May, 1949), 209-10. Concise demonstration of O. Henry's broad knowledge and use of standard Greek and Roman myths in his stories.

FORMAN, H. J. "O. Henry's Short Stories," *North American Review,* CLXXXVII (May, 1908), 781-83. Important as first serious critical recognition in America of O. Henry's artistry.

GALLEGLY, J. S. "Backgrounds and Patterns of O. Henry's Texas Badman Stories," *Rice Institute Pamphlet,* XLII (October, 1955),

1-32. Scholarly proof that real Texas desperadoes were more brutal than O. Henry's fictional versions of them.

GATES, WILLIAM B. "O. Henry and Shakespeare, "*Shakespeare Association Bulletin* XIX (January, 1944), 20-25. Traces O. Henry's familiarity with and varied use of well-known Shakespearean phrases in his stories.

GOHDES, CLARENCE. "Some Letters by O. Henry," *South Atlantic Quarterly*, XXXVIII (January, 1939), 31-39. Group of nine letters, previously unpublished, throwing significant light on O. Henry's predicament shortly before his death.

HENDERSON, ARCHIBALD. "O. Henry—A Contemporary Classic," *South Atlantic Quarterly*, XXII (July, 1923), 270-78. Typical example of excessive praise lavished upon O. Henry by critics of the 1920's.

JUNG, MARGETTA. "O. Henry in Manhattan," *Southwest Review*, XXIV (July, 1939), 410-15. Brief account of O. Henry's relationship with his sister-in-law, Nettie Roach, in New York.

KERCHEVILLE, F. M. "O. Henry and Don Alfonso," *New Mexico Quarterly Review*, I (November, 1931), 367-88. Useful discussion·of O. Henry's intimate knowledge of and fondness for using vernacular Spanish in his stories.

LEACOCK, STEPHEN. "O. Henry and his Critics," *New Republic*, IX (December 2, 1916), 120-22. Good example of heated controversy stirred up by early attacks on O. Henry's influence.

LOMAX, J. A. "Henry Steger and O. Henry," *Southwest Review*, XXIV (April, 1939), 299-316. Chatty reminiscences of Steger's anecdotes about his relations with O. Henry.

MCALLISTER, DAN. "Negligently, Perhaps; Criminally, Never," *South Atlantic Quarterly*, LI (October, 1952), 562-73. Strong but obviously biased defense of Porter's innocence; intemperately brushes aside all contradictory evidence.

NARCY, RAOUL. "O. Henry Through French Eyes," *Living Age*, CCCIII (October 11, 1919), 86-88. Good example of earliest favorable reception of O. Henry's stories on the continent.

NEWBOLT, FRANK. "Letter to a Dead Author," *Nineteenth Century*, LXXXII (October, 1917), 825-34. Sustained but tiresomely breezy love song in praise of O. Henry's writings.

O'QUINN, TRUEMAN. "O. Henry in Austin," *Southwest Historical Quarterly*, XLIII (October, 1939), 143-57. Impartial discussion of Porter's activities in Austin prior to and during his trial.

PAGE, A. W. "Little Pictures of O. Henry," *Bookman*, XXXVII (June, July, August, 1913), 381-87, 498-508, 607-16; XXXVIII October, 1913), 169-77. Good example of literary publicity stimulated by O. Henry's growing reputation after his death.

PATTEE, FRED LEWIS. "The Journalization of American Literature," *Unpopular Review*, VII (April—June, 1917), 374-94. Some of earliest unfavorable criticism of O. Henry's methods.

PAYNE, L. W., JR. "The Humor of O. Henry," *Texas Review*, IV (October, 1918), 18-37. Excellent critical analysis of basic sources of O. Henry's humor and of his humorous devices.

PECK, H. T. "The American Story Teller," *Bookman*, XXXI (April, 1910), 131-37. Discriminating discussion of strengths and limitations of O. Henry's humorous American slang.

RICHARDSON, C. F. "O. Henry and New Orleans," *Bookman*, XXXIX (May, 1914), 281-87. Useful biographical data concerning O. Henry's brief sojourn in New Orleans and his use of that city as background in some of his fiction.

ROBINSON, DUNCAN. "O. Henry's Austin," *Southwest Review*, XXIV (July, 1939), 388-410. Valuable historical summary of Austin during O. Henry's residence there in the 1880's.

ROLLINS, HYDER E. "O. Henry," *Sewanee Review*, XXII (April, 1914), 213-32.

————. "O. Henry's Texas Days," *Bookman*, XL (October, 1914), 154-65.

————. "O. Henry's Texas," *Texas Review*, IV (July, 1919), 295-307. Excellent biographical and critical treatment of O. Henry and his writings, showing care for scholarly accuracy and for impartial judgments.

————. "Review of Clarkson's *Bibliography of William Sydney Porter*," *American Literature*, XI (1940), 107-9. Judicious praise of Clarkson's accuracy and exhaustiveness, though numerous important omissions also specified.

SAMARIN, ROMAN, "O. Henry—'A Really Remarkable Writer,'" *Soviet Review*, (December, 1962), 55-58. Good example of recent favorable expression of Russian critical opinion.

STEGER, H. P. "O. Henry: New Facts About the Great Author," *Cosmopolitan*, LIII (October, 1912), 655-63.

————. "Some O. Henry Letters and the *Plunkville Patriot*," *Independent*, LXXIII (September 5, 1912), 543-47. Earliest scholarly efforts to establish O. Henry's reputation as a great writer.

TRAVIS, EDMUNDS. "O. Henry's Austin Years," *Bunker's Monthly*, I (April, 1928), 493-508.

————. "O. Henry Enters the Shadows," *Bunker's Monthly*, I (May, 1928), 669-84.

————. "The Triumph of O. Henry," *Bunker's Monthly*, I (June, 1928), 839-52. Series of articles occasioned by recent movement to convert Travis County Jail into an O. Henry Memorial Library; important factual data on O. Henry's activities.

VAN DOREN, CARL. "O. Henry," *Texas Review*, II (January, 1917), 248-59. First-rate critical analysis of O. Henry's artistic strengths and weaknesses.

Index

Adams, Franklin P., 46
Adcock, St. John, 159
Adventures of Tom Sawyer, The, 54
Ainslee's Magazine, 37, 91
Alabama, 55, 105
Aldrich, Thomas Bailey, 138
Aliäs Jimmy Valentine, 46, 161
Anderson, Charles, 25, 26, 27, 33
Anderson, Sherwood, 163
Arabian Nights, The, 74, 146
Armstrong, Paul, 46
Asheville, N.C., 45-47, 66
Astor, John Jacob, 111
Austin, Texas, 23, 24, 27-30, 71

Beall, Dr. W. P., 23, 69
Benchley, Robert, 144
Bibliography of William Sidney Porter, A, 165
Bierce, Ambrose, 138
Bill Porter: A Drama of O. Henry in Prison, 162-63, 166
Bonner, Sherwood, 50
Bookman, The, 156
Bourget, Paul, 158
Brann, William, 27
Broadway, 154-55
Brooks, Cleanth, 137, 165
Brooks, Van Wyck, 137
Bynner, Witter, 38, 42

Cable, George W., 50, 61, 64
Caldwell, Erskine, 160
Caledonia Hotel, 44, 47
Caliph of Bagdad, The, 164
Chamberlain, John, 164
Chaucer, Geoffrey, 19
Chekhov, Anton, 160
Cisco Kid, The, 84, 90, 161
Clarkson, Paul S., 164-65
Coleman, Sara Lindsay, 21, 45, 46, 161
Collier's magazine, 46
Conrad, Joseph, 151
Cosmopolitan magazine, 156
Cotulla, Texas, 22, 23

Crane, James P., 27, 28, 29
Crane, Stephen, 72, 83, 84, 110, 122
Current Opinion, 156

Davis, Richard Harding, 92
Davis, Robert H., 164
Delineator, The, 45
Dickens, Charles, 38, 107
Dixon, Joe, 23, 24
Double-Dyed Deceiver, A, 161
Doubleday, Page, & Co., 46, 156-57
Dreiser, Theodore, 106, 109, 160

Estes, Athol, 26, 27, 31, 32, 162-63
Everybody's magazine, 41, 89, 91

Fagin, N. Bryllion, 135
Forman, H. J., 156
France, Anatole, 155
Friotown, Texas, 23

Golden Ass, The, 91
Gray, F. B., 29
Greensboro, North Carolina, 17, 20, 21, 23, 27, 33, 45, 57, 68

Hackett, Norman, 161
Hall, Gilman, 37, 39
Hall, Dr. James K. & Mrs., 21, 69
Hall, Lee, 22
Hall, Richard, 22, 23, 24, 25, 27, 33, 84, 90
Hampton's Magazine, 47, 62
Hancock, Dr. Charles R., 47
Hardin, John Wesley, 90
Haroun al Raschid, 38, 110, 124
Harrell, Joseph, 24, 25, 33
Harrell, Mary S., 44, 74
Harris, Joel Chandler, 50
Harte, Bret, 138, 158
Hawthorne, Nathaniel, 68, 158, 159
Hemingway, Ernest, 109, 160
Henderson, Archibald, 158
Homer, 19, 147
Honduras, Republic of, 31, 90-94
Hooper, Johnson Jones, 49

Houston *Post,* The, 29, 30, 44, 68, 69, 72-76

Iconoclast, The, 27
In Old Arizona, 162
In Our Time, 164
Irving, Washington, 38, 95, 138, 159
Izvestia, 109

Jackson Square, 150-51
James, Henry, 19, 104, 111, 136, 158
Jennings, Al, 31, 35, 89, 92-93, 162

King, Grace, 50
Kipling, Rudyard, 72, 156, 158

Langford, Gerald, 33, 36, 76, 137, 143, 160, 165
Leacock, Stephen, 157-58, 159
Lewisohn, Ludwig, 164
Little Church Around the Corner, 47, 103
London, Jack, 109
Longfellow, Henry Wadsworth, 72
Lotus Land, 90-94
Lycidas, 67

McAllister, Ward, 43
McClure, Phillips and Company, 42
McClure's Magazine, 38, 41, 91
Maddox, John, 23, 24, 25
Madison Square Garden, 150
Maupassant, Guy de, 43, 51, 85, 138, 156
Maurice, Arthur B., 164
Melville, Herman, 138
Men Without Women, 164
Mencken, H. L., 163
Morte d' Arthur, 110
Motion Picture Magazine, 162
Munsey's magazine, 41
Murfree, Mary Noailles, 50

Narcy, Raoul, 159
Nashville, Tennessee, 59, 60
Newbolt, Frank, 158
New Orleans, 30, 31, 58, 61, 150
New York *Herald Tribune,* 109
New York *Sunday World,* 38, 41, 42, 44, 68, 76, 89, 96, 119, 121
North American Review, The, 44, 156

O. Henry, *see* Porter, W. S.,
"O. Henry," pseudonym, first use of, 35, 87, 169
O. Henry Biography, 157
O. Henry Memorial Award Prize Stories, 158
O. Henry Television Playhouse, 161
Old Creole Days, 64

Page, Thomas Nelson, 50, 51
Parker, Dorothy, 144
Partlan, Anne, 39, 47, 108
Pattee, F. L., 135-36, 151, 157, 163
Perelman, S. J., 144
Peters, Jeff (the "Gentle Grafter"), 35, 52-55, 74, 87, 148
Pittsburgh *Dispatch,* 37
Poe, Edgar Allan, 61, 135, 136, 138, 158, 159
Porter, David, 18
Porter, Dr. Algernon Sidney ("Dr. Al"), 17, 18, 57
Porter, Evelina ("Miss Lina"), 18, 19, 20, 21
Porter, Margaret, 27, 32, 34, 37, 39, 45, 162
Porter, Shirley, 18, 20
Porter, W. C. ("Uncle Clark"), 20, 21, 57
Porter, W. S. ("O. Henry"), ancestry, birth, and childhood, 17-20; attitude toward "Old" vs. "New" South, 46, 48, 56, 57-58, 63, 65-66; Caliph of Bagdad role, 36-39, 100-1, 109-13; contracts with *Sunday World* and other N. Y. magazines, 38-42; descriptive technique, 150-52; early efforts as professional writer, 27-30, 70-76; early training in literature and drawing, 18-21; experiences as bank teller, 27-28; experiences as draughtsman, 21, 23-24, 26; fatalism, 75-76, 88; first courtship and marriage, 24-26; flight to Honduras, 30-32; fondness for words and dictionary study, 23-24; humor, irony, and the tall-tale tradition, 48-55, 57, 63-66, 90, 92-94, 136, 144-48, 152-55; in-

mate of Ohio Penitentiary, 34-36; Irish dialect stories, 119-20, 128-29; knowledge of cattle raising, 22-23, 79-80; knowledge of pharmacy, 20; linguistic skill in foreign tongues, 23, 141-43; mastery of local color story, 55-63, 66-67; mastery of plot manipulation and surprise ending, 74-76, 85-86, 127, 137-41; playwriting, stage, and motion-picture adaptations, 46, 161-63; pre-occupation with crime and outlawry, 34-36, 87-94; residence in and love for Manhattan, 37-41, 95-99, 115-17, 131-34; romantic escapism, 40-41, 90-91, 93-94, 100-3, 109-15; second courtship and marriage, 44-45; treatment of restaurants and food consumption, 38, 122-26; 128-30, 132-33; treatment of the rich and poor, 109-15; treatment of shop-girls, showgirls, and menaced maidens, 103-8; trial and conviction for embezzlement, 28-34; variations on themes of adventure and pretense, 124-32; variety of character types, themes, and plot situations, 81-84, 95-96; ventures into book publishing, 42-44; verbal trickery, allusions and word coinages, 140-49; world-wide fame and declining reputation, 157-60, 163-65

WRITINGS OF:

"According to their Lights," 113-14
"Art and the Bronco," 80
"Assessor of Success, The," 115
"Atavism of John Tom Little Bear, The," 87
"Best Seller," 64, 66
"Between Rounds," 119
"Bexar Scrip No. 2692," 26, 71
"Blackjack Bargainer, A," 21, 43, 56
"Blind Man's Holiday," 31, 56, 58-59
"Bulger's Friend," 60, 61
"Buried Treasure," 82

"Caballero's Way, The," 84-85, 88, 90, 142, 147, 161, 162
Cabbages And Kings, 31, 42, 90-94, 142
"Caliph and the Cad, The," 30, 75, 127
"Call Loan, A," 85
"Call of the Tame, The," 132-33
"Chaparral Christmas Gift, A," 82
"Chaparral Prince, A," 85
"Cherchez la Femme," 31, 64
"Church with the Overshot Wheel, The," 40, 60, 61-62
"Complete Life of John Hopkins, The," 117
"Compliments of the Season," 114
"Cop and the Anthem, The," 43, 114
"Country of Elusion, The," 127
"Cupid a la Carte," 87
"Day Resurgent, The," 119-20
"Defeat of the City, The," 101
"Departmental Case, A," 84
"Diamond of Kali, The," 103
"Discounters of Money, The," 112
"Door of Unrest, The," 30, 60, 62
"Double-Dyed Deceiver, A," 83, 147, 161
"Duel, The," 133-34
"Duplicity of Hargraves, The," 56-57
"Easter of the Soul, The," 119-20
"Elsie in New York," 106-7
"Elusive Tenderloin, The," 44
"Emancipation of Billy, The," 36, 56, 57, 58
"Enchanted Kiss, The," 30, 35, 85
"Enchanted Profile, The," 108, 110
"Ethics of Pig, The," 54
"Fog in Santone, A," 36, 80, 85
"Fool Killer, The," 113
Four Million, The, 42, 43, 44, 96
"Fourth in Salvador, The," 92, 93
"Friends in San Rosario," 27, 37, 80, 85
"From Each According to His Ability," 113, 127
"From the Cabby's Seat," 102
"Furnished Room, The," 43, 101, 115-16, 122, 137

Gentle Grafter, The, 35, 43, 44, 52-55, 87, 142
"Georgia's Ruling," 26, 35, 85
"Gift of the Magi, The," 42, 101, 104, 115-16, 122
"Girl and the Habit, The," 138
"Green Door, The," 127-28
"Guardian of the Accolade, The," 56, 57
"Guilty Party—An East Side Tragedy, The," 122
"Guthrie Wooing, A," 87
"Halberdier of the Little Rheinschloss, The," 102
"Harbinger, The," 119
"Harlem Tragedy, A," 119
"He Also Serves," 46, 93
"Head Hunter, The," 146
Heart of the West, The, 35, 43, 44, 87, 142
"Hearts and Crosses," 81, 82
"Hearts and Hands," 87
"Hiding of Black Bill, The," 85-86
"Higher Abdication, The," 83
"Higher Pragmatism, The," 114
"Holding Up a Train," 89, 92
"Hostages to Momus," 50, 54
"Hygeia at the Solito," 82-83
"Hypothesis of Failure, The," 103
"Indian Summer of Dry Valley Johnson, The," 81, 82
"Jeff Peters as a Personal Magnet," 52
"Jimmy Hayes and Muriel," 80, 85
"Last Leaf, The," 104, 105
"Last of the Troubadors, The," 80, 84, 90
"Law and Order," 80, 83
"Let Me Feel Your Pulse," 20, 46, 48, 64, 66-67
"Lickpenny Lover, A," 108, 138
"Little Local Color, A," 132
Lo!, 46
"Lost on Dress Parade," 75, 124-25
"Love Philtre of Ikey Schoenstein, The," 20, 99, 102
"Madame Bo-Peep of the Ranches," 45, 82
"Madison Square Arabian Night, A," 110

"Mammon and the Archer," 109
"Man Higher Up, The," 53
"Marquis and Miss Sally, The," 82
"Marry Month of May, The," 113
"Memento, The," 40, 105-6
"Midsummer Knight's Dream, A," 102-3
"Midsummer Masquerade, A," 53
"Miracle of Lava Canyon, The," 32, 83-84
"Moment of Victory, The," 82, 147
"Money Maze," 37, 91
"Municipal Report, A," 21, 43, 48, 56, 58, 59-60, 67, 162
"Newspaper Story, A," 121
"Night in New Arabia, A," 75, 101, 109-10
O. Henry Encore, 44, 164
"October and June," 60, 62
"One Dollar's Worth," 84
"One Thousand Dollars," 101, 112
Options, 35, 43
"Out of Nazareth," 64, 65
"Passing of Black Eagle, The," 37, 83, 90
"Past One at Rooney's," 40
"Pendulum, The," 117-18
"Philistine in Bohemia, A," 128
"Pimiento Pancakes, The," 82
"Plunkville Patriot, The," 70
"Poet and the Peasant, The," 127, 152-55
"Princess and the Puma, The," 81
"Psyche and the Pskyscraper," 129
"Purple Dress, The," 108
"Ramble in Aphasia, A," 20, 126
"Ransom of Mack, The," 139-41
"Ransom of Red Chief, The," 43, 54-55
"Reformation of Calliope, The," 83
"Renaissance at Charleroi, The," 31, 60, 61
"Retrieved Reformation, A," 35, 38, 46, 60, 61, 161, 162
Roads of Destiny, 35, 43
"Roads of Destiny," 30, 38, 142
"Roads We Take, The," 88-89
"Robe of Peace, The," 75
Rolling Stone, The, 27, 28, 29, 33, 69-71, 72, 76, 157

Rolling Stones, 43, 70
"Rose of Dixie, The," 21, 50, 64, 65-66
"Rouge et Noir," 37
"Ruler of Men, A," 93
"Rus in Urbe," 132
"Sacrifice Hit, A," 103
"Service of Love, A," 104-5
"Shearing the Wolf," 53
"Simmons' Saturday Night," 74
Sixes and Sevens, 43
"Skylight Room, The," 106-7
"Snow Man, The," 47, 87-88
"Social Triangle, The," 127
"Sphinx Apple, The," 82
"Springtime a la Carte," 108
Strictly Business, 43
"Strictly Business," 104
"Supply and Demand," 93
"Technical Error, A," 88
"Thimble, Thimble," 60, 62-63
"Third Ingredient, The," 108, 147
"To Him Who Waits," 131
"Tobin's Palm," 38
"Tommy's Burglar," 121
"Transients in Arcadia," 75, 125
Trimmed Lamp, The, 43, 44
"Trimmed Lamp, The," 106
"Two Renegades," 93
"Ulysses and the Dogman," 121
"Unfinished Story, An," 40, 43, 106-7, 162
"Unknown Romance, An," 75
"Vanity and Some Sables," 114-15
"Venturers, The," 129-31, 133
"Vereton Villa," 48, 72-74
Voice of the City, The, 43
"Voice of the City, The," 131
Waifs and Strays, 43, 65
"What You Want," 112
"While the Auto Waits," 30, 38, 75, 124
Whirligigs, 43
"Whirligig of Life, The," 64-65, 143
"Whistling Dick's Christmas Stocking," 31, 60-61
"Witches' Loaves," 103
"World and the Door, The," 46, 92, 94

Quiet Lodger of Irving Place, The, 165
Quinn, Arthur Hobson, 164

Red Badge of Courage, The, 72
Roach, Nettie, 39
Roach, P. G., 26, 27, 28, 32, 34, 37, 47
Rollins, Hyder E., 70, 138, 143
Roughing It, 72

Shakespeare, William, 19, 145, 146-47
Sheridan, Richard Brinsley, 145
Sinclair, Upton, 35, 162-63, 166
Smart Set, The, 91
Smith, C. Alphonso, 20, 24, 123, 157
South Atlantic Quarterly, The, 164
Southwest Review, The, 164
Spirit of the Times, The, 49, 52
Steffens, Lincoln, 35
Steger, Harry, 46, 70, 156-57
Steinbeck, John, 109, 160
Stockton, Frank, 62, 138, 143
Stowe, Harriet Beecher, 72
Swaim, Mary Jane Virginia, 17
Swaim, William, 17

Tarkington, Booth, 54
Tennyson, Alfred Lord, 19, 94
Texas Land Office, 25, 26, 27, 71
"The Lady—or the Tiger?" 62
Thomas, Dr. John M., 34
Tolstoy, Leo, 158
Tourgée, Albion, 21
Twain, Mark, 54, 72, 109, 136, 143
Twice Told Tales, 68
Tyler, George, 46

U.S.S.R., 100, 109, 159-60

Valentine, Jimmy, 35, 162
Van Doren, Carl, 40, 62
Vieux Carre, The, 150-51

Wagnalls, Mabel, 39
Wallack's Theatre, 161
Warren, Robert Penn, 137, 165
Wells, H. G., 158
Winesburg, Ohio, 163-64
Worth, David and Eunice, 17